THE MUTT

10 ReganBooks
Celebrating Ten Bestselling Years
An Imprint of HarperCollinsPublishers

THE MUTT

HOW TO SKATEBOARD AND NOT KILL YOURSELF

RODNEY MULLEN

with Sean Mortimer

ALSO BY SEAN MORTIMER

HAWK: OCCUPATION: SKATEBOARDER

HarperCollins books may be purchased for educational, business, or sales promotional use. For information please write: Special Markets Department, HarperCollins Publishers Inc., 10 East 53rd Street, New York, NY 10022.

FIRST EDITION

Designed by Paul Brown and Kris Tobiassen

Printed on acid-free paper

Library of Congress Cataloging-in-Publication Data has been applied for.

ISBN 0-06-055618-8

04 05 06 07 08 ❖/RRD 10 9 8 7 6 5 4 3 2 1

FOR MY MOTHER,
ANN P. MULLEN

CONTENTS

ACKNOWLEDGMENTS

Without the help of these talented people, I could have never completed this book. My incredible wife, Traci Maria, has been an endless well of inspiration, strength, and reason. I particularly want to thank my friend and coauthor, Sean Mortimer, whom I've driven bananas. He is the main engine that powered this project. I also owe thanks to his lovely wife, Francesca.

The person I have become clearly has much to do with my father. It was incredibly hard drudging up painful times with him in order to show what blossomed out of them. Without his discipline and strength, I could have never gotten this far. I thank him for all that I have.

I will never be able to repay Steve Rocco—even though he still owes me one hundred dollars—for becoming the brother I never had. Also, thanks for the support of my friends and family: Sara Mullen, Barry Zaritsky, the Fragas and Hollowells, Matt Hill, Gary Valentine, Daewon Song, Stacy Peralta, Mike Ternasky, Daniel Sturt, Tony Hawk, Bruce Walker, Marc McKee, Daisy, Scooter, and Marley.

Thanks to the photographers who spent so many hours watching me fall: Grant Brittain, Seu Trinh, Phil Chiocchio, Jody Morris, Socrates, and also Miki Vuckovich, who had awesome pictures that a deadline screwup prevented us from using.

I especially want to thank our primary editor, Stephen Barbara; also, thanks to Renee Iwaszkiewicz who supported this book at the beginning.

Most of all, I thank My Lord, Jesus, for all He's done for me.

INTRODUCTION

A crack echoed across San Diego's Del Mar Skate Ranch reservoir and was absorbed by the surrounding crowd. The onlookers were watching the 1983 world championship freestyle skateboarding contest. It was a summer afternoon, and the California sun bounced off the white polished cement, making me squint to keep the glare out of my eyes. I was sixteen years old, in the middle of my last run of the finals, and had just snapped the tail of my skateboard against the reservoir's surface. I was already mentally on to the next trick when I heard the crack that announced the one before it. The best freestylers in the world surrounded me, and any of them could slide into first place if I missed a single move.

Five years of skating alone in a rural barn twenty miles from the nearest skateboarder were helping me focus now. Hundreds of hours had gone into practicing this run alone with nothing to distract me but an occasional cow meandering across the acres of grassy hills behind my barn. Marathon skating sessions with farm animals as your only company can tweak you, and in the past year I had gotten a little weird with my practice regimen—doing my run over and over with my eyes closed, like a bad Karate Kid imitation. Now it was taking all the concentration I could muster to drown out the crowd's outbursts while I made it through my run—just like being alone, back in my barn.

The remaining tricks snapped into place. I had packed this run with the hardest tricks I knew, at least three of which no one had ever seen. I hadn't fallen, hadn't sketched on a single move as I slowed down and wound up for the 360s that punctuated the end of my routine. I leaned my body to the left and lifted my front wheels as I wound up. For the first time in my run I stopped thinking about what was next—there *were* no more tricks left. My mind stumbled, like the pigeon-toed walk that had haunted me with slipups and skinned knees throughout my childhood. Now no tricks clicked into place in a neat row in my mind; nothing dictated what would happen next. That realization hit me for the first time, crushing any other thoughts—a mental sledgehammer swung by my father when he'd ordered me to stop skating for good. This was my last contest.

In the past few months, I had focused everything on skating just to avoid thinking about life without it. My isolation nurtured and honed a double-edged ability to concentrate. I could hold my skating in such tight focus that everything else that keeps people "normal" and balanced receded indiscernibly into the background. This, my father declared, was why I forced him to take skateboarding from me. It was for my own good. Two weeks after that declaration, I lost the only professional contest of my career after over twenty consecutive wins. The thought of leaving skateboarding a loser had haunted me all the way to that moment.

As I spun around faster and faster there was no escaping it. *The End.* As the outside world blurred by in whirls, I was alone within my spin. Tears welled up in my eyes, and then I felt them pull off my cheeks as my head whipped around and around. I began to trip out, feeling as if I was stationary, in my own vortex, while my worries and fears and energy spiraled out of control around me.

In less than twenty-four hours I'd be walking off a plane and heading back to that giant house in the Florida countryside, back to my chores. My father had ordered me to finally "grow up," to quit hanging out with pot-smoking degenerates, to cease mocking my 4.0 GPA, to stop wasting my talents on a slacker sport—he had multiple variations on that theme.

To him, my life was consumed by skateboarding, and I was only sinking deeper into the mire. Every consecutive World Title trophy, every package that arrived at the house stuffed with free skate gear, every phone interview, every time he saw me skating until midnight instead of focusing my abilities on what he deemed worthy—all this piled up until he couldn't take it anymore. He seemed to search for any misbehavior on my part that would give him a reason to force me to stop skating. And finally, in frustration and disgust, he had simply ordered me to stop skating. I was made to promise to never step on a skateboard again after this contest.

I could already feel the panic and depression soaking in as my spinning slowed and my run wound down. It wasn't exactly a new feeling, but the indifference I suddenly felt was. My passion, my desire, my energy—all were growing cold. I knew I'd already won this contest, but it didn't matter anymore; I was the biggest loser in skateboarding. I tucked harder, trying to keep my spin going, but it was futile. I pulled my arms in as tightly as I could, until I had nothing more to give and after about thirty spins, it was over.

It felt as though my spirit drained out of me, and I was left a dizzy, disoriented shell. My ears popped as if I were descending too quickly in a plane. The eruption of cheers from the people whom I respected most rushed in, flooding the silence that I'd brought with me from that barn. I heaved my board up and held my head down to hide tears I couldn't hold back. For five months I had tried to keep it a secret, but the word of my forced retirement had leaked out. I wanted out of that reservoir so badly, to run and get away from everyone staring at me as I broke down. But they were all streaming down, surrounding me, holding me. The first was one of the owners of *Transworld Skateboarding* magazine, Louise Balma. She grabbed my face and I looked up to see that she was crying worse than I was, and I somehow forgot my own embarrassment. She kept telling me that it wasn't really over, that I'd be back. I smiled and nodded as I tried to relax and memorize everything about the moment. I had to burn it into my mind, make it tangible so that down the line, when my life would spiral out of control without the stabilization of skateboarding, I could hold onto this moment in the hopes that it would be enough to keep me steady, to help me make it through.

I had duped myself into thinking that this moment was all about a result—winning the contest. Best in the world meant nothing to me, anymore. I would have traded it for being worst in the world, if only it meant that I could still skateboard.

That night, many of the symptoms that would intensify over the next few months showed up. I had no appetite and didn't eat, nor did I eat after I returned home the following day. My weight would eventually sink into the double digits. Sleepless nights would ink black bags under my eyes. I spoke less and less, withdrawing to the point where much of my speech was barely more than mere mumblings to myself. I began fantasizing about how peaceful death would be. I never realized that skateboarding was my life preserver until it was taken away from me. I fully depended on it to get through the pressure I felt at home. Now I was lost.

Today, over twenty years later, I can look back with a wiser (or at least older) perspective on the many ways skating has helped me grow as a person. For one, I've learned how to deal with everybody from stoned skaters to the LA bomb squad (though I'm still learning how to deal with my own stress: I once gave myself such a gnarly case of asthma that I came within a few hours of suffering brain damage.) And after starting one of the most successful skateboarding companies in history, I've become well versed in copyright law, as most people would be after facing legal threats from the odd trifecta of the Hell's Angels, the Walt Disney Company, and the Church of Scientology. I've also developed an acute sense of irony—blowing my knee out on the same day I won *Transworld*'s 2002 Reader's Choice Skater of the Year Award. It hasn't always been smooth sailing, you see, but one thing has kept me sane all these years—my nightly skating session, when my ideas and feelings somehow get translated into the motions of my board, and I feel alive.

My father always said skateboarding would ruin my life. Instead, it gave me freedom.

CHAPTER 1
LIVING NOWHERE

THE CADILLAC CUT THROUGH THE THICK AUGUST HUMIDITY AND PARTED

swarms of nickel-sized horseflies. We were cruising up and down the rolling hills of farmland and forest in central Florida, with the bustle of the city miles behind us.

It was 1966, and according to the fashion of the day, young men rocked a slightly hippie wardrobe—flared pants, colorful shirts, and long hair. My father, though, wore pressed pants, a crisply ironed button shirt, and a short, neatly brushed crop of hair with not a disobedient strand in sight.

Sitting in the driver's seat, his six-foot frame was ramrod straight. He was instantly recognizable from five hundred yards as a man who had enjoyed his time in the military. In the passenger seat, my mom's blond-streaked hair flowed down to her hips at a respectable hippie length, but all the signs of the free love era ended with her hairline. She was a southern belle and an ex-beauty contest winner with a Scarlett O'Hara flair. Considering that she'd given birth to me just a few days earlier, she probably wasn't going to be wearing any elaborate dresses for a few weeks.

Fifteen minutes outside the city of Gainesville, the Caddy turned, climbed our steep driveway, and came to a stop. My father hopped out and ran around the car to help me and my mom out. He gently took me from my mom and proudly grinned a thousand-kilowatt smile that didn't dim for days. After having two girls who were already four and six, my sisters Sara and Vicki, he had finally had a boy. I was the final piece of the dream he'd cultivated for years, a dream that included a big colonial house two Cadillacs in the driveway, and a perfect family.

For someone like my father, who had been in more fights than Steven Segal in a TNT marathon, having a male to pass those true-blue American bare knuckle qualities down to was as good as it got.

We lived in a rural area that was being developed within the city limits. My father, who always seemed to love the isolation and freedom of country life, thought this location would provide the best of both worlds. He was close to his successful dental practice in the city and enjoyed the calmness that comes with having few neighbors close by. This idealistic lifestyle didn't last long, though. A year or so after our huge custom home was built, houses began sprouting up like weeds on our block.

But even as the area around us became more populated, our house still stood out. It was massive—a southern plantation-style house, twice the size of an ordinary house. My mom's award-winning rose garden, the twelve-foot-deep swimming pool, the billiard house, the weight room, the basketball court, and the sunroom that looked out across our big, rock waterfall all made it look more impressive. Even the doorknobs and light switches were ornate.

My father worked hard, and he always figured out inventive ways to make more money. He looked at the money game in the same way that he looked at a lot of things—as a contest to be won. Even back in college, he had helped pay his way by cleaning up at poker parties he arranged with his classmates. He later branched out to larger games with older players so heavy he had to hire a bodyguard for protection.

During the Korean War, my father was a bombardier in the navy. He was part of an elite group that was chosen to drop nuclear weapons, and he boxed in his spare time all through the service. After being discharged, he earned a dental degree—this on top of the pharmaceutical degree he'd received before entering the war.

After getting his second degree, he married my mom and quickly figured out another way to make money aside from scraping teeth. He bought an office complex, renovated it, and sold it for a profit. This project turned out to be so lucrative that he made a second job developing real estate.

GIGGLES

My father had so many construction projects going on that we'd often take family trips to the job site. These also doubled as my father's weekly meetings with his contractors.

The same scene played out often. I'd be sitting in the backseat of the Cadillac, the windows up, the air-conditioning humming, watching my father through the square window above the dashboard, as if I were watching TV with the volume off. My father would begin talking to the foreman civilly enough, but then something would always seem to irritate him, and next thing I'd know the conversation would escalate.

My mom would sit there in the front seat, nervously. Sometimes she would turn the radio up in an attempt to distract herself from the noise of my father's shouting. But I could never distract myself that way; I would squirm so much that I often appeared to be performing a restricted break-dancing routine in the backseat. The last thing I wanted to see was my father in such heated conversations.

My mom and I would stress out over these meetings, but for my father they were pure entertainment. I never saw him more gleeful than after he had intimidated another person, and when he got back in the car after showing up a foreman or contractor, he seemed overjoyed. He'd supply me and my mom all the details on how he had made the other person back down. These times brought about a distinctive, unabashed giggle, similar to the pure joy of a child unwrapping a cherished present.

I probably wouldn't have thought too much about my father's confrontations if his blowouts only occurred at construction sites, but they happened at home, too. The climate around my father could abruptly shift from warm to absolute zero, from everybody laughing to nobody moving as we all waited to see who would get it. When my sisters sensed that my father was angry about something, they stayed out of sight, and I picked up on their wariness by osmosis. By the time I was five, I had learned to hightail it to my room to avoid a scene. So it was everybody for themselves.

My father lived by an extremely strict code of conduct, and as the head of our family he made us live by it as well. Yet there were subjective lines to these rules that bewildered me. Something as obvious as sassing would definitely get you in trouble, but subtleties in your words or actions could be interpreted as insincere or disrespectful slights. My father was tough and prone to tantrums, which was something we all grew to fear. I hated upsetting him almost as much as I did getting in trouble. I became more and more fearful of him, always wary that some situation could blow up.

But my father wasn't an ogre who stomped through the house looking for family members to harass. He was a disciplined, driven, and incredibly strong man who worked his ass off to provide the best for us all. As I got older, I started to feel that there were times his volatility bothered him as much as it did us.

TORTURE BOOTS

I grew up thinking that one of my father's goals was to create the perfect family, one whose picture you'd find in a store-bought frame—everyone with 8 percent body fat, teeth like piano keys, strong, smart, and totally disciplined.

Looks were a part of the picture, naturally, and our family was trim, perky, and ready to hurdle past anything in our way. As a member of the Mullen family, your days were full of physical activities. My sisters danced a few times a week, ran, and rode horses. My mom played tennis and swam. My father boxed, lifted weights, and ran every day. And I was born with crooked feet—Tiny Tim in a track and field family.

"Pigeon-toed" doesn't even come close to describing my crazy gait in those days. When I walked it looked as if my big toes were massive magnets pulling my feet toward each other. I couldn't control the way my legs moved, no matter what I did. Still, I did develop a steady running rhythm of five strides, one trip, five strides, one trip, five strides, one trip—until God would decide that he'd had enough fun and just make me fall all the way down.

Things didn't improve much when I was horizontal, since I had to wear special boots every night to correct my tweaked feet. It was just a few months after I had turned two that my nightly routine of being shackled began. The devices used were the size of large wrestling boots and attached at the heels, so that they pointed out in a V shape. The sick bastards who designed my nighttime footwear must have cured the leather with Kevlar, because no matter how much I wiggled my toes or struggled to pull my heels apart, I couldn't make those boots flex.

After a while I got used to sleeping strapped, but I noticed that nobody else in the house slept in boots developed by the R & D department of the Spanish Inquisition. By age four, I already felt defective, a freak in a family full of superior athletes.

My father didn't help me erase this thought, either. If we were walking down the street in public and my legs started their crazy dance, he'd sternly order in a loud whisper, "Walk straight! Walk straight!" He said it so much that whenever my toes strayed across my middle line I'd hear his instructions echoing inside my head as if yelled from a bullhorn, even if he wasn't around. Unfortunately, I couldn't think of any way to correct my walking problem, though I tried with all my might to keep those uncooperative feet pointed straight.

Gradually I adapted to my Mr. Bojangles legs by walking with an awkward gait, and by age six the wrestling boots from hell were finally discarded, but I was still the most pigeon-toed kid in Florida.

TORTURE BOOTS. THESE WERE DRAWN BY MARC MCKEE, WHO HAS PLAYED A HUGE ROLE IN THE SUCCESS OF WORLD INDUSTRIES.

CHAPTER 2
NURTURING A NERD

THE GHETTO OF MULLENVILLE

My parents were always cool about one thing: they gave me and
my sisters a private space to rule over. In that way, we were treated
like adults, and our rooms were treated as independent states. For
Sara and Vicki, and especially for me, the bedroom was a virtual
parent-free zone. Whenever something irritated my father and his
anger wound up into a tornado looking for a place to touch down,
I bailed to my room.

My two older sisters lived down the hallway, but the three of
us were like guests in a hotel. They were always off dancing or
riding horses or playing with their older friends, while I stayed in
my room building model airplanes or attempting to construct
something out of scraps of wood.

Because they led such busy lives, it wasn't uncommon for them
to miss a meal, or ten. Without that nightly dinner ritual, I often
went days without seeing my sisters. In fact, sometimes whole
weeks would pass where Vicki and I didn't exchange a word—not
even a "pass the salt." The two of us never really clicked, in part
because our personalities resided on opposite poles. I was hyper-
sensitive, and she was just plain mean. I was a lot closer to Sara,

though it wasn't like we'd spend days hanging out together. Our age difference sent us in separate directions.

If you walked through our house in the early 1970s, you'd see my mom's immaculate piano, thousands of dollars worth of furniture arranged as pieces are arranged in a showroom—and then you'd walk up to *my* room and wonder if you were still in the same house. It was the ghetto of Mullenville: paint was gobbed up on the quality carpet; oil stains gave a greasy leopard skin pattern to my floor; patches were worn through the carpet; and the walls were dinged up.

I was obsessed with construction materials, particularly brick, wood, paint, and concrete. With all the new houses being built around us, I often went on scavenger hunts after the workers had gone home, and I'd dig through the scrap piles looking for treasures.

I had a real thing for concrete, especially after I had taught myself how to pack it into balls. Whenever possible, I checked work sites for discarded paper bags of that magical powder. In my mind, concrete balls seemed the perfect weapon for booby traps, and I was obsessed with rigging my bedroom so that nobody could surprise me. As a concrete ball was hardening, I'd press several two-inch nails into it and thirty minutes later I had a spiked orb of death waiting for any interloper. It wasn't enough that it was my own private area; I had to make it a capital offense if anybody entered my safety zone.

I still don't know what the hell I was thinking then. I rigged booby traps in my closet, which doubled as a storage shed for my tools, so that if someone opened the closet and tugged on the light cord, a spiked ball would hit the person with a vicious uppercut, thrusting nails into his or her neck and jaw. And I built a second chunky, spikeless deathball and jimmied the door of my room so that if somebody entered my room at night, I could pull a string from my bed and release another ball of doom above the door.

But these protective devices were only employed in my bedroom. I was far from the budding psycho who prowled around the neighborhood in search of cats to burn. In fact, I never wanted to hurt anybody or anything; my deathball fixation centered around my obsession with self-protection. I hated seeing any living thing in pain, and I assigned myself a daily hour to patrol our pool and save all the bugs that had fallen in the water. For sixty minutes each day I'd carefully pace around the pool, playing insect lifeguard, my head bowed, scanning the surface for wiggling, frightened bugs trapped in the water. I guess that I felt a connection with them.

I would often get lost in my construction projects, my young brain focusing so much that it forgot natural instincts such as hunger. After a while my mom got used to this, and if I failed to make an appearance at the dinner table after repeated calls, she'd drop off a tray of food at my door.

I would always show my mom whatever new thing I had built; for instance, a lopsided workbench. She'd step over the matted carpet and slalom around the piles of splintered wood, broken bricks, never uttering a complaint, always proud of my projects. I also wanted to show my work to my father, and he sometimes came along with my mom to see what I'd built, even though I was always a little scared that he might notice another stain on the carpet.

My room finally got so disgusting, though, that my parents had to do something about it. So my father bought a new piece of carpet to lay over my ghetto floor, and I clearly remember interpreting this as an act of acceptance on his part. In my mind, he was proud of my projects, because he never mentioned the mess, and because he'd worked hard to buy me such a nice new carpet. He rarely handed out praise to me though, so I had to decipher his actions to get it—or imagine it—wherever I could.

NURTURING A NERD

Both my parents came from serious brain banks. My father was smart enough to earn two university degrees, and—just to keep himself busy—he often invented gadgets like our self-propelling pool vacuum.

My mom wasn't a dummy either. She graduated from high school at fourteen, entered college early, and earned two degrees herself (her subjects were English and physics). In her free time, she was crowned Miss University of Florida and played piano at concert recitals. After graduating from college, she began teaching at a high school, though she was only a few years older than her students.

My grandparents had also been teachers. My grandfather went to Columbia University, and at the time he was tested as having one of the highest IQs on the school's record. I spent my early years surrounded by all these ex-teachers, and they encouraged my budding interest in science. I couldn't have asked for a better educational environment to grow up in.

I can recall vividly my mom showing me my first electromagnet. I was five at the time, and the experience blew my mind. Suddenly, so many things around me could be broken down and understood (or at least understood in *my* mind). By teaching me this one concept, my mother had transformed the world into a puzzle waiting to be solved. Switch on a light, and I'd try to figure out how the electricity ran through the wires, how the positive and negative charges worked together to light a bulb. One discovery led to another. I realized that every single thing around me could be broken down into a series of comprehensible steps, and I wanted to learn them all.

A DOG'S LIFE

Some of my favorite family members were our dogs. We had a series of them, all named Sasha. The first Sasha was a German shepherd; the other ones were Samoyeds. These dogs offered me unconditional love. I could play with them, use them as pillows, talk to them. They were my closest friends. Once, in a desperate attempt to strengthen my bond with them, I scooped out a few fingers of dog food—the wet kind glistening with gelatin, with chunks of pulped pink meat poking out—and ate it. I'm glad my father didn't walk in at that moment. I can only imagine how it would blow his mind to see his son on all fours, gagging as he scooped dog food into his mouth.

The second reason I loved hanging out with the dogs was because they had a killer pad. Their little area, which was connected to the side of our house, was only four feet long. It had a dirty, cement floor with planks laid across it.

I used to quietly sneak through the doggy door on all fours and lie down on the planks. It became my panic room if things felt threatening in the house, or if I wanted to be sure to avoid my father. I'd curl up on the planks, comfortable with the dirt and dog hairs. Nobody ever found me in there.

I had another panic room. This was the small closet in our poolhouse, which was used as a changing room off the rear of the pool. We stored the pool chemicals and chlorine in that closet, and I'd move them around so that I could squeeze in and shut the door. The closet's darkness and isolation never failed to relax me, sometimes so much so that I drifted off to sleep in there.

HORSES SUCK

When I was six years old, we began taking long car rides every weekend to a second house that my father had bought out in the country, where we had a stable and horses.

My fear and hatred of snakes almost rivaled my feelings toward horses. I hated horses even before I was forced to ride one. And at our country house, each of us had our own personal horse. Mine was a pony, small and compact, but filled to the brim with evil. I could barely stay on top of the thing, and because I was so frozen by fear once I sat atop the animal, I couldn't drive the thing either. Stopping, steering, accelerating were all nonissues. Stopping would quickly *become* an issue, but for the first couple of rides I just wrapped the leather reins around my white knuckles and closed my eyes, trying to erase the gory images of death-by-horse that played in the movie theater in my mind.

The only thing I learned about my pony was that it took its lead from the bigger horses. One weekend, my pony—apparently bored at getting absolutely no direction from me—decided to follow my sister Vicki's lead. I saw this coming and pleaded with my sister to *stop* galloping fast. She looked at me, smiled, and took off like Crazy Horse going into battle. My pony tried to catch up.

After speeding up enough to ensure that it would cause some quality damage, the beast put on the brakes and hit the eject button. He threw me into a nice hard area of packed clay, aiming for a huge tire tread divot, where someone must have spent an afternoon spinning donuts with a tractor.

I didn't land on my head and crack it open, assuring a quick and painless death; instead, my short but direct flight was interrupted by my shoulder, which absorbed the whole impact of my fall. As soon as I hit the ground, the waterworks opened, and I started that little kid hiccupping cry, as tears and snot bubbles ran down my face. My father caught up with me and told me to stop crying, gave me the whole big boys don't cry deal, and added the whole John Wayne *be a man!* speech. John Wayne looked like he was taught at one point how to ride a horse, but I wasn't going to argue that point.

The last thing I wanted to do was get back on that demon steed. Actually, the second-to-last thing I wanted to do was get on that demon steed; the *absolute* last thing I wanted to do was piss off my father, but it was a close contest.

I forced myself to stop crying, wiped the snot off my face, and was helped back up on the horse. Every hoofprint that pony made shot a blast of pain through my shoulder.

When we were done riding, and my enemy was put into its stall, my father told me to take off my shirt. After a ride, I always stripped down and was hosed off. I tried to lift my arm to pull it through the sleeve, but I couldn't move it more than a few inches. I looked like I was trying to escape a straitjacket as I wiggled. My mom and my father knew something was wrong and took me to the hospital. An X-ray revealed a fracture in my shoulder. I think my father always felt bad about that day, but he never said anything about it.

It turned out that breaking my shoulder was a small sacrifice to pay, in the long run. I'd have done it earlier if I knew what the payoff would be—that my days of riding horses were over. I spent most of my weekends for the next year with my grandparents on my mother's side, while the rest of my family stayed at the ranch house.

My grandparents were always teaching me, working as special forces under my parents. They had already taught me to read before I entered kindergarten by making various deals with me. If I read six books, I was rewarded with a pocketknife that had its point and blade dulled; if I did some math problems, I'd get another treat.

Thanks to the tutoring I received from my mom and grandparents, I had no problems when I started first grade, even though I entered school a year early. Well, I did have problems, but not *academic* ones. I went to P. K. Yonge, which was a progressive school that taught students from grades K–12. It was a laboratory of the local university. Because I had a head start, I always cruised through the mandatory teachings and finished the extra assignments before any other classmate.

Schoolwork wasn't a problem, but my schoolmates were. They petrified me. The teachers and kids were always good to me, but I didn't connect with any classmates my entire time at school. I didn't break this pattern until college.

One teacher, a hippie sort of guy that I liked, took me aside during my free time and taught me to play the recorder, which is a simple flutelike instrument. Whenever I finished my work early, I was given free rein. I often walked outside and climbed a tree beside the school. I'd crawl up, getting as deep into the leaves as possible, and lean against the trunk. Hidden in the foliage, with no noise except windblown leaves, I'd play my recorder until I was called back in.

Another teacher took me aside and told me he was concerned about me. I had no idea what he was talking about.

When I was seven, my father took me to the local sporting goods store, where he bought a customized twenty-gauge pump action shotgun for me. The gun had to fit my tiny body, so they added extra padding to the end of the stock and made me wear two hunting vests with even more padding on the shoulder area to absorb the recoil action of the gun. They stopped short of duct-taping a pillow to my shoulder. I can only imagine what people thought of me as I exited the store in that full-padded costume with my pigeon-toed walk. "Look dear, how cute! A little boy funk dancing on his way to his first *Guns and Ammo* photo shoot."

Now that I looked the part, it was time to *be* the part. My father and a group of his buddies took me out to the country for some good old bird hunting. I was too young to realize what was going on and just trotted along happily behind them. We hiked for a little while until we came across an area infested with quails. One of the men spotted them and put his fingers to his lips to shush us.

My father and I quietly walked to the front of the group. I could feel the heat of his pride shining on me like never before. He loved hunting, he loved being a man, and he loved having a son. For him, walking through the wilderness in the middle of a hunt was a good way to bond with me.

I got down on one knee and braced the twenty-gauge against my padded shoulder. My father pointed toward a spot where a few quails were standing. At the sight of those quails, all the training my father had given me clicked into place, and all I could think about was hitting my target.

The quails heard us and flew up in the air—right in front of me. I followed the flight of one, leading it with my gun as I'd been taught, and squeezed the trigger. I don't remember the noise, just the mess. Feathers shot into the air, and a cloud of blood materialized in front of me, a red mist so fine it looked like spray paint. Then my hearing came back. The men were hooting and hollering behind me.

I felt as if I was about to short-circuit. I had killed it. Until the feathers and guts filled the air I had never thought about what I was doing. My father was so proud of me, and I desperately wanted his acceptance. But a part of me wished I could hit the magic rewind button and undo what I'd done.

I was haunted by the image of that quail all week. My father bragged to his friends about my killing skills, but I cursed myself for them. I wanted to do things with him—fun things that put him in a good mood. With hunting, it was a fairly safe environment regarding his mood swings, and I enjoyed our bonding time together, but the killing part . . .

For the next few months, whenever he took me hunting, I lined up birds, squirrels, or whatever was small and living and in my sights and aimed to the right of them and pulled the trigger. I could hear the men behind me shaking their heads as I blasted away like a miniature Mr. Magoo.

My father couldn't understand what the hell had happened to his son, Dead Eye Rodney. After a few months of scratching his head over my cross-eyed crosshairs, the hunting trips decreased in frequency, until one week I simply wasn't invited.

I was cut off from another thing, too—visiting my grand-mother. One Sunday I was at her house when I heard my grandma screaming into the phone. I'd never heard her explode like that, and I began pacing nervously.

She didn't say much after the call. She was quiet the rest of the evening and as I was leaving she told me she loved me and gave me a long, tight hug. It struck me as odd, because she wasn't a very affectionate person, and I wondered what exactly had tran-spired on the phone. That was pretty much the last time I ever "officially" saw my grandma. After my father had slammed down the phone on the other side of the connection, Grandma was offi-cially blackballed. I still have no idea what that conversation was about, but it was clear that she and my father didn't see eye to eye on something.

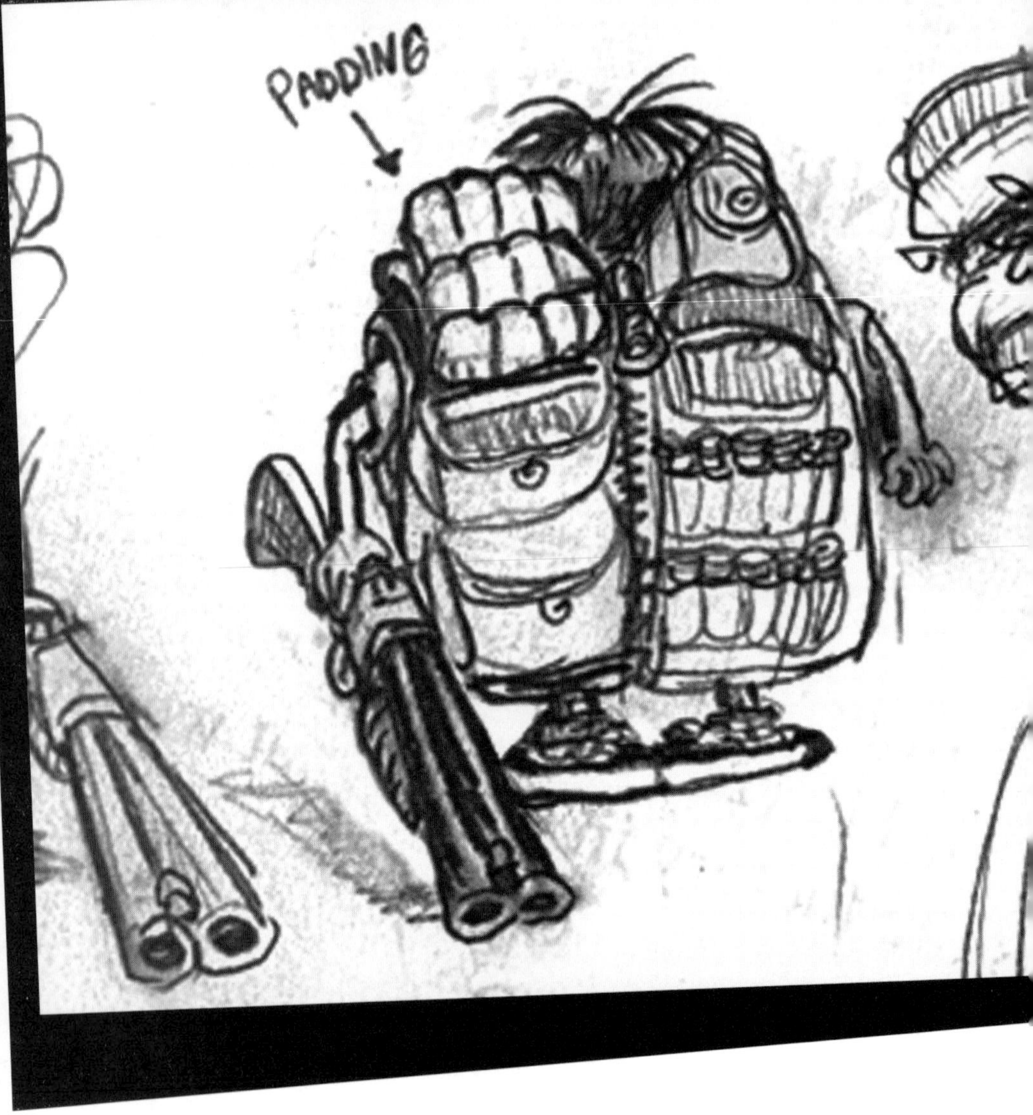
PADDING

MOM TIME

I usually got picked up after school by a driver in one of the family Cadillacs. Our drivers were people in their twenties, generally, and they did a variety of chores for us, such as shopping or dropping the kids off.

On Wednesday afternoons, though, my mom personally wheeled her Cadillac into my school pickup loop to take me to her country club for the afternoon. Those three hours in the middle of the week that I'd spend with my mom, away from our house and the rest of my family, were my favorite. We'd sit by the pool drinking sodas or go swimming or just doze off in the sun. It was like taking a hot air balloon ride above the unpredictable episodes at home. My memories of those Wednesdays burn a lot brighter than the days actually did, but they sparkle just because of the contrast.

My mom was a tennis nut and played every Wednesday at the club. I noticed a change in her attitude once she walked onto the court. She became looser, happier, and more assertive as she fired tennis balls over the net; a different mom from the one I knew at home. Her eyes would burn with focus and determination. She was good at tennis, and she knew it, and nobody could take that away from her while she was on the court. I got a true sense of who my mom was when she played at the club, and some of my fondest memories are from those Wednesdays.

I tended to horde any one-on-one time with my mother, and the other way I found it was through the piano. It was her favorite pastime. Her love for it was obvious—she poured it into the keys for hours at a time. When I was seven, my mom sat me down on the polished wood bench and taught me how to plunk away.

She never explained her attachment to the piano, but anybody close to her knew how essential it was in her life. Gradually, as the years passed, she began treating the piano differently, almost as a friend with whom to talk over her worries and problems. If she was feeling down, she'd avoid the light, snappy pieces, and I'd feel a deep sadness coming through whatever melody she was playing.

These beautiful haunting pieces would drift up to my room and soak into me. She wouldn't have to say anything; I could tell how she was feeling by her musical choice.

I didn't play long, but it was fun while it lasted. I turned the rows of black and white keys into numbers and the songs into puzzles needing to be solved. One of my favorite songs to play was the peppy theme to the movie *The Sting*. It was so upbeat that it never failed to cheer me up. It didn't put a smile on my father's face, though. What the hell kind of tough guy plays piano? What's next, cake decorating? He told my mom to lay off the piano teaching and took matters into his own hands. By next Tuesday I'd be learning how to break stacks of cinder bricks with my forehead and punch holes in people. My father had signed me up for karate.

I hated karate, and every Tuesday and Thursday before class I got a stomachache. I was surrounded by guys who were eager to learn how to correctly unload prepackaged fists of fury on anyone who displeased them. I was stuck in a bad version of the *Karate Kid* movie, and I couldn't turn it off.

My father wanted his only son to carry on his tradition of physical toughness. He wanted me, like him, to be able to open a can of whoopass on anybody I pleased. But what did he get? A piano player who rescued bugs. Rodney Mullen, patron saint of distressed insects.

Fortunately, my karate school went out of business. And while I never pursued the piano again, I did discover something else that would push every other interest out of my life, whether or not my father liked it. I was turning nine when a new neighbor on my block, Jack, showed me his purple metal Bonzai skateboard, and that discovery changed everything.

CHAPTER 3
SKATEBOARDS AND WEED

WITHOUT WHEELIES I MIGHT NEVER HAVE STOOD ON A SKATEBOARD. BY

age eight, I could lean back and balance on the rear tire of my bike and ride for hundreds of feet past the neighboring houses that had been built in the past few years on my block. I would cruise the neighborhood on my bike until dinner, enjoying the freedom. I rarely played with my sisters, who were now teenagers and off making out at the mall or doing whatever girls do at that age. On weekends, I stayed out all day until hunger reeled me back in.

The mad scientist of our block was Frank, a fifteen-year-old kid referred to as "The Wizard." While I had a workbench with some tools to play with, he had a massive two-car garage filled with tools and spare parts dedicated to his projects, such as a double-decker bike.

Like every kid on the block, this lanky teenager who already stood over six feet tall and laced up a size fifteen shoe had a Jones for wheelies. But unlike us, the Wizard took it to a scientific level and carefully measured and spray painted marks on a sidewalk every twenty meters. Groups of kids would gather at the wheelie strip and have contests.

The Wizard's front tire always touched down near the one hundred meter mark, the longest in the neighborhood—except for mine. The coolest guy who hung out at the wheelie strip, though, was fourteen-year-old Jack Iversen, the James Dean of the block. He wasn't popular like the jock quarterback who can knock a beer can off your head with a football at three hundred yards, he didn't swagger like a hallway hero, he was cool in the true sense of the world—he didn't care, or didn't seem to. Jack did whatever he wanted. He wore his hair or clothes however he wanted, instead of looking like he was popped off the high school assembly line. And he was a skateboarder.

Jack would usually skate in front of his house by himself. Skating fit him perfectly. It was the ultimate loner activity. There were no rules, no coaches, no teammates—you skated when and how you wanted to.

Jack was so mellow and unconventional that the two of us clicked naturally. I think his father was a brain surgeon, a very domineering man, and Jack, by regularly getting into trouble, never helped their relationship. I never got to know his mom too well, mainly because she freaked me out. She only spoke in Elizabethan English inside her house. It was as if she had learned to speak by watching a PBS Shakespeare marathon. It took me a while to understand that "Wouldst thou enjoy a feast of swine?" was her way of offering leftover ham.

Jack was the guy I wanted to be. His aloofness was like a Teflon coating allowing all weird household problems to slide off him without doing any damage, superficial or otherwise. The fact that he smoked more pot than a colony of Rastafarians might have helped him develop this calm. His family life was so tilted that he could puff away all day and his parents never suspected that their kid was a baker. I didn't think there were too many potheads a couple of centuries ago in England, so I didn't blame his mom for not noticing.

Almost every afternoon after school I bailed to Jack's house. I never hung out with my schoolmates. I couldn't relate to any of them—they were trading baseball cards while I was setting death traps in my room.

Jack had been skating one day, and he offered to let me try. I took up his offer and immediately recognized the freedom it offered. There wasn't really an established "right" way to skate, no set rules as there are in baseball. Nothing in my life up until then had allowed such total creativity. It's difficult now to try to explain what skateboarding meant to me without it sounding like cheesy movie dialogue, but I felt then the unlimited possibilities that it offered. I was generally nervous and self-conscious, but once I stood on the board those traits evaporated. I suddenly understood the transformation in my mom when she stepped on the tennis court.

This is why I have a hard time calling skating a sport—it lacks a defining structure, and it's constantly changing and evolving. It's so fulfilling, and it pushed me so hard to be creative that it felt more like an art to me. I'll read biographies that describe how different artists and composers would stay up through the night working, a feverish energy burning inside pushing them forward—and that was exactly how skating affected me from the start.

And that passion hasn't diminished over the years. The unlimited possibilities for inventing skateboard tricks continue to propel me forward as if I'm chasing the horizon—there's never going to be a finish line. Skating still has the power to wake me up at night with the thought of new possibilities and steal my attention when I see something like a fork bounce. *How could I make my skateboard flip that way?* From that first time I began riding Jack's board, only one thought obsessed me: how can I get better?

Anyway, the purple Bonzai Jack had was one tweaked-looking skateboard, something the Wizard himself might have cooked up. Back in the late 1970s, skaters were experimenting with new materials and new ways to improve skateboards. The Bonzai theory was to make the board out of metal and give it a kicktail on both ends. On the double kick front, they were about twenty years ahead of the game, though the metal idea never caught on.

Jack never let living in Florida get in the way of his becoming a cool Southern California skater. He was obsessed with having a surf style on his skateboard. At the end of the 1970s, in fact, skating was all about surf style. You had to look good just rolling down the street; no stiff arms, no squatty cockroach stance. Instead, you had to flow as if you were casually cruising down a wave. The Z-Boys defined style at that time, through their exposure in *Skateboarder* magazine, which was Jack's umbilical cord to what mattered in the skating world.

The Z-Boys were a gang of rowdy kids from the sketchy areas around Santa Monica, and they surfed and skated in the same way—aggressively. Tony Alva, Jay Adams, and Stacy Peralta were the main skateboard stars of the Zephyr surf shop team—hence, the skate gang name—and they were also the most popular skaters in the world. From what we could read, and *Skateboarder* was our only communication with "progressive" skateboarding, it didn't get better than the Z-Boys.

Jack would bomb down the hill by our house, squatting low, his lead arm thrust outward as if he was getting barreled in a monster wave, even though we lived forty-five minutes inland from the beach. But as far as I was concerned, he was the Z-Boy of the block.

REEFER MADNESS

When you're ten, age difference is a big deal. In some ways, the five years separating me and Jack might as well have been dog years. But we soon formed a third connection besides dominant fathers and a growing infatuation with skateboards.

Jack and his friends smoked weed pretty much every day, and after a few weeks of hanging around with him I was picking out seeds from my own stash, licking the Zippo paper, and sparking up. I was only ten, remember, and I hadn't done any drugs before; I hadn't been one of those kids siphoning vodka from his parents' liquor cabinet and filling it back up with water. In fact, I should have been petrified that pot smoke was even wafting near me, because if my father had ever learned that I was spending weekend afternoons sucking on the tailpipe of a bong and scoring dime bags, his anger dial would have been cranked up past ten. But I wanted to fit in.

JUST SAY NO

I spent more time studying skating than doing it in the summer of 1976. This wasn't my choice; since I didn't have my own board, it was the best I could do. I'd steal a ride on Jack's board whenever I could, usually before, during, or after a smoking session. In those brief intervals, I mainly learned how to balance on a moving object. I didn't think I'd have a problem getting my own board once I decided that I really wanted a one. After all, my parents had always been supercool about buying me or my sisters most of the stuff we wanted, so long as they didn't think it would be detrimental to us.

My parents respected that their kids did their best, and they generally rewarded us for our efforts. In our house, every matriculating Mullen aced school. It was expected that we would all come home with rows of As lining our report cards. My grade point average throughout school was higher than 4.0, because I used my nerd superpowers to complete as many extra assignments as possible.

I didn't realize my father had already formed an opinion about skateboarding. One night while we were at the dinner table I casually asked my father if I could have a skateboard.

"*Hell* no!" he boomed, as he finished chewing his food. "Not just 'no,' Rod, but *hell* no!"

This was my father's standard answer whenever he wanted someone to know that a particular conversation was not open to debate. "That's not going to happen," he snapped, as he took another forkful of spaghetti off his plate. "I just worked on a kid who smashed his head and knocked out his teeth after falling off one of those damn things."

I cursed that untalented, uncoordinated sissy-boy and his entire genetically flawed family for their weak teeth. He, they, had just ruined my life. Why couldn't he have smashed his head a little harder and gone straight to the Emergency Room, bypassing my father and his dental drills altogether?

Back in the 1970s, downhill skating was a craze. Skaters found the biggest hills, hiked to the top of them, and blasted down. Scary stuff nowadays, but back then it was even freakier: you had some seriously rickety boards with crap wheels, small wheelbases, and sketchy trucks that would loosen on their own. You didn't wonder *if* you'd get speed wobbles, you wondered *when*. And pads were more of a joke than anything else. Designed for volleyball players, and with no protective plastic shield on the front to skid on, they were just square blocks of foam wrapped in an elastic gasket that fit snugly on your leg. You might as well have licked a package of Kleenex and stuck it on your knee. You could use your pads as a compress after you fell though, so perhaps they did serve some purpose.

Still, I was unprepared for my father shutting me down. But I saw a slight glimmer of hope behind his rejection. I had asked him causally, so he couldn't be aware of my growing infatuation with skateboarding and probably hadn't given it much thought. I knew that what my father said was law, but I also knew that his "hell no" was mainly a knee-jerk reaction based on a patient he had treated.

But his rejection made me examine how much skating meant to me. I realized for the first time that skating affected me in a way I hadn't comprehended—and in many ways still can't. The nerding out with the Erector sets and booby-trapping deathballs had been preoccupations of mine, but skating was becoming an obsession.

I couldn't understand why I was getting so emotional. I somehow felt that I *needed* skating, not just *wanted* a skateboard.

Suddenly, my construction projects seemed to me like relics of a past life. That night, my life was split into two periods: B.S., before skating; and A.S., after skating.

I had to devise a plan. My mom and sisters and I had constructed a sort of underground railroad over the years, in order to avoid pissing off my father if we wanted to do something forbidden. Shopping, for instance, was a passion of my mom's. She had mink coats in her closet, expensive shoes lined up in rows on the floor, and plenty of hidden treasures stashed away at my grandma's house. These "hidden treasures" were items that my mom felt would cause a Mt. Vesuvius–sized eruption from my father, and those eruptions would have been pretty well justified—my mother bought some ridiculously expensive things, such as a bed that supposedly belonged to a long-dead king of Spain.

But skating wasn't anything I could hide at my grandma's house. There was no way to get a board and begin skating without my father's permission.

I needed somebody to help me work on him, somebody on the inside. My mom recognized that skateboarding was different from any other athletic activity I had tried. I had done karate, horseback riding, even baseball—a favorite sport of my father's—and she knew that I wasn't into any of them.

Jack pumped up my skateboard madness when he gave me an old copy of *Skateboarder* magazine with Greg Weaver carving a grind on the cover. I read every word in it, down to the fine print of the subscription card. Then I'd start again from the beginning. The longer I went without my own skateboard, the more obsessed I became. I smoked on the weekends and reread my magazine every night before I went to sleep, counting down until New Year's Eve, the date that my mother and I had decided to approach my father again.

My mom thought that my father would be in a festive mood on the last night of 1976. She had been dropping subtle hints about my love for skateboarding, adding her own opinion that it was a positive physical activity, and that if I wore safety equipment I probably wouldn't get injured.

This night had almost four months of planning behind it.

At around 10 p.m., when I noticed that my father was wearing a big smile, happy to be in his nice house surrounded by his nice family, I breathed deeply a few times and waited for a gap in the conversation. Then, sensing my chance, I jumped in headfirst.

"Hey, Dad, do you think if I was really careful, the most careful I've ever been, that maybe I could have a skateboard?"

There was a pause, a silence in the room. My mom knew how much this meant. She was probably holding her breath, too.

"If he's careful, I'm sure it'll be safe," she said. I flinched nervously. Should she have said that? Perhaps she had overplayed our hand. He might now wonder if we had been talking about this behind his back; he might be led to think that we were conspiring somehow. If he thought that, any chance of me getting a board would be killed.

I wanted to say more, to plead my case. I needed some way to tell him how skating made me feel. But I couldn't explain it, because I didn't even understand it myself.

The pause stretched on. I hadn't seen anybody in the family ever ask my father for something twice. I looked at him for clues. Was his jaw clenching? Was his stare narrowing into a glare? Were his eyes doing that thing when he got superpissed, when they appeared to change color from blue to green?

"Okay," he said.

I went numb. I hadn't expected that answer; I hadn't expected any answer, to tell the truth. I was too scared. My knees crumpled and I landed in a loose heap, exhaling hard. A little hyperventilating laugh chirped out of me, I was so happy.

"This is our deal," he continued. "You wear pads all the time. I mean all the time. If I ever catch you without pads, it's all over. No discussion—that will be it for your skateboarding."

I nodded eagerly. Then he let me know that I hadn't scored a complete victory, only a temporary one.

"First time you ever get seriously hurt, Rod, you are done with skateboarding."

I thanked my father like a death row inmate who's just been pardoned and excused myself to be alone. The rest of the night went by in a haze. I don't remember bringing in 1977 with hoots and whistles and banging pots; all I remember is silently sitting by an upstairs window that was cool to the touch and staring out at a streetlamp, my mind like a calm lake because I was going to be a *skateboarder.*

I still don't understand why skating meant so much to me at the time. I had no way of knowing then that a little over ten years later, skating would pull me out of a quagmire of depression, sleeping and eating disorders, paranoia, and suicidal urges.

CHAPTER 4
THE BEGINNING OF THE END

ON THE FIRST DAY OF 1977, I OFFICIALLY BECAME A SKATEBOARDER.

My father had made a binding agreement, and he honored it. He drove me down to Inland Surf Shop, the local skate and surf store, and watched as I meticulously picked out the components of a board. I'd been going to Inland for the past two months, and I had every detail of that shop burned into my brain; I had studied that shop as if I were cramming for a test. You could have asked me which board was the third down in the second row and I'd have piped, without hesitation, "G&S Stacy Peralta Warptail."

Naturally, I bought the same style of board I'd been obsessing about, the only one I really knew, a black Bonzai. It was a smaller model than Jack's: twenty-four inches long by six inches wide, and it had the funky double kick at the nose and tail. Without knowing it, I picked out the safest wheels I could at the time, big fat orange no-name wheels, almost as wide as the tires on my father's Caddy. They were at least three times as wide as wheels today, and so soft that it'd be almost impossible for new skaters to comprehend them. Stick a pair of bearings in a marshmallow, bolt them to your board, and you'll get an idea of how soft these things were. I could have pushed off from the top of a San Francisco hill and slowed to a stop halfway down. They lowered my statistical chances of injury significantly, since, if you don't move over three miles per hour, it doesn't hurt as much when you fall. My father bought me ACS 500s, trucks that don't exist anymore.

I'm sure my father figured that I'd goof around on this board for a year or two before moving on to something else.

SOLITAIRE

Once we got home, I padded up. The mandatory safety equipment was part of the bargain, so I strapped on my Cooper hockey helmet that had a 1970s free love hippie rainbow screened on it. The hard plastic chinstrap immediately rubbed against my neck and made a nice glowing rash. My helmet rocked back and forth, banging the hard foam and plastic edges into various sections of my head. I pulled my volleyball pads up to my knees. My gloves were so oversized that I looked like Mickey Mouse's stunt double.

I didn't immediately take my new board over to show Jack. Unlike most skaters, I didn't seek out skatemates. I wanted to relish being on my own board, concentrate fully on skating, and not be distracted by talking or looking over at somebody else. From the start I was a skating monk, relishing the solitude it afforded me. This was the first thing in my life that didn't have other people's fingerprints all over it, the first thing that completely removed me from the anxiety I felt surrounded by. I trusted skating completely and purposely lost myself in it.

I skated until bedtime, for almost seven hours, without a break for dinner.

Again, the next day, I skated all day long. When the school week started, I padded up as soon as I got home and skated until dinner. By the end of the week, I could do almost two 360s and had copied the exact body position of skaters carving grinding pools from my issue of *Skateboarder*—except I skated on flat ground, off the end of my porch.

ON THE CHAIN GANG

I skated whenever I had a spare minute. But from age five on, I had been taught that free time came after "The Chores." My parents gave us heavy doses of freedom anchored by responsibility. If we needed something, they bought it for us, or handed over a few bills, but my father also believed that salvation lay in hard labor— for men at least. My sisters had to do household chores, but

SKATING FULLY PADDED WAS THE AGREEMENT REACHED BY MY FATHER AND ME. THE SOCKS PULLED UP TO MY KNEES WERE PURELY MY OWN PROBLEM.

because we had maids at the time, they were given fairly easy duties. Since we followed a strict, old-school rule in our house, I never had to load a dishwasher or do any of their chores.

I would have gladly swapped with my sisters though. By age eight, one of my chores was mowing the lawn, and I'm not talking about a postage-sized stamp of green, either. I piloted a sit-down mower and drove back and forth until you could use our lawn as a putting green. I had to use a push mower for the hard-to-reach places, clean all the dog crap, weed the garden, and finally wash down the cement areas. It took me over three hours from start to finish, and then I had to trim the edge of the lawn, which took me almost another hour.

In addition to lawn purgatory, there were other "projects" to which I had to dedicate the majority of my childhood Saturdays. Of course, my sisters were never included in these projects; they were a manly sort of thing. My father and I were supposed to bond through sweat and sawdust as we built something together, but usually the thought of it made me stress. I didn't look forward to helping him because sooner or later I knew I was going to screw up.

These projects weren't dinky jobs, like building a coffee table; we're talking about contractor-grade projects. We might spend a month of Saturdays building a weight room off the side of the house, doing everything but installing the electrical wiring.

TRICKS ARE TREATS

Aside from Jack, there was another skater in my neighborhood, Clint, who I barely knew. Clint had built a mellow sixteen-foot—well, I guess you could call it a ramp. It's true that wood and nails had been used on this thing, but it was more like an art project than a legit ramp. He had painted a bright blue frothing wave on his quarterpipe, and at least a third of the seven hundred nails pounded into every conceivable joint of the thing poked out, just in case it wasn't dangerous enough already. You could get injured just walking past this monstrosity. I'd occasionally retreat from my skateboard monastery, take my life in my hands, and pretend to carve this huge wooden wave. Up and down I'd carve, sometimes making ocean sounds, but for me this was the beginning of the end of copying surf style. Skateboarding was branching off and coming into its own.

Two years after receiving my first skateboard, and only twenty-three hundred miles away in San Diego, Tony Hawk's brother Steve would give him his first skateboard. Tony and I would eventually be given credit—sometimes *blamed*—for popularizing technical tricks over style. Both of us were even tagged with the same behind-the-back nickname of "Robot." It wasn't a premeditated plan to overthrow vert skaters who did gnarly grinds, or freestylers who did ballet routines; it was just that technical tricks interested the both of us.

By the late 1970s, the battle between style and tricks had already begun in the skateboard world, but for me there was no question. In 1978, after coming across a picture of a skater doing a rolling handstand in *SkateBoarder*, I knew I was only interested in tricks. Even before I could do a lot of them, I began dissecting them like one dissects a frog in science class, to see how it works.

After four hours of practice, I learned stationary handstands on my board. And after two weeks of "officially" becoming a skateboarder, I could slalom between plant containers, do a few 360s, and scare the crap out of anybody watching as I wobbled around like a drunk gymnast, performing handstands on my creeping skateboard.

I had no problems in my first few months of skating, at least not with my father. He always placed an emphasis on dedication and seemed impressed by how much time I spent on my board. He became a little concerned about the collection of small scabs and bruises that covered my body from falling while down-hilling, but since it was never anything major, he shrugged it off, impressed that I never complained about my injuries.

One Saturday he surprised me by announcing that our next project was to build a ramp in the driveway. Nowadays kids can mail-order a portable kicker ramp that weighs about fifteen pounds. None of that wimpy, no commitment crap for my father—he had plans for a ramp that could double as a hurricane shelter.

So we spent all weekend measuring, cutting, and hammering until we finally had it finished. I still can't believe my father built this ramp for me. For a man who took so much pride in the appearance of his house, planting a gargantuan ramp in the driveway must have run a close second to parking a car on the front lawn. But he saw how much I loved skating and was excited about working on the ramp with me. One of my fondest memories of my father is of him building that ramp for me.

This thing was huge! (Most vert ramps at the time were only three or four feet tall.) It stood seven feet tall at the end of our driveway, which happened to be fairly steep, so that it was perfect for gaining speed before hitting it. Just in case the driveway itself didn't provide enough speed, my father also built a starter ramp at the top of the driveway.

Once the ramp was completed, other skaters began showing up to skate. Jack and I never became the skate buddies I once imagined that we'd be before I had my own board. Occasionally, I'd still smoke out with him, but even that was growing old, and it was starting to dawn on me how low I had sunk, lying to my parents to get money for weed.

One day, I simply decided I was through smoking weed and was determined to make a clean break from it. After rehearsing my speech to Jack and his older stoner friends in front of a mirror, I walked over to the usual spot where we all hooked up. I was sweating it. I knew how it would all go down: I'd respond with a clear and loud "No" after being offered a joint. Then, everybody would pause midinhale and look at each other suspiciously. These guys were all older, and even though they were always mellow toward me, I figured once I rejected their "lifestyle," they'd take it as a huge insult and beat the crap out of me.

But I was prepared with a plan, one that would no doubt make my father wince from embarrassment. I'd blurt out my decision and then curl up in the fetal position as quickly as possible, keeping my head covered with my hands at all times. Perhaps the thick fog of drug smoke that'd surround us would provide cover, so that they'd be unable to locate me for the stomp-down. Or, even more probable, perhaps they'd decide to pound me but then forget about it and just go watch TV and eat a few bags of potato chips.

I should have worn my safety equipment, I thought as I stood in front of Jack.

He exhaled a thick line of white smoke and passed the ganja to his friend. Then I told him I was done with weed. I stood nervously in front of him, lightly bouncing up and down.

"Yeah, it's probably the best thing for you, Rodney," he said, nodding.

I tightened my gut, ready to receive a wicked uppercut to the kidneys.

"You know, you're getting better and better at skating. I bet you'll get supergood at it, and smoking weed is just going to get in the way. Maybe you'll even be in *Skateboarder* one day."

The joint came back around to him. Obviously he wasn't too concerned about appearing in *Skateboarder*.

I couldn't believe it! I didn't even get a bloody nose or a bitch slap out of the whole situation. Instead, I got encouragement.

SARA THE SURFER

Once Sara got her driving license, home became little more than a pit stop for her, a place to grab the occasional meal and get some sleep. She had started surfing and lately spent her weekends at the beach. I understood why she wanted to split so often, and sometimes I wished I was driving around on some highway instead of being at home where anything could happen. Occasionally, Sara's surfer friends would come by to pick her up and throw down a session with me on the ramp. My father was worried about getting sued, so he had liability-release forms typed up and made anybody who skated in our driveway sign them. Sara's friends began

AS YOU CAN SEE, MY SOCIAL SKILLS HAVE ALWAYS BEEN AS SMOOTH AS BUTTER.

showing me simple tricks, like edgers where you pivot at the top of the ramp on one wheel, and a few other basics. I practiced every day after school and in less than a month I could do all the tricks they'd shown me.

One time my father watched me skate. "You're better than all those older guys," he said. It was one of the raddest things I can remember him saying to me.

CHAPTER 5
RUNNING AWAY FROM CONTESTS

THE MORE I SKATED, THE MORE I NEEDED SKATEBOARDING IN MY LIFE.

Riding a ramp and memorizing issues of *Skateboarder* wasn't cutting it anymore. I begged my sister or mom to drop me off at Inland Surf Shop whenever possible. Since it was only fifteen minutes away, I could usually bum a ride off somebody.

On Saturdays my mom would drop me off for an entire day of surf shop day care. I'd hang out at Inland, talking to the guys in the shop, drooling over the boards hanging on the walls, and skateboarding in the parking lot. I still mostly skated alone, but I needed the skate atmosphere around me. Bill Murray, the owner, was an awesome guy. He was a middle-aged man who used a cane and never, at least not to my face, complained about me camping out all day. He basically quasi adopted me, even letting me hang out in the back of the shop.

Keith, a nineteen-year-old sex addict who frequented the shop, was responsible for coming up with my nickname. Hardcore surfers sometimes called each other "Surf Dogs." One day, he was standing behind the counter, lounging, while I studied Bill's collection of stickers.

"Man, don't you ever get tired of lookin' at those things?" he asked in his Florida drawl. "You're like a little skate mutt." He thought that was pretty funny and started laughing. I loved the attention and the nickname fit perfectly, because of my shaggy hair and small stature. From then on, Keith called me "Mutt," and soon nobody at Inland called me Rodney.

All Keith would talk about was sex and surfing, and he was smooth enough to satisfy both needs. He always wore these smoked sunglasses and talked in the most chilled-out voice I'd ever heard. One time he drove up to where I was skating and rolled down his window.

"Check this out, Mutt." He looked at his watch. "It's only noon and I've already had sex twice with two different girls." He smiled and nodded to me. "That's right, two of them."

I smiled, happy for him.

"Mmmm, tasty." I could see his eyebrows rise behind his sunglasses. He parked his car and went to work in the shop, and I practiced some more 360s.

I had another habit that I picked up shortly afterward, thanks to my new nickname. I was still such a tweaker about talking to groups of people that I'd occasionally bark back at a person instead of answering a question with words.

FIRST SPONSOR

Bill always made sure that I was safe, and he'd always encourage me, as I'd spend the day in his parking lot, trying to spin one more 360 and learn another new trick. 360s taught me more about the essence of balancing on a skateboard than any other move. You need to be centered to stay balanced and to keep spinning. Being centered helps with every aspect of a trick. I remember not being able to do more than five and a half 360s after months of trying. Every day I would struggle to increase my record by a single spin. Then one day I nearly doubled my record. Immediately, I feared that I'd lose my spinning ability, but within a week, I was at twenty.

That was my first breakthrough in learning a trick. I had wasted months until I finally stumbled across the "secret" to 360s, of simply finding my center. I was angry at myself for wasting so much time. From that point onward I focused on the mechanics of each trick: every motion would be taken apart and cycled over and over in my head, whether I was on my board or lying in bed, from foot placement and weight distribution to where I held my shoulders and eyes.

Nine months after I bought my first board, Bill walked out to the parking lot and watched me land an old-school kickflip. (Back then you stood with your feet together in the middle of the board, hooked your toe under the board, and flipped it over.) He watched me do a few more tricks and then spin over fifteen 360s.

"If you keep progressing like you have been, Rodney, you could be the best in the world."

I thanked him, but shrugged it off. My father had always warned me never to put much value on compliments.

"How about riding for the shop?" he asked. "I'll give you a 30 percent discount on anything on the shelves and enter you in contests."

I nodded okay and thanked him. I didn't know what had just happened, but, armed with my 30 percent discount, I bought a new G&S Stacy Peralta Warptail with Road Rider wheels. Stacy, a world champion skater, was one of my heroes, and this board was a huge improvement over the Bonzai. It was designed by an actual pro skater, so it was a lot easier to learn tricks on.

After finishing my chores, I spent most Sundays, and, depending on the size of my father's weekly project, part of my Saturdays at the skate shop. I'd skate in the parking lot for a few hours, take a break, and then watch a movie like *Star Wars,* which I saw over and over, partly because I loved it and partly because it played in the theater for over a year. I'd eat popcorn, soda, and candy bars during the movie and have enough of a sugar rush to skate until the sun went down and my mom picked me up.

I'd do everything possible to bring the outside world of skating close to home. Like any skate rat—or skate mutt, as I was now known—I had a serious sticker Jones. Any leftover money went into collecting stickers. I could spend close to an hour staring through the glass display case at the cluttered rows of stickers. At night, alone in my room when I was supposed to be alseep, I'd lay my board on my bed and try out different sticker patterns. Then I'd "practice."

Somebody at the skate shop had made a mini skateboard deck out of a scrap piece of surfboard fiberglass. It was sanded down so that you wouldn't get splinters, and some of the shop workers would occasionally goof around with it when bored. I became fixated on it, and once the guys realized how obsessed I was, they gave it to me. That night, I broke apart a Hot Wheels car and Shoo Goo'd the dissected axle and wheels on my board. Out of cardboard paper and balsa wood I constructed a ramp. I clipped coat hangers and used them for the coping.

Playing with my homemade fingerboard and ramp was one of the ways I survived Monday Night Football. My father had a TV in his room, and it turned into a boys' club every Monday. No girls were allowed in the room during the game. I'd sit on the bed and play with my board and ramp as my father clapped or yelled at the TV. At commercial breaks he'd yell "go for the long bomb," and I'd run across the room and catch a pillow pass.

Every night I'd stay up with a flashlight under the covers of my bed "skating." But it wasn't all playtime—I began figuring out what might be possible, how to make the board move, how subtle shifts of weight could make the board react. Sometimes, I'd spend hours with my face inches from my miniboard, studying it, thinking, dreaming, not realizing until I looked at my alarm clock that it was midnight or 1 a.m. I'd flip my board a certain way and try to duplicate the movements over and over, memorizing a pattern for later, when I could try it on my real board.

From age ten onward, I slowly evolved into a night owl, spending more and more time awake in the hours when everyone else in my house was asleep. Sneaking around in the calmness of night, I could totally relax and do whatever I wanted—so long as I didn't make too much noise.

GREEN ACRES

One day I was skating on my ramp when one of our neighbors stormed past me to complain to my father about the "damn racket" I was making. Since I was brought up to always be respectful of my elders, I stopped skating and nodded, while our neighbor continued to bitch at me and my father. Not the correct approach, but this guy didn't know my father. He kept shouting—and then my father snapped. This was his property, his son was skating on a ramp they'd built together, and no sloppy neighbor with an overhanging belly was damn well going to step on his driveway and tell him what to do.

"You got a problem with my son skating on my driveway?" He looked at me. "Rodney, go in the house."

As I was walking inside, I heard my father say, "Let's settle right here, right now."

I believe there's a survival instinct in all of us. It kicked in for our neighbor once he saw that my father was ready to rumble. It wasn't a bluff; my father wanted to fight. It was on. Our neighbor was bigger, but he knew he was about to get destroyed. Not only that, he could see that my father *wanted* to destroy him. The guy quickly shut up and walked back to his house, and he never spoke to any of us again.

My father got the giggles later that night, recalling how he'd shut that guy down. But while we may have won the battle, we lost the war. We had to tear down our ramp.

My dad had been irritated by busybody neighbors and the growing congestion in our neighborhood. It wasn't long before he bought a big chunk of land in an area nicknamed Rattlesnake West. The new house my father built was massive, larger than our old house. It sat on more than fifty acres of property and was surrounded by farmland. It was about twenty minutes from Gainesville, the closest town, and our only neighbor was two miles away and already using the senior discount at Sizzler.

I had two concerns about our move, but I could only address one of them. I needed a paved area to skate and figured I could convert our three-car garage into a skate area. But the isolation we now lived in was a problem I had no control over. Even though I didn't hang out much with the neighbors on my old block, there was still comfort in having people close by. Now I was on my own.

If I thought I had it bad with chores *before* the move, I was in for a rude awakening. Lawn duty doubled. At ten years old, I could drive that mower like a bootlegger tearing through the backwoods. Put a couple of football fields together and that's what I had to mow every week.

On weekends, I'd get up with my father around seven and get working early so I could skate by two in the afternoon. Skating at the shop was the carrot dangling in front of my nose; if I could make it through the week, I knew I could hang out where everybody was relaxed and loved skating, and where Keith might tell another one of his Kama Sutra stories.

One weekend, Greg Wilson, an Inland employee, asked me if I wanted to hit a skatepark with a few of his buddies. It was in Kissimmee, about two hours away. I had often stared at pictures of skateparks in my editions of *Skateboarder.* They had seemed like smooth Martian landscapes to me, not just in shape and design, but distance as well. I had never actually entertained the thought of going to one of them.

As we pulled into the parking lot of the park, my face was glued to the window. The park was full of cars and skaters who were drinking soda and fixing their boards. As we walked in, I couldn't stop looking around—I'd never seen so many skaters in one place before. The sun was shining, the humidity was in the nineties, and everywhere I looked somebody was skating. I was so used to skating alone that I could literally feel the energy from this mass of skaters. It was like some sort of weird skate radiation blasting me.

At home I was constantly aware that chores or a construction project had to be done, and that I could get in trouble for not doing something that should have been done, even if I hadn't been told to do it. I had always felt tied to an invisible leash, one that reminded me that skating was a privilege, not a right, and could be taken away at any time. This skatepark was the first place to allow me to give myself up to skating and, at least for the time being, forget about any stress from home.

Compared to a modern park, the one Greg and I went to was mellower and more surf orientated, with lots of flowing banks and bowls. At the time, it was perfect for me. I skated nonstop for over three hours and stopped to buy a soda. As I sat drinking, I remember saying out loud, "This is heaven!"

Bill Murray and Greg Wilson had ulterior motives for taking me to the park. I loved skating in the park and on my driveway ramp, but by default I'd focused more on freestyle skating, since it can be done on flat ground. No matter what, I knew that I'd always be able to find a patch of concrete or a quiet section of a parking lot. Skating banks and bowls was fun, but they weren't always accessible. Bill must have known that every Sunday the skatepark held a freestyle contest, because once it was announced over the loudspeakers, Greg told me to get ready to skate—he had entered me in the contest.

When I heard my name announced, saying it was time for my run, I ran away and hid. I was too freaked out about skating *against* people. Greg found me and told me to just have fun, to go out and skate my best, but I just shook my head. He shrugged after a while and dropped it.

Greg turned out to be as stubborn as I was, but I think he knew I might warm up to the idea of skating in a contest if I had a week to muse over it. He signed me up for a contest taking place the following week.

I can never figure out my nerves at contests. Sometimes I'm relaxed, and sometimes I could swear I'm in the middle of a nervous breakdown. At my first contest, my hands were shaking as I walked out onto the freestyle area.

We're not even talking about a serious contest here; this was a handful of local kids. But I took it as seriously as a world championship. I had been raised to do the best I could, to "never walk away as a failure," as my father would say. Add to that the competitiveness my father had always ingrained in me, and you can see why I was so high-strung. I had wanted to enter that first contest, and I'd felt like a wimp for bailing out on Greg, so I had practiced

TIM SCROGGS CLOWNING AROUND. HE WAS MY EARLIEST PROFESSIONAL MENTOR AND A FREESTYLER HIMSELF.

all week for this contest. I landed everything in my forty-five-second run and won.

The prize was a small, molded steel skateboard necklace. It was awesome. What better prize could there be? As I was accepting it I had a weird epiphany; I realized, *this is a contest! This is what you have to do in freestyle contests.* Even though I had prepared for it, I wasn't sure if what I had been doing was right.

More important, I also watched Tim Scroggs skate that day. He was the first pro skater I ever saw in real life. Even though I knew he was from Florida, I assumed that he lived in some unattainable location, far away from me. Tim could spin 360s forever and had style and even sound effects—he'd whistle while spinning,

ME AND TIM SCROGGS (RIGHT), IN FRONT OF THE MIRROR I USED TO WATCH MYSELF IN AT SENSATION BASIN. WITH US ARE BARRY ZARITSKY (LEFT), AND SOME UNKNOWN DUDE.

and it would make him sound like a siren. Forget the difficulty of regular kickflips, Tim landed double ones and even double M-80s, where you landed a kickflip and quickly turned 180 degrees. I was too shy to talk to him, but I followed him around, my brain stuck on a single phrase, "That's a real pro!"

It blew my mind to see a person skating at such a high level—and live, in the flesh, not just in a magazine. It's probably incomprehensible for kids to understand how skaters got information before the mid-1980s. There was no Internet, no video magazines, and nothing on TV. My umbilical cord to the "real" skate world in those days was a few magazines that weren't even current. They usually lagged at least three months behind what they were covering, so that skaters stuck in the middle of nowhere—like me—lived in a time warp.

But the lag time wasn't the worst part—not by a long shot. I had to look at single photos in *Skateboarder* or the newsprint *Skateboard News* and try to imagine how the skater got himself and his board into that position. The sequences never captured the motion of the trick with any real detail. Most of the time, it was like finding one piece of a jigsaw puzzle and imagining what the finished picture would look like. Worse, *Skateboarder* later became infamous for publishing photos of tricks that skaters hadn't landed. But my attempts to "solve" these pictures, and my late-night fingerboard sessions, flexed my imagination about what was possible on a skateboard and in the long run made me think outside of what other people were doing. From the start I didn't look to other skaters as models to copy; I looked at my board and fantasized about what was possible.

The magazine photos and written coverage gave me a serious case of California fever. That state has always been, and continues to be, the skateboard mecca, populated with empty pools and skateparks on every block—or at least it seemed that way in my decade-old mind. My days were full of dreams of hanging out with famous pros like Stacy Peralta.

CHAPTER 6

WITH A LITTLE HELP FROM MY FRIENDS

A FEW WEEKS AFTER MY FIRST VICTORY, BILL TOLD ME ABOUT A

serious contest coming up at Kona Skatepark in Jacksonville, which was about an hour from Inland. This would be heavy—a pro event with skaters from all over the States competing. It was as if the pages of *Skateboarder* were going to come to life for me.

My mom drove me out to Kona, dropped me off, and spent the day shopping in some of her favorite stores nearby. While she was shopping, I was hoping to see some of my favorite pro skaters. At age ten, if you could have granted me a wish of meeting anybody in the world, any actor, artist, or astronaut, I would have picked Stacy Peralta.

The cool thing is that, at least back then, it was fairly easy to meet a pro and say hi or get an autograph. All you had to do was go to a contest. I didn't have the guts to talk to any of the pros though. I stood there, frozen, staring at them all as they skated. Dennis Martinez from San Diego was there, wearing his trademark hat, a fedora similar to the one Indiana Jones wears, skating as smoothly as an ice skater.

At times like that, I try to shut down every distraction around me and zero in on whatever I'm focusing on. You could have yelled in my ear and I wouldn't have heard you. Oddly, I wasn't most impressed by the tricks the pros were doing, but by how comfortable they were on their boards. You could tell they were in a different league just watching them cruising around doing nothing. They had skating so wired that they didn't appear to relate to their boards as separate objects. There was a unity of board and skater.

One guy who made a strong impression on me was Jim McCall, a smooth skater with hair down to his shoulders. He skated for Walker Skateboards and did my favorite trick at the time—a one-handed handstand. He didn't win, though; Dennis Martinez won, mainly because he did stationary space walks, a trick he was famous for, and played with his hat while he skated. At certain points in his run he'd take it off or flip it, as if playing with a hat constitutes a skateboard trick. There was an element of showmanship to freestyle skating that skaters had no opportunity for in other styles.

I still had an amateur contest to skate in, so I began practicing my run. I was entered in two of the most cursed styles of skating, slalom and freestyle. Slalom is simply going as fast as you can and weaving in and out of cones; the latter requires a lot of tricks and spins on flat ground. (It's odd to have to explain these, but I feel I have to, because both of them only exist today as fringe elements. Except for a few fossilized boards on eBay, freestyle equipment is nearly extinct.)

I tried to warm up for my contest, but it was about as hard as trying to skate in the middle of an LA freeway. There were so many skaters around that it was impossible not to get in somebody's way. I was upside down, practicing my handstands, when I heard the whizzing of wheels get louder. I tried to look up, but before I could react a skater hit me, sending me sprawling onto my back.

I looked over from the ground to see who had just used me as a speed bump and froze once I saw the straight blond hair that draped over the skater's shoulders. I knew that hair. I'd memorized pictures of it from magazines and even saw it on the TV show *Charlie's Angels* for a few minutes when a guy with a bit part whizzed by on a skateboard. There was only one person in all of skating who had hair that famous—Stacy Peralta.

"Hey, man, sorry about that. Are you okay?" he asked as he helped me up.

I nodded my head vigorously. I was better than okay. Body-checked by my favorite skater, personal contact—it doesn't get better than that! It was the next best thing to a hug, only we had used elbows and knees and at full speed.

I kept nodding, unable to speak.

"Sure you're okay?" he asked.

I nodded, silent.

"Okay. Take it easy, man."

As he skated away, I watched him, rubbing my bruised arm. I'd been wrecked by my hero and he was a cool guy!

I skated decently that day and placed third. It was my first major contest, and I was happy. Nationally sponsored amateurs had traveled to Kona from around the States (including California) to compete, and I saw some of the best skating I had ever seen. Right after the barrel jumping contest, I stalked Stacy until I worked up the nerve to ask him for an autograph. In my entire life, I've only ever asked for two autographs. The second was Henry Hester's, though I have no idea why I asked for his.

I was so awed by everything, especially that moment Stacy had crashed into me and apologized, that every detail of that day was seared in my memory. For the next year, I played it back in my head as if I was pressing repeat on an answering machine.

Another good thing came of my skating at the Kona contest. During my run, I had impressed a fellow Floridian, Bruce Walker. Bruce owned the small company Walker Skateboards, which Jim McCall skated for, and he asked me if I'd ride for him. Walker was the local skate and surf guru, and he had achieved deserved cult status in my home state. (Later on, he also coached Kelly Slater, arguably the best surfer in history.) His small but very influential company was huge in Florida. Unfortunately, it didn't have the same impact on the rest of the country.

I was totally retarded about board sponsorship. How did it differ from shop sponsorship? Bruce explained that he'd send me free Walker products and coach me for contests. Nowadays, a lot of skaters are overinformed about sponsorships and about turning pro. From what I can see, many of the fringe benefits of a professional skater's life get promoted, while the basic reason why we skate—for the joy of it—goes ignored.

Until the early 1990s, there was no real skate fashion, no rich pros adorned with pounds of "ice," and fame wasn't based on much of anything outside of your skating and your personality. But I'm glad I was clueless then, because otherwise I'd feel robbed now. I discovered skating without all the commercial hype and baggage. My personality dictated what direction I took my skating, and even though it was the total opposite of other skaters, we appreciated one another.

Bill at Inland was bummed that I was going to ride for Walker. "I can't compete with what Walker could offer you," he said. "But I'm happy for you. You should do this." I'll always appreciate that Bill encouraged me to skate for Walker. He called Bruce up to make sure it was a good deal for me, and that I would be taken care of properly. I still skated at Bill's shop most weekends, so that my relationship with Bill never changed.

I guess my mother and father were cool with my Walker sponsorship, but it wasn't as if they were Little League parents, standing at the sidelines of every contest screaming their heads off. My mom was proud that I had placed third in a big contest, but she really had no idea about sponsorship. She hauled me to contests all over Florida but never got more involved than that. She was happy if I was happy. My father didn't pay too much attention to my skating. Sometimes he'd watch me skate for a few minutes if he was walking by, but we rarely talked about it.

During the week I was stuck in the middle of hundreds of acres of farmland, with a farmer I never met as my neighbor. But I skated every night in our garage, hour after hour, sometimes imagining that I was skating with the pros.

SKATE COACH

Bruce Walker made a huge impact on my life. Every three months or so, I'd take a five-hour bus ride to his house in Melbourne to skate with him and other team riders. My father didn't want me to slack on the chores, so I would finish them during the week if I knew a trip to Bruce's was coming up.

I've always been lucky to have mentors pop up throughout my life, and Bruce was the first serious one to devote a lot of energy to me. He was old school, a "coach" in a way that doesn't exist anymore. When I began skating, teams were smaller and tighter than they are today, and almost always somebody on the team helped with everything from personal problems to landing tricks to planning contest runs.

Bruce helped me think about contests in a more strategic way. I soaked up all the knowledge I could from him. More important, those trips to his house were minivacations. I bunked and skated with the other Walker teammates, like Jim McCall, and it felt like a skate camp, where you ate, slept, and dreamt of skateboarding.

I saved everything from my trips to Bruce's house: bus tickets; candy bar wrappers; receipts from stores; soft drink cups; broken shoelaces. In my room I cleared out a drawer and made a mini-shrine for all my souvenirs. Whenever I was feeling low, I'd pull out my drawer and go through my organized piles of trinkets, getting lost in the carefree feeling I had felt at skateparks or at Bruce's house. These little scraps were like batteries from the outside world that recharged me.

HIP PADS

I entered a few local contests that skate shops or skateparks put on, never as big a deal as Kona had been, but I liked having a way to mark my improvement as a contest skater. At one of these tiny local contests I met Barry Zaritsky, a skate shop owner who was dedicated to making skating safer. He was a skinny guy, around six feet tall, with a bushy mustache, and he was the most energetic person I had ever met. He threw his seemingly inexhaustible powers into everything he did.

Barry watched me skate with my full safety equipment on, and if there was anything he loved, it was seeing somebody wearing full pads. He was a zealot about preventing injuries and was always researching innovative rehabilitation methods. He introduced himself to my mom, thanked her for having me wear full safety gear, and awarded me a pair of his SIO Barry padded shorts. They were handmade and had foam sewn into the hip. He announced that they were a prize for wearing a helmet while freestyling.

CONTESTS

Bruce's coaching helped me structure a contest run, and he had such faith in me that I thought, *Wow, he thinks I can do this?* And that made me skate harder.

I won the third major contest I entered against other sponsored skaters from Florida. I had absorbed my father's attitude toward goals, and after I won that contest I knew that if I fell behind I would only have myself to blame. It was the same as my attitude toward school; after earning straight As, even an occasional B on a quiz would sting.

DANCING MONKEY AND THE ORGAN GRINDER

My first demo was a bit surreal—more like a dancing monkey show than an organized event. Sara and her surfer friends took me to a surf industry trade show in Melbourne, a city on the coast of Florida about three hours away from our house by car. Sometimes I went with Sara to the beach, but I never surfed. Instead, I cleared rocks out of the parking lot and skated. The trade show was more like a surf fair: shops had set up booths; a few pro surfers autographed pictures; and surf movies played in a small theater.

At the show, my sister and her gang dragged me to one of the surf movies. Halfway through the movie, one of the reels broke, and the guys pushed me up on the stage and told me to skate. I was nervous at first, but once my feet hit my board, my anxiety faded and I just wanted to land tricks. After a few minutes of skating, I stopped to catch my breath and heard clapping. I looked out into the crowd and saw that everybody was hooting and cheering for me.

People patted me on the back, and later some people in the crowd told me how much they liked my skating. I stared at my Vans and nodded into my chest. They were praising me, but I couldn't deal with it and mumbled thanks without making eye contact.

Skating was becoming my main form of communication—it was much easier for me than talking. I was at the point where I had learned all the basics and could make up my own tricks, and, little by little, my own style was starting to come through. No two

BARRY ZARITSKY HOLDING A SAFETY SEMINAR WHILE USING ME AS A PROP.

skaters look the same on a board, and I've always felt that style comes from within a person and to a certain degree is a reflection of his or her personality. Watch a skater sometime, and you'll be able to get a sense of who he or she is, just by following the style. A skater like Kevin Harris, a freestyler on his way to becoming Canadian champion at the same time that I was coming of age, was smooth and mellow on his board, just as he was in person. On my board, I was like a computer spitting out technical tricks, the exact opposite of Kevin.

CONCAVE BOARDS

Clearwater, a skatepark about three hours from my house, announced that it was holding a major pro contest. I went, and this time, though I felt awed by the pros, I studied their tricks and watched how they practiced. Instead of being blinded by idolization, I was like a sponge—soaking up everything I could.

The first pro I saw was Tony Alva, arguably the most famous skater in the world at the time, and a former world champion. I was riding a standard flat Walker board at the time, and I noticed that Alva was cruising on a warped-looking board, its side edges rising higher than its middle. It took me a while to realize that this was the first concave skateboard I'd ever seen. Nowadays it's a standard design, but back then it was cutting-edge.

I had been entering the monthly Kona contests and winning them, but it was strictly a bush league affair. They were basically events to keep skaters interested in their park, and after I had won five in a row, the organizers wouldn't let me enter anymore, because they felt it discouraged other kids. They'd let me skate, but my runs weren't scored.

But Clearwater was different. This was a major contest that would be written up in *Skateboarder,* and it had been organized by the professional skateboard circuit, so all the big guns had come to compete. I was so excited at the chance to just skate with them that I didn't even feel nervous.

WITH A LITTLE HELP FROM MY FRIENDS **57**

Some of the skaters I had competed against—or hadn't been allowed to compete against—in the Kona contests entered the amateur freestyle contest, so I entered the pro. In my mind, I wasn't really pro, and I told the contest organizers that I didn't want to compete for prize money, and they were cool with it. Back in the 1970s and even through most of the 1980s, there were lots of pro/am contests where amateurs could compete against pros yet remain amateur.

My run went fine, but I never expected to place in the top ten. I didn't care, either; I was just amped to be skating with so many of the pros I looked up to.

Amazingly, I placed third, right after Tim Scroggs and Jim McCall, two skaters whose talents I looked up to. From then on, contests became my only reference point, because I'd only really skated in isolation at my house and didn't know if the tricks I had been inventing were weird or innovative or just plain goofy looking. I wondered what other skaters would think of me trying to do these unorthodox tricks.

Tim Scroggs was a ripping skater, and in my mind he had the edge over everybody else, since he was sponsored by the newly formed Powell and Peralta. Stacy had quit G&S Skateboards and partnered with George Powell, who was known then for making fast wheels called Bones. Powell immediately created cool offbeat ads that promoted the arty attitude of the company. Stacy had already recruited some of the best skaters in the world, and he was quickly surpassing his abilities as a skater by becoming the greatest talent scout in the history of skating.

Powell instantly became the coolest company in skateboarding, in my mind, not only because Stacy was my favorite skater at the time, but because it was the vanguard of the "new" skating. Suddenly, the other companies seemed stale, as if they were a few steps behind. Powell created an image that was an explosion of art, humor, and new skating. Everybody could sense that skating was going through a metamorphosis—though, unfortunately, this was happening at the same time skating's popularity was dropping. The foundation of skating, surf style, was evolving into a more trick-based style, and this might have contributed to the dramatic drop in participants, along with a generational swing in terms of the audience. Older skaters were moving on to other things, and the new skating generation wouldn't get interested for another few years. By 1979 though, the new, more technical style of skating was emerging. Talented skaters like Tim Scroggs were inventing their own tricks, and I knew there was a lot I could learn from them.

THAT'S MY MOTHER AND FATHER LEANING AGAINST THE WALL AS MONTY NOLDER ACCEPTS HIS TROPHY AT ONE OF THE FIRST PRO CONTESTS I EVER ATTENDED.

CHAPTER 7

THE KARATE KID SCHOOL OF SKATING

BARRY ZARITSKY WAS OFFERED A JOB MANAGING A NEW PARK NEAR

my house called Sensation Basin, and, after accepting it, he moved into an apartment near Gainesville. Barry was now in the hood, only fifteen minutes away from me. Tim Scroggs also got a job at the park. At the tail end of the 1970s, being a top pro skater didn't always mean that you actually made a good living at it.

Sensation Basin became a retreat for me, a place to concentrate on nothing but learning tricks. It totally replaced my sessions at the Inland Surf Shop parking lot. Even though there were lots of skaters at the park, I usually stayed by myself, and I was too nervous to start a conversation with Tim.

A big surprise came from Barry. After a week of watching me skate—fully armored, of course—he approached me for a chat.

"Rodney," he said, nodding, "you are going to be the best, and I'm gonna help get you there."

Immediately afterward, he began giving me pointers. Barry wasn't a coach like Bruce Walker; he was more like Mr. Miyagi from the *Karate Kid* movies, in that he changed the way I thought about skating—often using metaphysical lingo I didn't understand. As it was, I was making progress, but Barry pushed me to another level. He adjusted my mental outlook by talking to me about vibrations and ways to affect people on a subconscious level through my skating—really far-out stuff. He even tried to change my diet. Every time I bought something with sugar in it, he'd slap his hand down on it before I could pick it up. "I'll buy that back from you for double the price, Rodney." But I liked my sugar.

After two weeks, Barry planned a workout regimen for me. I was happy to do it, and it seemed natural after all the athletic influence my father had exerted. It began with running three laps forward, then three backward around a small pond in the center of Sensation Basin. The excitement jacked up a few levels after an alligator moved into the body of water. The thought of tripping into the pond and being served up as a meal made those backward runs end a little quicker.

Barry had this idea about not relying on your eyes, which was akin to the *Star Wars* invocation to "use the force." He ranted

APPARENTLY I'M BUMMED ABOUT SOMETHING. PROBABLY HAD SOMETHING TO DO WITH BARRY NOT LETTING ME EAT MY FOURTH CANDY BAR OF THE DAY.

RODNEY MULLEN

about how much I overused my eyes, and next thing I knew, everything from tying my shoes to jogging had to be done without looking. Finally, I had to do entire contest runs looking straight ahead. I was scolded if I looked down at my board.

Having a supporter like Barry, who was as amped about my skating as I was, really accelerated my development. Whether he was talking about the evils of sugar in peanut butter, or the importance of skating with your head up, he radiated passion, as he still does today.

The time between the two contests, the 1979 Oceanside amateur contest and the 1980 Oasis pro contest (roughly the span of a year), was the most stressful and creative time of my entire life. It began when I was still twelve, and it ended just after my fourteenth birthday. My father had begun hinting that he thought my energy was being misdirected by skating, and the pressure of those words acted like rocket fuel to propel my skating after my thirteenth birthday.

OCEANSIDE

I now had two coaches—the metaphysical Barry and the seasoned Bruce Walker—to guide me toward my future as a professional skater. Bruce knew that I had to get out of Florida if I wanted to compete against more-experienced skaters. I had already competed against some California amateurs at the Clearwater contest, and this had given me a hint of what to expect. Bruce told me in May 1979 that one month from then, in June, the biggest amateur freestyle contest of the year was going to be held in Oceanside, and that I needed to get to the West Coast to see if I was ready to compete at their level.

There was one problem: I had a grocery list of obstacles in front of me. Who would chaperone me? I was only twelve. Who would buy my ticket? Who would pay for the expenses of the trip?

I talked to my mom about it, not to try to convince her, but just to let her know that I was going crazy dreaming about entering this contest, since I couldn't skate in any local contests. I didn't want to turn pro; I just wanted to keep skating, to keep taking it further. She understood my problem but couldn't think of a solution.

The surfer who lived down the hall from me, Sara, was responsible for altering the course of my life. She was graduating that summer, and in a few months, she made it clear, she would be moving out of the house. Listening to Sara talk, I had an image in my mind of her coming home in a graduation gown, kissing us good-bye, then peeling out of our long driveway and speeding off.

Sara did something that I'll always be grateful for—she chose a trip to California as her graduation present and offered to take her little brother along for the ride. Now, that's love. At home, we were still the antimusketeers, each one of us acting for himself or herself, but Sara had always been in my corner. On weekends, she'd occasionally drop me off at Sensation Basin and watch me skate for a while. And whenever we were out of the house and were together, she was as supportive as anybody has ever been to me.

She arranged the date of her trip to coincide with the Oceanside contest, and when the day arrived, my mom drove us both to the airport. I had never been on a plane before and could not believe that I would be landing in California in less than seven hours. I had studied *Skateboarder* magazine for years and knew of many of the hot skating spots, but I couldn't imagine what it would really be like to set foot in the mecca of skateboarding.

CHAPTER 8

WINNING BUT REALLY LOSING

I INHALED AS DEEPLY AS I COULD AFTER STEPPING OFF THE PLANE.

I smiled like an idiot as I walked down the metal stairs onto the Los Angeles International Airport tarmac and plodded toward the terminal. Inhaling the polluted Los Angeles air made me feel deliriously alive.

Sara rented a car, and we drove an hour and a half south on Freeway 5 toward Oceanside. I must have scared more than a few drivers we passed, because my face was almost smashed into the window as I stared at the side of the highway.

I couldn't get over how free people in Oceanside appeared to be. Girls in short shorts roller-skating, surfers waiting for waves as they bobbed in the water—everybody seemed so carefree. I constantly said to myself, "These people are *living*!" They all appeared to be doing exactly what they wanted to be doing.

The contest was held at an outdoor amphitheater about twenty feet from the beach. *Skateboarder* magazine later reported that the skaters came from approximately twelve states and a number of foreign countries, including Belgium, Brazil, and Canada. The day before the contest, Oceanside was packed with contestants going through their runs. You could barely skate more than five feet without having to dodge somebody. I managed to find a little area away from most people and worked on my tricks.

I had no idea what to expect. It had been over six months since my last contest, and that had been against less-seasoned competition. I was bummed because Oceanside had also been a pro contest for the past four years, but a conflicting contest at the Del Mar Skate Ranch, a famous skatepark twenty minutes to the south, forced Oceanside to go strictly amateur. But a few pro freestylers would be judging tomorrow, among them Steve Rocco. At the time, he was generally considered the most progressive freestyler.

Freestylers were considered the nerds of skating. Freestylers developed smaller boards than vert skaters, making them easier to maneuver and flip around. Most skaters choreographed their routine to music and made sure they did the required maneuvers. That's right, you read correctly—*required* maneuvers. An example for the pros was a mandatory two "upside-down tricks," such as headstands on a board. For every requirement you missed, points were docked. Besides the required moves, though, freestyle was left to the skater's imagination. Some skaters cruised around doing weird gymnast tricks, like front-flips off their boards.

Over ten thousand people watched the Oceanside contest, but it was evident that skating was sliding in popularity. Most of the spectators just happened to be at the beach and were curious to know what everybody else was watching. *Skateboarder* magazine wrote, "The fad may be dead but as this Championship has shown, the sport has matured and the level of skating continues to increase at a phenomenal pace."

Everybody else entered in the contest appeared to know what was expected. I was nervous because my skating was so different, and I assumed I was behind the progressive California skaters. There were so many different styles that I don't know how they were judged. The guy who won the sponsored men's division had his face painted up like a mime. Worse, he was riding a Powell board and wearing a yellow Powell T-shirt. My dream team was being violated before my eyes by a guy who looked like a slumming circus performer.

The other contestants also confused me. Many were doing strange runs that ended with them actually stepping off their board and doing some kind of disco dance step. For some reason I thought they were doing their freestyle runs the "correct" way.

The only guy who blew me out of my safety equipment was Steve Rocco. He was only goofing around during practice, but still—it was like seeing the future of freestyle skating. He was already years ahead of anybody else. I stalked him around the contest so that I wouldn't miss anything he did. I wanted to ask him for an autograph, but the guy scared the crap out of me. He was loud and constantly made sarcastic remarks.

The only person I met at Oceanside was an amateur freestyler. He was a fellow nerd, and we talked about math. He casually pointed out a striking lady in a red pair of shorts that used about as much material as a single sock, who had a chest that defied gravity.

"Man, there's lots of hookers here today, huh?" he asked.

I nodded, uncertain of what else to do. I stared at the lady thinking, *Oh, so that's what a prostitute looks like.* The hooker traffic was pretty light in the farmland where I lived.

I skated in the sponsored boys division, 11–13 years old. My nerves settled after I got in contest mode, hearing Barry's words in my head. My age group was the minor leagues—there were still three age groups above me, and the skaters in those groups were considered the heavy hitters that industry people watched.

I stayed on for my entire run and won the thirteen and under category. I had the best cheerleader I could have asked for in Sara, who did everything but wave pom-poms from the sidelines. After I received my trophy, she was beaming with pride. She kept saying, "That's my brother! The champ!"

Sara called our parents and told them that I'd won. They were fine with it, they congratulated me, but they didn't get nearly as excited as my sister. I didn't really want to spend time talking on the phone anyway; I wanted to focus on absorbing everything around me. We walked around Oceanside that night and Sara got hit on by a few marines stationed at the nearby Camp Pendleton. Early next morning we left for San Francisco.

NOR CAL

I was relaxed. The California attitude soaked into me, but deep in the back of my mind, I heard the whisper, *this is all a temporary freedom, Rod, don't start fooling yourself.* I absorbed everything, knowing that when I got back home I'd need these California

I LIKE THIS PHOTO. I ACTUALLY LOOK NORMAL IN IT.

memories stored and sealed so that I could open them and cheer myself up.

It was about a seven-hour drive from Oceanside to San Francisco. "The City," as San Francisco is known to people in the area, has a totally different vibe than Southern California. Everything is packed in tight, creating a fusion that energizes you.

Once we checked into the hotel and ate, I went out to skate. I found a quiet spot in the parking lot and skated for an hour and then cruised around checking out the city. I'd stop every few blocks and skate some more. I made it to the famous Embarcadero and skated down the row of piers that line the bay. There's also a walkway that goes around the bay, and it's usually filled with people looking out at the waterfront.

I was concentrating so hard on my tricks that I didn't notice people had gathered around me until a half-dollar coin rolled past me. Once the first coin hit the ground, other people began tossing money. I skated for another fifteen minutes, and by then the sidewalk was clogged by the growing crowd. I didn't want to stop skating, since that meant I might have to deal with some of the people trying to talk to me. I buried my head in my tricks and blocked out most everything else. But it got too weird and I stopped after a while. A few people complimented me, but luckily nobody wanted an extended conversation.

Once people knew the show was over, they tossed even more money. I had a pile of change that made my shorts sag down after I'd filled my pockets. My first job! I had made money skating, and by the "official" rules of various governing skateboard organizations, I was not allowed to make cash skating unless I was pro. I wasn't worried, though; I just thought it was funny. Anyway, skating was becoming deader by the day, and these organizations were going out of business due to lack of members.

Sara and I stayed in San Francisco for a few more days. Every night after dinner I'd skate around, and everything about California seemed magical to me. Even the trash blowing around on the streets seemed better than Floridian garbage.

The plane ride home sucked. I was saturated by depression; the closer we got to our departing gate, the crappier I felt. As we walked through the San Francisco airport, I saw a spent copy of the *San Francisco Chronicle* lying on a chair. It reminded me of everything I was leaving behind.

I stared out the small plane window as we sped down the runway and lifted off. The houses shrank, the people became smaller and smaller, until finally they shrank out of sight. Were they savoring every minute of the existence in California, I wondered? Were they worthy of living in such a paradise?

Once we cut through the clouds and had officially left California I sank back into my seat, slipping into a depression coma. I hoped there'd be a mechanical problem or some sort of delay forcing us to turn around. Waiting on the tarmac for hours was better if it meant we were still in California.

THE END

It didn't take long to find out why my dad was so unusually happy about my contest win. He said, "I'm glad you won, Rod, you've proved all you need to prove—you're the best. Now it's time to stop and concentrate on another sport, something worthwhile, like golf. That's a sport where athletes *really* compete." His reaction was the opposite of Sara's, which made me miss her even more now that she had moved out of the house.

My father consistently told me that I had lots of "native ability," but praise was only part of his message. Obligations are bound to every talent—that was a strong part of his code. Once skating became an integral part of my life, he saw that it was pushing other sports out.

It seemed like the Oceanside contest was the rock that loosened the avalanche, and from that point on skateboarding became the central focus of his frustration anytime I "screwed up." Suddenly, a lawn edge that looked sloppy or a forgotten chore seemed to him a symptom of the same problem. "It's all you think about," he'd often yell when he spotted a misdeed. "That goddamn skateboarding. Instead of thinking about your job, you're daydreaming about that waste of time."

I spent at least one day a week on one new chore—sanding or filing some part of the mower or other tractor attachment until the flaky rust was gone. Next I had to slather a coat of yellow paint on the metal and watch as the rust ate through *that*. Naturally, most of the damaged sections were hard to reach or in nooks and crannies, which broke the pace and made me look even slower and more "distracted." The good news was that, according to my father's code, I was allowed some freedom if I was diligent in meeting his expectations. After I finished the list of chores he gave me, I could do whatever I wanted. At least, this was true for a little while.

In the two months following the Oceanside contest, I started to sense that my skating life was endangered. My father knew that *I* knew he wasn't a skateboarding fan, and every day when he got home from work and saw me practicing, it increased the tension. I tried my best to avoid angering him the only way I knew—staying out of his way.

I fantasized more and more about escaping to the outside world, where I'd feel calmer and safer. I couldn't figure out how to stop irritating my father and continue skating at the same time. And the more I thought about it, the more frantic I became and the more I clung to skating. It was the only thing I had.

I only had two other interests: studying math problems and reading the Bible. My family was never overtly religious, though we went to church at times when I was young, particularly on the holidays. Eventually only my mom and I would go, and my father said the reason I went was to avoid my chores. I began casually reading a children's Bible on my own when I was seven, and after a few years I was flipping through a few pages of the adult version each night. I had a Casio digital watch with a timer and I made sure my reading sessions lasted twenty minutes. Like skating, reading the Bible was an escape for me—something complex that I could examine from different angles and think about on multiple levels. I didn't have any close friends to talk with, and for the most part problems weren't really discussed around the house. The Bible provided support for me.

My days were all about skating though. I'd find a way to Sensation Basin as often as possible. Barry had begun arranging demos at any place that was interested in skating, and the two of us would go, me skating and him conducting a safety seminar.

Barry not only looked the opposite of my father—loose, grinning, with fuzzy red hair and a big mustache—but he was also my father's opposite regarding passion for my skills on a board. He was always pumping me up Rocky style, nothing but positive energy blasting from him. "You can do this! Go for it!" he'd say. I had always been on my own before, and here was a friend who was a manic cheerleader. I couldn't believe that somebody would care for me that much.

My mom invited Barry over for dinner one night so my father could check him out and make sure he could trust him to take care of me, since we were starting to take bigger and longer trips together. From my dad's point of view, I knew Barry would be the oddest guest to ever grace our table. We'd occasionally have some of my parents' professional friends over for dinner, but they were doctors or lawyers. Barry was from another world, and he allowed his mellow hippie attitude to flow. But if there was one thing about Barry, it was that he didn't bullshit: he called it like he saw it. Considering that Barry and my father represented opposite poles of the social spectrum, I feared that this dinner party could be the last supper for me and skateboarding, but it passed uneventfully, thank God. (A few years later, when Steve Rocco sat down at the same table, things really got exciting. I hightailed it to my room after my father challenged the both of us to a fight.) Barry charmed both my parents, naturally, and even though my father had a problem with him being a "hippie," he didn't strike him as one of those "bad" hippies. In fact, my father respected Barry's straightforwardness.

WINNING BUT REALLY LOSING 71

Because my parents trusted Barry, they gave me a lot more freedom to do demos or to skate at the park until it closed at midnight on the weekends. Some weekends we'd have three or four demos booked and I'd leave on a Friday night and not return until Sunday night, the two days spent frantically driving from one location to the next. Barry would demo anywhere—we even drove over twenty hours to a demo once. He had a beat-up camper van that blew this blue smoke all over the state, as we traveled to demo after demo. Always scrimping on cash, we survived on boxes of whole wheat crackers and jars of peanut butter. Jay Jr., Barry's dog who rode shotgun, usually ate more than his share.

Our little exhibitions weren't like demos nowadays; they weren't carefully planned events with crowds of thousands and advertisements on TV and radio. These were budget events. Kevin Harris, the Canadian freestyle champion, screened his own sign and organized demos at his local mall for whatever money he could get, sometimes fifty bucks, but usually for free. Like him, I was also in heavy rotation for school demos. Every other week I skated in school gymnasiums to the applause of kids my age. Because of my GPA, and because of the experimental nature of my school, I had no problem cutting certain classes.

My favorite demos were for kids. Usually all the students would come into the school gym and sit around its edges as Barry gave a speech about skateboard safety and explained what I was doing while I skated. The sole part of the demo I hated was when he demonstrated the importance of pads. He'd bounce an egg on some pads to show how much impact they absorbed, and it was my job to catch the egg when it bounced up. But an egg is oblong, so I could never predict what sort of bounce it would take. It was like throwing a football on the ground and trying to catch it. I never broke an egg, but I silently cursed every time he dropped one of those damned things on a pad.

Young kids are so open to whatever is happening around them. They'd cheer and clap like a pack of overjoyed monkeys. They'd look at what I was doing and decide whether they liked it or not.

There were no "cool guy" filters, and I can't remember anyone ever mocking me, as strange as some of those demos were.

I also skated in occasional parades, which were always *surreal*. I skated forward ten feet, stopped, did a few tricks, and waited for the Shriners, the generous geezers on the miniature motorbikes suited up in dress jackets and Arabian fezzes, to catch up with me. The horses sometimes crapped as they walked along the parade route, and one time as I was concentrating on a rolling handstand I plowed through a steaming pile.

A RARE PHOTO OF ME AT SENSATION BASIN WITH MY HELMET OFF, ON BREAK FROM DEMO PRACTICE.

RECRUITMENT

Like a lot skaters of the time, I was mad with Powell and Peralta fever. Everybody knew this company was different. Stacy and his buddy Craig Stecyk were turning Powell into a successful art project, and they had the best skaters in the world.

As much as I appreciated what Bruce had done for me, we both realized the limitations of Walker Skateboards. Bruce had a huge name in Florida, but compared with Powell, his company was small and couldn't afford to do much more than give me free product and coaching.

Bruce knew this before I did, and I think he realized that the more he pushed me to improve, the closer he came to losing me. Going to the Oceanside contest, after all, was his idea. He stressed that I needed to keep entering contests in California if I wanted to keep progressing.

Tim Scroggs had already joined Powell and Peralta. He was famous in the wordwide skating community, and that world was shrinking by the day.

After a few months of skating at Sensation Basin, I got to know Tim, and he eventually asked me if I wanted to skate for the Scrogg Squad. Powell's skaters were called the Bones Brigade, so I assumed that Tim was inviting me to join a farm team of sorts. I didn't care, though—I was panting just to get flowed Powell product.

It's funny how, as a kid, you can't see outside your local area. Until writing this book, I believed that "the Scrogg Squad" was a legitimate group or company under Powell. When I mentioned this to a friend of mine recently, he stared blankly at me, a quizzical look coming over his face. As far as I know now, nobody outside of Florida, probably nobody outside of *Sensation Basin,* had ever heard of it. But apparently Tim had spoken to Stacy and hooked me up in a casual way. I was basically on the B team, which was sponsorship-lite. I got some free gear, but it was up to me to show Stacy I had what it took. I was on a probation of sorts; I wasn't officially on the team, and there were no ads or contests to travel to.

Unfortunately, my father believed I had what it took—and wanted to put a stop to it before it spun further out of control. When I turned thirteen, my father decided he'd had enough of my skating.

A few months before he laid down the ultimatum, I began to sense that our relationship was eroding. His threats of enrolling me in military school came more and more frequently now. It was harder to avoid staying out of trouble, and impossible to do anything 100 percent right in his eyes.

One weeknight, after skating in our garage, I walked inside the house and saw my father in the kitchen, fuming about something. He noticed me come in, and I did what I always did—smiled and bowed my head slightly to avoid eye contact. I nervously played with a wheel as he faced me.

"You don't do anything right. You're always thinking about skating," he said, staring holes through me. I didn't know what I had done wrong. A long pause followed, and, whenever there was a long pause from my father, I knew the firing pin was about to drop. "This is going to stop soon," he said and turned away.

I couldn't move. My body temperature dropped and I felt dead. There had been no wiggle room in that comment. I had done everything I could to keep my skating from being taken away, but it was no good, it was impossible. To him, skating had no future, and I was just dithering my life away.

A few days later he continued our conversation at the dinner table.

"Rodney," he said evenly, calmly beginning a speech. My mom ate quietly; she knew that there was no point trying to stop him, which would only make whatever was going to happen worse. My head dropped automatically as I listened. "You can keep skating until the end of next summer, but once school starts, after you turn fourteen, it's time to move on. You're growing up, and you need to start thinking about your future," he said.

He couldn't blame every minute mistake of mine on skating, and I think he knew that. If anything, I was doing a better job at my chores and at school than I had been doing before skating, because I knew what was at stake.

But in a way, I had seen it happen before. Sara had been given the same deal with dancing. If there's a line that runs through our family, it's dedication. My mom enjoyed raising roses: she was head of a rose gardening club and won multiple prizes over the years for her roses. My father excelled at his moneymaking ventures, and, of course, his dental practice. And Sara had been a dance nut—as passionate about dancing as I was about skating. By her teenage years, she was spending three or four nights a week going to classes, and in the summers she studied dance in New York. She ended up playing the starring role in the local dance company's production of *The Nutcracker,* but all that ended for her when she turned sixteen and my father made her quit.

He said he was worried about her feet and her future. She freaked out, naturally. To put it simply, she was "devastated"— that was her word for it. For months afterward, she withdrew into a shell, gained weight, and shut down, trying to figure out a way to cope with having this huge part of her life torn out of her.

Now, it was my turn; I would go through a waiting period before I suffered the same fate. I knew my time was up, so I doubled and tripled my efforts toward skating.

My routine changed. I'd come home from school, pad up as quickly as possible and literally run into the garage and start skating. On the weekends, after spending hours on my chores, I'd rush over to Sensation Basin. The second I stepped on my board I'd start the timer on my Casio digital watch, not a moment sooner. On every pee, drink, or food break, I stopped my watch timer. I told myself I wasn't finished until I had skated ten hours on the weekends and two each weeknight, down to the second.

The first half hour of my weekend routine was dedicated to warming up, doing tricks but not worrying about consistency. For the next three hours, I'd break a contest run I was working on down into threes. Since contest runs lasted two minutes, I'd work on them in forty-second segments, practicing them over and over until I could do each segment without looking at my board. Barry had a serious fixation on the number three, so we used it as a foundation for everything we did. I broke my run into threes, I stretched three times, ran around the lake three times, landed tricks three times, and then landed tricks three times without looking at my board. The last ninety minutes of my sessions were dedicated to learning new tricks.

Those last minutes were often the most intense. But they were also the most enjoyable of my skating sessions. Contests were a necessary evil for me; my real attraction to skating has always lain in the innovation.

Over the next few months, I invented rail flips, helipops, and 50–50 Caspers. Stuck in my garage, I had no idea what freestylers around the world were doing. But I assumed that whatever it was, it would be better than anything I was coming up with. With less than a year left to skate, I felt I needed to push myself harder.

I began keeping a skating notebook. I jotted down ideas for tricks and noted observations I'd made on how my board flipped, how different foot placement affected tricks, or how long it took me to fix problems and derive variations off new ideas. Then I'd rate the entire session, giving myself a grade as though it was a school report card.

SKATING WITH TIM SCROGGS. IF IT WEREN'T FOR HIM, I MAY NEVER HAVE MET STACY PERALTA.

CHAPTER 9
TURNING PRO

IT WAS GETTING OBVIOUS TO ANYBODY WHO SKATED IN 1980 THAT

the sport wasn't going to last much longer unless something changed. Sensation was open until midnight, but it survived mainly by catering to the next fad—roller skating. On Friday and Saturday nights Sensation was infested with roller boogie couples groping each other as they cruised around the alligator pond. Sensory overload was achieved by hiding multicolored lights in tree moss.

Occasionally there were complaints about a shaggy little kid running backward around the pond against the flow of roller-skating traffic. And occasionally the more distracted couples would spot me too late and be forced to dive into the weeds to avoid a collision. That little kid was followed by a jogging hippie shouting metaphysical phrases and every so often screaming an encouraging, "Faster! Faster!"

Most complaints went unvoiced, especially after the roller skaters noticed that the manager was the mustachioed man doing the chasing. Off the loop stood an area where skaters could do stationary moves, and, since nobody used it, I staked my claim and practiced there.

Phil Chiocchio, the owner of Sensation, bought full-length mirrors and lined the back of the building where I skated with them. After I had learned to do a trick without looking at my board, Barry made me learn how to do it while looking at myself in the mirror. His goal was to have me do my final, hardest move staring right at the judge. When he spoke of this look, he sounded as if he were comparing it to a sniper's bullet. He pumped his fist and shouted, "You'll crush that judge!"

PRO? WHATEVER.

Stranded in Florida where skating was slowly dying, I was clueless; I didn't even know what role a sponsored skater played in the skateboard industry. Barry knew that the biggest professional freestyle contest of the year was taking place in a few months at Oasis Skatepark in San Diego, and he told me I was going to enter that contest; that was why we were working on my "killer" routine. I didn't have a way to get to Oasis, a way to survive once I was there, or even a sponsor who would enter me, but that didn't bother him.

ROLLING FINGERFLIP. BACK IN THE LATE 1970S, YOU HAD TO ADD THE ADJECTIVE "ROLLING" TO A TRICK NAME. WE'VE COME A LONG WAY.

I was going to enter the pro contest because Barry said so. Never mind the fact that I was on the Powell B team—not even a legit team—I was going to enter as one of Powell's pros. Barry was confident that I skated at the level of Tim Scroggs, whose interest in skating seemed to be waning. And anyway, with skating so depressed, it wasn't really that big of a deal: if I sucked, nobody would notice, just as nobody noticed if you ripped, these days. Being pro didn't mean squat. Most pros didn't make as much money as the guy bagging groceries.

Scroggs helped me out by talking to Stacy, letting him know that I was skating well and was interested in entering the Oasis contest. This helped, because even though I had won contests in the past, getting noticed—especially out in the Floridian boonies—was next door to impossible. Having that indirect connection changed my skating prospects for the better.

Tim was like a big brother to me, and we got along well. There was friction between us only once, when he got a little weird and accused me of stealing his tricks. Freestylers were always weird about "their" tricks. Vert skaters invented tricks and then every-body who had the skills learned them, and I had never heard about anybody complaining. But freestylers were like spoiled kids hord-ing candy, when it came to their tricks. I had even heard stories of pro freestylers spying on each other. But in any case, Tim's tempo-rary bitterness was, I think, a matter of transition; I was on my way up at the time, while he was a seasoned pro moving on to other things in life. Probably he was just in a bad mood for a few days, because soon afterward he returned to normal. It didn't take long before I realized how much he had begun boasting about me to the "outside world" on the West Coast.

Barry may have been scheming to get me to the Oasis contest, but I wasn't doing anything about it, except maybe daydreaming. My father had already set down the day I'd have to quit skating, and I had only made it to the Oceanside contest because of Sara, who was long gone by now. What chance would I have of getting my father to pay for me to go to California and enter a skateboard contest?

My parents trusted Barry to take me around the state for demos, sometimes bringing me home days later, and Barry hatched a plan around these circumstances. One day, after having me run around the skatepark's lake three times, he laid it all out for me.

"Rodney, you know it's never a good thing to lie to your parents, but I know what you can do at this contest! You're already light-years ahead of everybody else, doing tricks that nobody has even thought of, never mind seen yet. I'll sell the furniture in my apartment, and that should be enough for one plane ticket so you can go alone. Tim has already arranged with Stacy so that everything will be taken care of once you get to California. We can tell your parents we're going away for a long demo and you can go win that contest."

I couldn't believe that Barry would empty his apartment just so I could go to a contest. His motivation was purely enthusiasm for my skating, since he didn't know the full story of my home life and didn't pity me or anything. The only person outside of my family that I ever confided in was Tank, a worker who helped around our property on the weekends. I usually spent a part of my chore time doing heavy work with Tank, like digging holes for our never-ending fence line. He was a massive black man with a truly awesome belly laugh, and he put a smile on my face every time that huge laugh of his boomed through the air. Because Tank occasionally caught a bit of my father's temper, the two of us were natural confidants. "Watch out for him, Rodney," he warned me one day, after my father had yelled at us. He was driving the tractor while I was lining up the drill bit that bored holes in the ground. "Your dad is like a rattlesnake; you never know when he's going to bite you." Then he let loose his deep belly laugh.

With Barry encouraging my skating and my father crushing it under his foot, I had opposing pressures in my life. I thanked Barry and told him I would think about it. It would equal high treason in my father's eyes, but I loved skateboarding and the finish line was coming up so soon. If I skated at Oasis and won, perhaps it would make losing skating a little bit easier.

Stacy Peralta called me a few days later, on a Saturday, and I remember it as one of the strangest days of my life. It was as if God had wanted me to go to the Oasis contest and was doing everything possible to line it up for me. For some reason, I woke up early and *wanted* to do chores that day. I was so excited that I sanded down a massive portion of the tractor's mower even before I ate breakfast, and immediately after breakfast I started painting the thing with gusto. An hour later, I mowed and edged our football fields of lawn, washed the courtyard, cleaned out a closet, and helped Tank put in some new fences. When I was finished, I skated for two hours.

My parents were in the kitchen when the phone rang. My mom answered it and told me that Stacy Peralta was on the line. I started hyperventilating.

"Really? Stacy Peralta! He's calling me!" I was so excited I literally began hopping up and down, but I was almost too nervous to pick up the receiver. The last time I'd spoken to Stacy was after he'd smashed into me at Kona.

"Hey, Rodney, how's it going?"

"Good. Really good."

"I heard from Tim that you're skating really well. I think it'd be a good idea if you could find some way to the Oasis contest. Once you're here, we can take care of everything."

"You mean it?" I blurted.

He laughed. "Yes, Rodney. I mean it."

My mom saw how thrilled I was, and she used my excitement as a crowbar to open up a conversation with my father about the Oasis contest. Even though I didn't talk to my father much about skating, he heard me babbling about it and knew how much I idolized Stacy. Stacy was *the man* in my mind. My father may have been controlling in my eyes, but in his mind he was never intentionally malicious. I don't think he ever meant to cause me or any family member anguish. He was just trying to guide our lives the best way he knew.

I asked Stacy if I could call him back, hung up the phone, and yelled: "Stacy Peralta called me!"

"Why not let this be a last fling for Rodney?" my mom suggested, as I bobbed around with a smile on my face. "This could be a nice way to end skating for him and also a birthday present."

"Okay," my father said, shrugging.

Just to celebrate, I skated for over nine hours the next day and got so tired that I woke up in the morning and realized that I had forgotten to take off my pads and helmet the night before.

Barry was overjoyed when he heard the good news, probably because he wasn't going to need to use cardboard boxes for furniture anytime soon. Almost immediately, we began working on improving my contest run. It finally hit me that I was going to be skating against professionals at the biggest freestyle contest in the world. The best skaters had been practicing all year for this contest, even Steve Rocco. I imagined the insane levels of skating that I'd witness at Oasis—it'd be like a nuclear blast of new tricks. I knew that I had learned a lot in the last year, and I wasn't even a pro. I figured that if I had learned three new tricks, the pros must have learned nine new tricks. I doubted that I'd even place in the top ten, but the chance to actually skate against the pros would be a perfect way to end my skating life.

I was most nervous about letting Barry down. I had never known anyone so passionate about my dreams. I could deal with screwing up or just plain sucking, but my skating had become a part-time job for Barry, and I figured it'd be a huge blow to him if I didn't perform. He told me just to do my best and give it my all— nothing could be worse than not going full bore, he said.

THE Z-BOYS' HOOD

Before I left for California, I went shopping with my mom for a new pair of corduroys, dress shoes, and a golf shirt. My mom wanted me to be presentable when I met Stacy. She also bought me a new Sherlock Holmes book, which was my favorite series at the time.

I flew to California with Tim Scroggs, and we met Stacy at the airport. He was wearing a pair of loose old jeans and a Hawaiian shirt, and the 1970s-era straight blond hair that used to drift past his shoulders now looked shorter and shaggier. Immediately, the freedom that I had breathed in one year earlier in Oceanside filled me; I felt as if I were entering back into a favorite dream.

The dream only got better on the drive to Stacy's parents' house in Santa Monica. To me, just looking out the window was like entering one of the classic Craig Stecyk articles that mythologized the Z-Boys in *Skateboarder* magazine. This was the home turf of that famous crew of rowdy skaters, and one of them was a few feet in front of me, steering his Volvo through traffic.

Stacy traveled a lot, but his parents were so cool that he continued to live at home even though he was a world-famous skateboarder and a company co-owner who could afford to buy his own house. His parents were awesome; they made me feel relaxed the minute I stepped through the door. They were older than my parents but greeted me with hugs. It was obvious they were supportive and proud of everything their son had accomplished. They created such an inviting atmosphere that I felt as if I was returning to a favorite relative's house for the weekend. After I dropped my gear in Stacy's old bedroom, we went out to skate.

I started warming up on the street outside his house. Stacy came out to watch. This was it, my audition! I had dreamed of having Stacy watch me skate and, at least in my fantasies, he had watched with excitement, getting more and more stoked. As I popped off trick after trick, I watched Stacy out of the corner of my eye, trying to make sure that he was watching me and looking for his reaction.

He watched intently, sometimes laughing. I did a helipop (or, as it's known today, a 360 nollie), one of the newest tricks I had invented. That one got a big laugh from him. I began getting nervous—did he think my tricks were so stupid they were funny, silly circus tricks that weren't real? I had no idea, because nobody else was doing tricks like them at the time.

I hit my tail and popped my board into the air using only my feet, then drove the nose down so that I landed on it and stopped. I didn't realize it then, but nobody had ever popped their board into the air without using their hands on flat ground. A few years earlier, Alan Gelfand, another Powell rider, had invented the ollie air (a no-handed aerial) on banks and bowls, but on flat ground nobody had figured out how to mimic his trick. I had been in my garage skating when I figured out that if you kicked with your rear foot and dragged your front foot upward, it lifted the board into the air. Once I was high enough in the air to level the board I just shifted my weight to the nose and pointed it down.

When I stopped skating, Stacy nodded at me and smiled. I discovered later that he was like this with all of his skaters. Tony Hawk told me that he'd show Stacy tricks he had invented and Stacy would just laugh at him, too. And like me, Tony could never tell if Stacy was ridiculing his tricks or was impressed by them. Bones Brigade skaters had to learn to translate the Stacy laugh.

Stacy had a dream garage. Stacks of boards were piled up in the corner, stickers filled clear plastic bags, and what seemed like hundreds of wheels sat in boxes on the ground.

"Hey, Rodney, do you need some wheels?" Stacy asked.

I didn't even think about taking any of the product; just looking at it was reward enough. Back then, being sponsored didn't mean the same thing it does today. Nowadays riders will receive skate shop–sized orders and set up new boards every week. I was still riding my cut-down Ray Bones Rodriguez skull-and-sword graphic board, the same one I'd skated on for the past two months. I loved it because it was heavier than an ordinary board, and it felt sturdier to me.

I didn't even think about my board's weight. I rode trackers with copers that were fastened on with plastic and metal washers. Talk about adding weight. . . . Then I had a tail skidplate screwed on and bolts that were at least an inch too long. (Today I ride a larger board that's probably 30 percent lighter than my old Ray Bones.)

Stacy dug through some boxes and unloaded the biggest present he had for me.

"Here you go, Rodney; have a shirt," he said and handed me a Bones Brigade T-shirt with a bomber plane on the back and two bombs on the left sleeve. These were only given to the elite team riders—legit team riders—like the guys in the ads, but I didn't know what getting one meant. A part of me thought that Stacy was being supernice to a weird little barking kid who tagged along with Tim Scroggs, who was a real freestyle pro for Powell and

ME WEARING MY CHERISHED BRIGADE T-SHIRT—TUCKED IN, OF COURSE.

Peralta. I never asked Stacy if I was on the team, though. What would happen if he laughed at me or said no?

THE CONTEST

Oasis was located beneath a major freeway in San Diego, and occasionally you'd see a bottle fly out of a car. Passersby liked to throw the bottles at skaters, turning them into homemade hand grenades in the process, with glass shards shooting everywhere. Tim cruised around, practicing his run, while I found a quiet corner in which to practice my routine.

After half an hour of warm-ups, I stopped skating and stared around me in awe. Steve Rocco, who was tearing the place up, pushing as fast as he could and doing his tricks at double the speed of anyone else, blasted everyone with his combination of smooth lines and technical tricks. The best freestylers in the world were skating around me now, and almost all of them were doing exactly the same tricks they had done over a year ago. Steve was the only one who seemed to have learned anything new and who was taking his skating to the next level. The skills of some of the pros had noticeably deteriorated over the year.

It bummed me out. I expected them to be on the fast track, learning tricks twice or three times as fast as me. At the contest, there were still some old-school skaters who mixed gymnastics and ballet, ignoring technical tricks altogether. One skater even wore a leotard gymnast suit.

Anybody could see that Steve was cutting-edge. He had this amazing ability to look cocky and aggressive while skating. He had a flow, a style, and the strongest tricks. He was unquestionably the best skater there.

My months of training with Barry had created an impenetrable shell around me, and I felt I could skate without any distractions. But everybody was skating differently, and this made me slightly self-conscious. I had no opinion about my style in comparison to theirs; all I knew was that I had chosen to skate in a different direction, but I didn't know if that direction was ahead, to the side, or behind that of my peers.

My mind was so regimented that my tricks clicked off one after another. I didn't move more than three feet at a time during my run, and there was no way I could change now—I had to do what I'd programmed myself to do.

Stacy didn't know what to do with me. He was an awesome coach, but I was too withdrawn, too freaky, for him to figure out. I had spent hundreds of hours with Barry, who would talk about sending out vibrations and hitting the judges on a subconscious level. "They'll feel it all right," he would say, "but they won't be able to understand it."

I practiced some more, and when I took another break, some of the skaters had stopped and begun watching me. Perhaps they

STACY PERALTA, ONE OF THE MOST STYLISH SKATERS EVER.

were watching because they were scared—and not necessarily scared about my skating. I had the normal Florida twang, and I thought people were weirded out by it. I also was the only one wearing a helmet. And elbow pads. And kneepads. And I could have stood eye to eye with the little people in *The Wizard of Oz*. I also looked years younger than the average fourteen-year-old. I must have looked like a nine-year-old wad of pads who fell off a farm tractor.

I didn't watch anyone skate once the contest started. Barry had drilled that lesson into me. He had told me not to watch the competition, and I obeyed him by sitting away from the crowd and facing in the opposite direction.

Stacy saw me, and he came up and patted me on the shoulder. "I wish I could help you, but . . . well, you seem like you're in your zone. I don't know what to say to you, but you look like you have it under control, so good luck and I'm always here for you. Can I get you anything?"

I shook my head no and told him that I was okay right now, but thanks. He smiled and walked away. I was nervous, and the only way to calm myself I could think of was to pray. I put my head down, pulled my helmet over my face, and closed my eyes. *Here I am God, at my last skateboarding contest—my last skateboarding anything; help me if that's what's best in your eyes. Thank you for this last chance.*

Then my name was announced, and I walked over to the contest area. Unlike the Oceanside contest a year earlier, which had drawn ten thousand spectators, Oasis looked pretty spotty. The beach crowd didn't get sucked in as it had at Oceanside, and with skateboarding's popularity hitting the bottom, there was hardly any crowd—maybe a hundred people all told, including the skaters. That helped to calm me.

My music came on, the low bass chords of the Talking Heads' "Psycho Killer" filled my head, and I began doing my footwork, everything clicking into place after hundreds of hours of practicing my run in front of the mirror at Sensation Basin.

The singer, David Byrne, began singing as I sped up my footwork. *I can't seem to face up to the facts. I'm tense and nervous and I can't relax.*

I did a helipop and raced into more fast footwork, skating as fast as I could.

I flipped my board onto its side, on the rail.

Then I fell on a simple rail trick. I got back on my board and finished my run. People clapped as I left the contest area, but I think most of them didn't know what to make of me.

I wasn't bummed, because one of Barry's strategies was to make me save my best for later in the show, since otherwise the judges will score the second run lower, even if it's identical to the first. If they've seen it before, they get less excited. I had spazzed out and gone full bore, but luckily I had fallen. I could still save the best for last, if I could just stay on.

Steve, on the other hand, nailed his first run. He landed everything perfectly and scored higher than me. But his run boosted my confidence. I had seen him lay it all on the table; that was the best he could do. Now I knew what the judges thought of my skating: I was in second place, one point behind Steve. I had worried that they might have thought my style too technical, lacking in that old-school flow.

A calmness flowed over me, and I thought, *I can beat him if I do everything I planned.* It was the best score out of two runs, and I had one run left, and I wasn't worried because Barry had prepared me for this moment. I said my silent prayer as "Psycho Killer" pounded over the speakers and began my run. I didn't even hear the song once I started. I nailed the first tricks, and the rest of my routine unfolded. One of my last tricks was a 540 shove-it, the hardest trick I could do. Basically, you spun the board one and a half times underneath you, jumped in the air, and landed on it. By its very nature, it's a risky move for a contest.

Skaters had been doing 360 shove-its for years, but few people had ever seen a 540 shove-it. Just as Barry had told me, I picked one judge out of the panel and made eye contact with him before my run. As I set up for the 540 shove-it I stared at him and kicked my board. He was watching my board, not me. I didn't even know why I did it, why I risked it at my first pro contest. I just thought, *this is the way it's supposed to be done.* I heard the crowd erupt and smiled, knowing that not only had I given it my best, but that other people appreciated my effort as well.

Stacy came over excitedly and shook me by the shoulders. After the judges tallied their scores, he got even more hyped. "You're in first place! You're in first place, Rodney!"

Steve still had one run to go, and I remembered that only the highest score counted. Again he landed everything perfectly. But the judges gave him scores of 94.33 and 94.00 for his runs, while I received a 95.33 and 95.00 for mine.

I didn't jump up and down or hoot; I felt totally serene. I smiled at Stacy, who was bursting with excitement. I was happier knowing that I hadn't let Barry down, and that I had this as my final memory of skateboarding. I had won a pro contest, and Stacy's reaction surpassed my wildest dreams.

Steve's reaction also surpassed my expectations, but in a different way. Fighting mad would be a nice way of saying that he was *pissed.* I figured that out by the subtle clues he dropped. One clue was him pacing around yelling, "He didn't win! Rodney didn't win! The guy didn't even move around!" I didn't know what to think. I looked up to Steve. He was the only freestyler I admired, and he was rabid at my winning. I was crushed. *If Steve says that I didn't beat him, then I must not have beaten him. Yeah, the scores say I beat him, but I'm sure I got extra points for being a shrimpy kid.* Stacy was overjoyed, and people congratulated me. But I began fixating on Steve.

As I accepted the trophy I remember thinking, *Wow, that worked out. I won a contest and now skating is over.* I hadn't been thinking about life after the contest.

An hour later, Steve was still fuming. But he was good friends with Stacy, and once he calmed down we developed a friendship.

Oasis Skatepark had various banks and bowls to skate in, and we walked around them, checking out the local skaters. I spotted a twelve-year-old kid who stood out even among the pros. I related to him automatically, because he skated differently from anybody else. He had developed a unique style because he was so light. He was a mixed mass of scabs, pads, torn shorts, and taped shoes. He was skinnier than *anybody* I had ever seen, except for maybe some kid I had seen in *National Geographic*. He was so narrow that he had to wear elbow pads on his knees, and his lack of mass hurt his skating because he didn't have the weight to create enough momentum to grab and blast an air. He could barely get above the copping.

We watched as he skated run after run, trying to solve his problem. He started ollieing into his airs and grabbing late, when he was already in the air. Every other skater grabbed the board early, before even reaching the top of the bowl. With that small innovation, skating would be taken in another direction and a new era of vert skating ushered in. I had been observing the young Tony Hawk.

We began talking to the kid with the hayseed hair poking out of his helmet, and he introduced himself as Tony Hawk. "You get way higher on your airs when you ollie into them," Steve told him, and you could tell Tony appreciated the compliment from a famous pro.

Before Tony was sponsored, before anybody knew anything about him, he made an impression on me. I related to the way he attacked his skateboard problems. He thought outside the box and was already on his way to leaving the current generation of professional skaters in the dust.

Years later he told me that he remembered watching the contest. "You were more technical," he said. "Most freestylers worked on their choreographed routines, and you nailed trick after trick"—a compliment I could easily have returned to him.

THE BITTER END

I wasn't feeling hyper about winning the contest. A calmness flattened everything out in me as I walked back with Stacy across the Oasis parking lot to his Volvo. I was quiet and stared out the window all the way back to his parents' house. Stacy was stoked, which made me happy, but I hadn't told him (or anybody) that my skating days were now officially over. I felt bad, as if I was deceiving Stacy. After all, he had picked me up at the airport, fed me, let me stay at his house, and, most important, he had encouraged me. My favorite skater in the world, the guy whose pictures were pinned to my wall, was stoked to have me around. *If I have to end it,* I thought, *then this is the perfect way.*

That night I called my parents from Stacy's. They sounded happy for me, but there was no excitement on the other end of the line. It was just like it had been after the Oceanside contest.

I didn't skate in California after that. There was no panicked desperation, no skating through the night to squeeze the last drop out of skating. It was over, and I had promised my father that I would stop. I wanted it to end at Oasis. It meant a lot to me that my last memory on a board would be of skating with Steve and Stacy, heroes of mine.

I sat in Stacy's old bedroom, staring at the glow-in-the-dark stars pasted on the ceiling. I was thankful that I'd been able to skate as long as I had.

The next morning, Stacy drove me to the airport. I was anxious, sweating it out, like a guy trying to get the courage to ask a girl on a date. I had one final, big, important question to ask Stacy. This was the last piece of knowledge I needed to stop skating at total peace with myself. I kept trying to work up the courage to ask him my question on the fifteen-minute drive to the airport, but it wasn't until we pulled up to the curb outside of Departures that I sputtered:

"Stacy, am I on the Bones Brigade now?"

He turned and looked at me and started laughing. "Of course you're on the Bones Brigade, man." Then he gave me a Bones

ALWAYS STYLISH, STACY PERALTA JOKING AROUND WITH HIS TEAM'S PER DIEM MONEY.

Brigade patch, a special one for team members. (I wasn't the only one who went through this, though. Stacy never told any skater on the Brigade that he was "officially" on the team.) He gave me his home phone number and told me to call him if I needed anything—decks or wheels—or if I just wanted to talk with him. He congratulated me again and told me how happy he was that I had skated so well.

I looked back and waved to him as I walked through the automatic doors in my new corduroys and dress shoes. Stacy waved and drove off. When I was sure he was far enough away not to see me, I stepped out onto the curb and watched as he drove off.

CHAPTER 10
STAY OF EXECUTION

I'D NEVER HAD A SMOOTHIE UNTIL I WENT TO CALIFORNIA AND SKATED

in the Oasis contest. The memories of drinking that fruit shake drifted through my head as I tenderly unfolded the receipt for it. I didn't want to bend it too much and tear the creases. I laid it out on my desk and unwrapped another receipt, this one for a blueberry muffin I bought the morning of the contest. I lined up all the stickers Stacy had given me on my bed with the receipts.

For the next forty-five minutes I emptied my package of California artifacts, such as my plane ticket and the tourist brochure I'd picked up from the airport. I meditated over each one, reliving the memory each talisman held. My skateboard stood in my closet, and I went over and skimmed my finger over the edge of the wheel. The last time it had touched the ground was at Oasis. Eventually I packed my souvenirs neatly in a paper bag and put them away in my drawer. Some kids hide porn mags under their mattress. I hid my bag of receipts and stickers.

I felt like an archaeologist digging up finds from another lifetime. I had come to accept that my life was going to be totally different from this point on, but I was clueless as to where to go, what to do now. It never entered my mind to sneak around and skate, argue with my father, or do anything but what I'd promised him to do.

I hadn't said much to my mom when she picked me up from the airport. We drove most of the two hours back to our house in silence. I stared out the window, depressed that only this morning I had woken up staring at the stars on Stacy's ceiling.

Once we arrived home I saw my father in the kitchen, and he asked me about my trip.

"It was fine. I had fun."

"Good," he said. "You won the contest and proved that you're the best. Now you can move onto something real." He looked at me and I could tell he cared so much that it was almost hard for him to properly get across how much he felt. He wanted the best for me so much that it killed him when I threw it all away. "Rodney, do you know how talented you are? You're so talented that you could be a pro golfer, you could excel at a sport where there is

THIS IS ME WEARING MY OASIS UNIFORM WHILE BALANCING ON MY RAILS DURING A DEMO AT THE UNVERSITY OF FLORIDA. I USED TO SHAVE DOWN FULL-SIZED VERT BOARDS TO MAKE CUSTOM SHAPES.

serious competition. Skateboarders don't have dedication or determination, not at any real level."

I nodded, and in a way I could understand why he felt that way. The fact that I had only been skating for less than four years, had just turned fourteen, and was world champion proved his point, in his mind. How could a kid so green beat older, more experienced men? They *had* to be a bunch of slackers.

For the next two days I zoned out, unable to do anything with the time in which I had formerly skated. I could still feel skateboarding inside me, my mind unable to get off the hamster wheel of brainstorming new tricks. I turned everything into a skateboard—pencils, erasers, broken sticks, folded paper. And I spent hours every day writing down my thoughts, recording every minute detail of my trip to California.

SKATEBOARD NEWS, MY SAVIOR

On my third day back, my mom called me downstairs to answer the phone. We'd just finished eating dinner and my father was reading the paper in the family room.

"Hello?" I said into the phone.

"Rodney? This is *Skateboard News* and we wanted to ask you a few questions for an article we're doing on you."

"Okay," I answered, and for the next fifteen minutes I was interviewed.

My father heard the conversation and was impressed. He called me to where he was sitting.

"Rod, who was that?"

"A skateboard magazine."

"A real magazine?"

"Yes, sir."

"They're doing an article on you? Just you?"

"Yes, sir."

"Who called last night?"

"Stacy Peralta called and Todd, too; he's the team manager for Powell and Peralta."

"Stacy, is that the guy who took care of you in California? He paid for everything?"

"Yes, sir."

He chuckled, a sign that usually meant he was in a lighthearted mood. "Damn, Rod, I can't believe that all these people are calling you from across the country. I like how you handled yourself in that interview—very mature. I'm proud of you. You know with all these people investing money in you, maybe you should keep skating. It wouldn't be right for me to tell you to quit, if they have all this money invested."

I don't think he gave a rat's ass about anybody losing money, but he must have rethought my contest win when he saw the reaction people had to it. Maybe it was a bigger deal than he thought, after all. Now, for the first time, he appreciated that part of the world was opening up to me, and he didn't want to shut that out.

Before, all he saw was an absentminded son who wasn't socially adjusted and who left reeking pads around the house. But these few phone calls allowed him to see me and skating in a different light.

"Thank you! Thank you!" I said. I began shaking, emotions exploding inside me like a string of firecrackers. I wanted to hug him, to show him how much I loved him, but he wasn't a big hugger, so I did the only thing he'd taught me to do: I stuck out my hand for him to shake. I skipped upstairs, clearing four steps at a time, and grabbed my skateboard out of the closet. As I ran past him out to the garage I yelled at him again, "Thank you!"

For the rest of that night I spread Oasis dirt and dust all over my garage.

RIGHT RUN, WRONG YEAR

After the Oasis contest, skating couldn't see its future, because it didn't look as if it had one. Sensation Basin was about as crowded as the moon, with Barry manning the sole outpost. Even though I loved the place, I only skated there about three times a week, on a weekday and maybe on Saturday and Sunday, depending on how time-consuming my chores were.

The best aspect of winning the contest at Oasis (and that skatepark closed shortly after my victory) was that it blasted me to the forefront of Powell's skaters. I still wasn't anywhere near as important as Steve Caballero or Mike McGill, two of the hottest

ME AND PHIL CHIOCCHIO.

vert amateurs in the world who skated for the Bones Brigade, but my name got around after winning that contest. *Action Now,* the surfing/BMX/skateboarding/music magazine that *Skateboarder* turned into to survive skateboarding's drastic drop in popularity, did a three-page article on the championship contest and had three pictures of me on the first page.

By the end of that year, *Action Now* wanted to do a full-length interview with me, and Stacy wanted to shoot an ad—and also get me out for a little vacation in California. That was the best part of the deal for me: more time in California. Freedom. Being chaperoned by Stacy, one of the most famous skaters in history, and having him introduce me to other pros was better than any fantasy I'd ever dreamed of at night while playing under the covers with my fiberglass miniskateboard.

Later I stayed with Steve Rocco, whose effect on me was more unnerving than any anxiety nightmares I had ever had. Steve was the flip side of Stacy, and I quickly learned that when he started grinning, the best thing to do was turn in the other direction and run.

LORD OF THE FLIES

Even though I had hung out him with a little bit at Oasis, Steve Rocco and I didn't have a real relationship. When Stacy drove me to his house, Steve met us outside and smiled, throwing a skateboard wheel up in the air and catching it. He was happy to see Stacy, and the two of them talked for a while. I suppose Stacy had wanted me to stay with another freestyler, figuring that we'd connect. He knew Steve was responsible—well, responsible compared with some of the other characters in skating. And at the very least, he felt Steve wasn't going to take me to a strip club or buy me a vial of crack.

The three of us skated around the beach strip. Steve lived with his parents and his brothers in a house on the beach, and we skated up and down the pier hitting all of Steve's favorite spots. That California sense of freedom slowly loosened me up, and I skated without pads for the first time. Then I slid out on some sand and skinned my knees.

Stacy, one of the most intuitive people I've ever known, sensed that this was a big deal for me. Stacy knew I had promised to skate full pads for the rest of my life, and he knew how emotional I could get around my father, because he'd called once after my father had raged about something and everybody in the house was running for cover. I answered the phone in a whisper and told him that I couldn't talk and had to get off the phone immediately. He asked if everything was okay. I had just mumbled, "Things are rough around here right now. Gotta go, okay?" Click.

He was more stressed about my skinned knee than I was. One thing I'll always appreciate about Stacy was how protective of me he was. I got the sense that he truly wanted to help me, and in ways that had nothing to do with skateboarding. He let me know that if I ever needed anything, at any time, I should not hesitate to call him. I assured him that the scrape was so small it wouldn't matter.

Absolute lawlessness ruled Steve's house. It was as if highly evolved monkeys, geniuses in mischief, had escaped from a lab and rented a house in Hermosa Beach. My ordered, respectful world was flipped upside down the moment I stepped through his door. Steve was the personification of a contained riot. Just being around him made me nervous, but in a good way.

Steve was six years older than me, an age gap that should have been insurmountable, considering how young I was. He could almost legally drink, and I had just started high school. He must have relished the prospect of toying with me and my kooky regiments, seeing how far he could push the "robot" with the Casio digital nerd watch, the strict skateboarding rules, and the weird eating habits: I would eat the same thing for months until I burned out on it.

There was an atmosphere of absolute freedom in his house, down to the fact that when you stepped out his front door you were right on the beach. Steve never scared me, because I always sensed that he was protective of me and beneath it all respectful, but he did enjoy rattling my cage. He never suffered from lack of ego. He knew what a talented skater he was, and he seemed to respect me even more for having beat him and having done tricks he hadn't at Oasis.

I did skate like a robot compared with Steve, who skated faster than any other freestyler. He'd mock me in a friendly way, telling me to move around when I skated. He never did it to hurt me, always to make me expand my style. My trucks were as tight as I

THIS IS EITHER A NOSESTALL OR A VERY POOR G-TURN. MY WIFE MADE ME PUT THIS IN.

could get them, and he forced me to loosen them so that my skating would be more fluid.

He was a famous skateboarder, world famous, and sponsored by Sims, a huge company. My attitude toward sponsorship was one of total gratitude; I figured you should be thankful you were getting anything at all. I never asked for anything surplus. Meantime, Steve's room was stuffed with racks of clothes. Racks! What couldn't fit on the racks was stacked in piles, still in the sealed plastic bags they were shipped in. I had one extra set of wheels at home, and I rode my board until the wheels had coned inward from too much use. But Steve had boxes of wheels—at least twenty sets! I found out why he was throwing a wheel into the air and catching it when Stacy and I arrived earlier.

Steve and his brother Sal had been running outside and pegging unsuspecting tourists with skateboard wheels. They continued after Stacy left. I hid inside—no way I was going to be a part of this. I'd hear angry screams and curses outside, as the two of them would come back in the house, giggling. To me they were throwing away some of the most valuable stuff on earth, and I considered sneaking out and collecting every single wheel once they fell asleep.

They had a nice house with tile floors that were, as Steve said, "perfect for skating." The floor of his bedroom looked as if stagehands had dragged gear over it for a decade. Chips were missing, and scratch marks covered the center of it, because he'd start skating whenever the urge hit him.

The way the Roccos expressed themselves was enlightening, almost *too* enlightening, in fact—they just said what they thought. There were no filters in the house, just a bunch of wandering, thundering ids. Throughout my whole visit, I never even saw Steve's dad. And once, I remember watching a fight between the brothers, an all-out scrap, and thinking, *I just landed on the island in* Lord of the Flies. I had just read that book about a plane crash that leaves a group of school kids on a deserted island, and how they eventually run amok and push a boulder on Piggy, the nerd of the group. While I was in the Roccos' house, there was no mistaking who the boulder would be dropped on.

Not to say Steve was a barbarian. He didn't graduate from high school, but he inhaled information on everything from science to history to math. That was another real connection for us. He often passed the time by solving accelerated number theory problems, and he always solved the "genius" problems in the back of *Omni* magazine. It tripped him out at first, when I helped him with some problems, but then he got excited and we really bonded.

We'd drive around in his Celica babbling about tweaked math concepts. My interest in math impressed him more than my skating. He was my first real skateboarding friend, and I felt the effects of his friendship deeply in those first few days.

I had another frightening introduction to get through after the Rocco family hazing. Stacy braced me for meeting Craig Stecyk, a powerful creative force behind Powell and Peralta. In the late 1970s at *Skateboarder*, Craig had penned articles and shot photos, helping to shape the image of skating. Stacy always respected Craig, and they both used Powell and Peralta as a canvas to express what they felt skating should be about. Craig always had the man-behind-the-curtain-pulling-the-strings mystique about him, and Steve worshipped the guy, so that automatically jacked him up in my estimation.

"I think he's going to really like you and he's going to be nice to you, Rodney," Stacy said before the meeting. We were going to shoot an ad, and Stecyk was the photographer. "He's not always nice to people," Stacy went on, "but whatever he does with you, it's going to be good."

I had no idea what was going on, or what to expect. But this lanky, older guy wearing a baseball cap and sitting in the Volvo passenger seat waved at me when Stacy pulled up. I crawled in the back of the car, and he turned around and began firing questions at me. Once he found out that I'd played baseball, he began asking me if I could throw a curveball or if I knew how to hold my fingers for a knuckleball. Immediately, just with how he moved, I could tell he was an artist, and not in a fake way. More so than with any other person I had met at that point, I could tell everything about him was artistic.

We went to a Coca-Cola factory and shot lots of funky pictures that I never saw again. Through their passion, Stacy and Stecyk showed me that skating was an art. As corny as that sounds, I understood what I always felt like when I created tricks—an artist. Whatever was going on in my life I'd channel into skating. During that trip, I experienced both the anarchistic and artistic sides of the "sport" I loved. I'd never have experienced skating in those respects in my Florida isolation.

CHAPTER 11

RAT ON A SKATEBOARD

WHILE AT STACY'S, THERE HAD BEEN SOME DISCUSSION OF A RODNEY

Mullen pro board. It really didn't mean anything to "work" on a pro board back then. I just had a shape and size in mind that I conveyed to them. I couldn't believe that they were doing a pro board for me in the first place.

I had never thought of skating as a career opportunity. My father constantly reinforced the value, the sanctity, of hard labor, and I remember thinking that the only real trade I was good at was digging holes and laying down fences. I thought that I'd continue to skate as I got older, but that it would become a hobby of mine, like crossword puzzles. Still, getting my own freestyle board was cool.

V. C. Court revolutionized skateboard graphics. He was the Powell artist who often wore all white and roller-skated around wearing John Lennon–style glasses. He brought his own style to whatever he drew, and he was responsible for the skull-and-dragon graphics that helped define Powell's image. He created the famous skull-and-sword graphics for Ray Bones, the skull-and-snake graphics for Mike McGill (after the fighter plane graphic), the dragon for Steve Caballero (after the skull propeller graphic), and for me he designed a robot dog performing some sort of kickflip.

In a single picture he summed up my skating life—I was the mutt who skated like a robot and did lots of technical tricks. Some skaters had tagged me as this, a robot, because I did trick after trick and was more consistent than most. They didn't mean it as a compliment, though. I find it funny now, because like I said before, Tony Hawk would soon blow up on the skate scene, creating trick after trick that nobody else was doing, and likewise he would be tagged a "robot," usually by disgruntled skaters who had no hope of pulling off any of the skinny kid's moves.

A box came from Powell a few months after my visit to California. I opened it, hoping for some cool new stickers, not realizing that my first pro model board was inside. I pulled out the board. It had a faded lime-yellow stain with a mechanical dog flipping a board under the word *Mutt*. I walked into the house with it and ran into my father.

"My first board!" I said to him, still not believing it.

"Oh, yeah?" he said, examining it. "What is that? What's that thing drawn on it?"

"It's a dog, a mutt; that's my nickname."

He handed the board back to me. "A dog is it? Looks more like a rat to me."

He was right. Some other people confused it with a rat, too. I took the board up to my room and studied it all night long. Skateboarding was just about dead and freestyle twice as dead and I couldn't imagine anybody buying my signature model board—and my first tiny royalty checks backed up that belief. I didn't care, though; to me it was proof that Stacy was proud of me.

Then I tried to ride it. As if by some cruel joke, the board designer had completely screwed up the shape. The nose was too short, the tail too high, the distance between the trucks too long. I never rode it and continued riding Ray Bones models that I shaved down on my own.

A few months later, when I had the guts to talk to George Powell, I asked him if I could move the nose back and make the tail mellower. It wasn't a problem, but I felt uncomfortable asking him. I felt that I should have been happy enough that they made a board for me.

My improved shape did little to improve sales. A couple of my royalty checks (they paid slightly under a dollar for each signature board sold) failed to break double digits, but every once in a while they'd send me an inflated check of a hundred dollars or so. I'd just glance at the amounts and give the checks to my mom, who deposited them in our joint bank account. I guess I wasn't too much of a businessman back then.

VERT DOG

Vert skating was more fun than freestyle. Out of the thousands of pictures I've had of me in magazines, only one is a vert picture. In it, I'm blasting a backside air a few feet out—decent enough for the time. Even though I freestyled all day long at Sensation Basin, I'd goof around on the halfpipes and bowls now and then. Gradually, I began skating vert more and more, doing basic tricks like slide 'n' rolls, handplants, lipslides, half-Cab sliders to fakie, inverts to tail, laybacks to tail. I loved airs-to-axle, a goofy trick where you did an air and landed on your axle, stopped, and then dropped back in.

In Florida—at least where *I* lived in Florida—it rained every afternoon during the summer. I'd go inside and play Asteroids until it dried up, usually an hour after it started. But one day while I was skating the halfpipe, it began to sprinkle. I stopped after my run and put my palm up to see if it was really going to come down or if I could get away with skating more. It was a light rain, one of those halfhearted showers that feel more like a mist than anything else.

I rolled in and went up the wall to do a frontside rock 'n' roll and whipped out. Did I land and break my arm? My leg? My collarbone? Of course not. Where else would the son of a dentist who had encouraged his son not to skate anything but flat ground land? Seven feet down, straight onto his mouth. I could hear my teeth crack and feel the blood swishing around my mouth.

I yelled. Not because of the pain—I didn't even feel that—but because of my father's rule that stated I had to quit skating once I really hurt myself.

"Owwwwww!" I screamed. "Muh teef bok!"

I was so scared of losing skateboarding that I didn't even think about my teeth.

I slowly walked to the manager's office, where Barry iced my mouth. (Barry is known as the Ice Man, due to his fondness for icing injuries.) My lips resembled ruptured hot dog wieners. I called my dad, snot now bubbling out of my nose and tears streaming down my cheeks. Every possible liquid from the neck up was streaming out of me.

"Huuuhhh—huuh—huuuuoooow." That was the first sentence my father heard as he picked up the phone.

"Rod?" He recognized my whining immediately. "That you? What the hell is wrong with you? Speak English!"

"Bwoke teef!" I moaned. More snot. More tears.

"Broke teef skawing." Now the hiccups started.

"You okay? You need to go to the hospital?" he asked.

"Nowh," I quickly answered. The stack of napkins I held on my chin was soaked with blood.

"Need a ride home?"

"Nowh. Can I swill swate?" I asked. Then I threw in a "sworry" for good measure. This was it. I knew he was going to say something about the promise I once made to stop skating if something like this happened.

"Goddamnit! Be careful!" was his only response.

I think my father was pleased that I took my faceplant like a man—except for the tears and snot and hiccups—and didn't grow scared of skating. I think it would have disappointed him if I'd backed away from skating because of a physical injury.

The next day, I sat in his dental chair as he looked into my mouth.

"Good job, Hot Rod," he said. "You killed it. Your two front teeth are cracked and the nerve is dead in one of them. I'm surprised you still even have that one."

He was right. To this day, if you look closely, you can see my two front teeth have the texture of a china cup that's been glued back together after having been broken into pieces.

MAGIC MOUNTIAN

My second pro contest was at Magic Mountain, a theme park outside of Los Angeles. This was at the end of 1981, and I was fifteen. The highlight of my whole year was seeing Stacy and showing him what I'd learned since my last visit to California. I practiced to win contests, but I learned new tricks just to make Stacy laugh. The approval I didn't get from my father, I looked for in Stacy. His acceptance meant everything to me. *Everything*. I focused almost all of my energy toward impressing him. He'd watch and laugh while I skated, shaking his head.

I went through my standard ritual at the Magic Mountain contest, skating by myself and saying a silent prayer before starting my run, and keeping my back to the crowd at all other times. I went on to win the contest, but it was a bittersweet victory—the level of skating I saw depressed me. Steve Rocco had lost most of his competitive spark and came in fourth, and a lot of freestylers seemed to be drifting away. I was out in the sticks, hitting my Casio timer buttons religiously every day, while it seemed as if most freestylers were skating less and less. The gap between me and other skaters was widening. I tried to add at least a few new tricks to each contest run I did, but most skaters were repeating the same runs they'd lost with back at Oasis.

Steve and I were becoming closer friends. The moment we hooked up in LA, we connected again as though I hadn't even left. In fact, he was the only one I really hung out with at the contest. We arrived at Magic Mountain early and rode all the rides before anybody else was admitted to the park. That part was more memorable to me than winning the contest.

During a conversation while riding on the front row of the Colossus—one of those rides where you whip around at seven hundred miles per hour until your eyes roll back and you vomit or pass out—Steve said to me, "You know, Rodney, nobody is going to beat you anymore."

I didn't so much care about the compliment; I cared that any competitive aspect was gone from our friendship. He had told me that I was on a different level, peerless, and that meant more to me than any other pro freestyler's opinion.

Kevin Harris, the current Canadian champion, and one of the rare freestylers who was improving, entered the contest as an amateur for G&S Skateboards. He later told me that he had been impressed by my skating at Oasis, but at Magic Mountain he saw that it was all over for every other freestyler. "The gap was too big by the Magic Mountain contest," Kevin said. "I knew if I practiced eight hours a day I wasn't going to catch up with the tricks you were doing." But Kevin had one thing I didn't—he could flow like water. In my mind, he'll go down as the smoothest skater in history.

Most of the other competitors were getting older and had started thinking about careers outside of professional skating. With its dwindling popularity, skating wasn't going to provide any sort of lifestyle now, unless you wanted to call a cardboard box home. I was so young that professional skateboarding didn't have anything to do with money for me. I didn't care too much about how much money I made, since I didn't really need money. Everything I needed was provided for at home.

PRO AT HOME

By the time I turned sixteen, in 1982, my life was regimented with little variation. I dedicated about fifteen hours a week to chores, aced my classes at school, and averaged three demos a month with Barry. Just like my father, I locked myself into a tight, often inflexible, schedule from which I rarely deviated. School. Chores. Skating. I had three contests to skate in that summer and wanted to introduce at least one new trick that nobody else had seen in each final contest run.

But something happened that no amount of regimenting could control: hormones. I was a teenager, and my body was carpet-bombing me with them. I'd meet girls at some of the demos Barry hooked up, but nothing serious ever happened. The odd one might write me once or twice before getting bored, but that was the extent of it. I was acutely aware that there was a life outside of skateboarding, one that involved girls and other amusements. I'd see kids going to movies, making out at school, holding hands. I can recall one Friday night when I was skating and suddenly stopped myself. I realized that thousands of other teenagers within a twenty-mile radius were out partying, having fun, actually *living*. I was stuck on this thought for a few minutes, my brain forcing me to consider the consequences of the path I was taking in life. I stood there, wondering what it would be like to be holding hands with a girl watching a movie.

What came from my twenty hours of skating a week? A few new tricks in a contest run? I didn't skate for money, and I couldn't have cared less about the pathetic amount I did make from skateboarding. I had fought so hard just to keep doing it, and what had I achieved? It was as if I had been training for an Olympic event and had suddenly been told that the event didn't exist anymore. Skating had about the same number of participants and level of mainstream popularity as yo-yoing.

But I also knew that if I didn't have skating I'd be socially bankrupt. I looked down at my Casio and made a mental note to cut three minutes from rest periods between sessions.

I became more dedicated to skating than ever before. It was now an essential ingredient in my life, something I needed, like food and water. Having a compulsive nature, I heaped more tasks onto my regimen. I ran a mile a day, and once a week I tried to beat my best time. Stupid. It was a perfect way to wreck myself. My legs would burn up, and after two months I'd get dry heaves and have coughing fits after running. But I did continue to beat my record for almost half a year.

No matter what stood in my way—chores, family outings, homework—I still skated two hours a day, and five hours on the weekends. If I started late, I'd skate in the dark. Even if I was at a contest, I reasoned that I really only skated for perhaps forty minutes, so I forced myself to make that time up later that night.

NOT ENOUGH SENSATION

Phil Chiocchio was forced to close Sensation Basin in 1982. Even though I didn't skate at the park as often as I used to, it was as if my personal clubhouse was being condemned. I enjoyed the park, but I wasn't attached to it because lately I had mostly skated at home to maximize my time on my board. Barry had helped me lay the foundation of my training, and, with my handy Casio, I was ready to handle the rest. We both had a sense of "mission accomplished" and felt that I didn't need any coaching at that time. Barry also felt it was time to move on from being a skatepark manager. He eventually married and relocated to the Bahamas, but he continued to study medicine and years later became the National Skateboard Association's medical trainer. We were also both prepared for the closing because for its last few months the park was usually empty.

YOU CAN ALWAYS COUNT ON KEVIN HARRIS FOR A SMILE.

CONTENTS
ACKNOWLEDGMENTS
INTRODUCTION
LIVING NOWHERE
ROCKY BEING A NERD
SKATEBOARDS AND WEED
THE BEGINNING OF THE END
RUNNING AWAY FROM MY FRIENDS
WITH A LITTLE HELP FROM MY FRIENDS
WINNING THE KARATE KID SCHOOL OF SKATING
WARNING, BUT REALLY LOVING
TURNING PRO
STAY OF EXECUTION
RAY GUN A SKATEBOARD
STORM WARNING
SMITH GRIND
SPRING-TIME LASER
WATCHING THE DREAM
TREAL LIFE AT THE UNIVERSITY OF FLORIDA
THE GREAT ESCAPE
A NEW COMPANY
JUMPING OFF FLORIDA
LOCAL SHARKS AND SKATEBOARD WAR
HICKEYS AND HOMECOMINGS
THE MOST ILL-EQUIPPED BUSINESSMAN
TERMINAL DIAGNOSIS
STARTING OVER
NERD LOVE AND DEVILMAN
PHONE CALL AND DEVILMAN
DOOMSDAY
ENJOI
ALMOST
PHOTOGRAPHY CREDITS

CHAPTER 12
STORM WARNING

"WITH ALL THE TALENT YOU HAVE, YOU COULD BE A MAJOR-LEAGUE

baseball player or a pro golfer," my father reiterated one morning, in one of his bad moods. Sometimes he made remarks like this, which seemed complimentary but were really double-edged. True, he was saying I was athletically gifted, but he was also emphasizing a very different message—that skateboarding was a waste of my time. He'd often tell me that Sara's surfer friends, who used to skate on my old driveway ramp, would grow up to be bums.

With my high school graduation only a year and a half away, my father began to have serious doubts about my ability to cope with the world as an adult. He wanted me to get on the "right path" toward being a doctor, dentist, scientist, or professional athlete. The parental leash tightened on me.

The scrutiny of my shortcomings suddenly returned, and once again skateboarding took the blame for any of my deficiencies. On the one hand, he was proud of my discipline, but on the other he was annoyed by my success, which was pressuring me to focus on what he believed to be the wrong pursuit.

In 1982, I went to California for the first of three summer contests, The Rusty Harris contest in Whittier. I opened my run with a new trick I had learned, the flatground ollie.

Alan Gelfand, another Floridian who skated ramps and bowls, had invented the first no-handed aerial in skateboarding's history back in 1977. It's impossible to overstate the importance of this trick, which was named after Alan's nickname, "Ollie." To be able to make your board do an air using *only* your feet was mind-blowing at the time, and skating might easily have petered out due to lack of progress if nobody had invented this trick. (This is the same trick that allowed Tony Hawk to get higher airs by grabbing later.)

I always liked the way the trick looked and was impressed by the unique thinking behind it. On ramps you could scoop your tail and keep your momentum. You still had to guide the board 180 degrees with just your feet, but I began dissecting the trick, taking it from a vertical plane to a horizontal plane. The trick didn't translate well, because the scooping mechanics of it totally fell apart when you had to go straight up from a flat surface. But I noticed that Alan drilled his rear trucks back so that he could hit the tail of his board quicker. Freestyle boards were so much smaller and lighter and the tail and wheelbase shorter, so that my tail already hit the ground fast.

Years earlier, I had invented a set-up trick that could get me into position on the nose of my board. I popped my board into the air and drove the front down so that I landed with the nose resting on the ground and my body leaning forward. That solved my scooping problem, because I realized that I could already pop my board up, but it was such a severe seesaw motion that I wasn't sure how to level it out at the top of the pop and land on all four wheels.

One Sunday afternoon, after trying different techniques, I just backed my front foot toward the tail, hit the tail harder, and dragged my front foot up the board to lift it higher and slowed down the seesaw motion of the trick, so that by the time I was descending, it was level. The seesaw motion was the essence of the trick.

It was easy. Once I had the foot placement figured out, I practiced doing the trick higher and higher. In less than an hour I could pop a foot off the ground.

I was happy that I had solved a problem, but I wasn't that impressed with the trick. It was neat, but it was also sort of boring. To me, it served as a key that opened the door to an unlimited number of new tricks. Now, if I could pop high enough and give myself enough time, I could complete tricks airborne—and that offered a world of opportunity. It was as if I'd been given a whole new perspective on skating because the plane on which I could skate had just doubled.

Years later, people credited the flatground ollie with sparking street skating, since it allowed you to pop up curbs and keep cruising down the streets uninterrupted. More important, the flatland ollie was a bridge between freestyle and vert, and when you mixed the two, modern street skating became possible. I was blown away when Tony wrote in his autobiography that "Rodney Mullen figured out how to ollie on the flat ground and street skating wouldn't exist without the ollie. Every time you ollie you should get on your knees and thank Rodney or take him out to eat if you see him skating around Los Angeles."

In 1982, nobody had even coined the term *street skating*. At first it was actually called *streetstyle*.

I never named it the flatground ollie, and when it appeared in *Thrasher* magazine as a Trick Tip, it was called an "ollie prop-pop."

I remember showing it to Stacy before the Whittier contest. He made me do it over and over again so that he could figure it out for himself. As usual, he laughed.

After winning the contest, Stacy congratulated me and asked me if I wanted to ride for Independent trucks. He had ridden for Tracker, as I was at the time, but he wanted to spread his team out between the two largest truck companies to avoid the impression that he was affiliated with one of them. I didn't care. Whatever Stacy wanted was fine with me, plus Indy made really good trucks.

He took me on a trip to San Francisco, where Indy was based. I had a chance to meet Fausto, the owner of Indy. (He was also the owner of *Thrasher* magazine.) *Thrasher*'s head photographer shot a picture of me popping an ollie, and in a few months it was on the cover of the most popular skateboard periodical in the world.

Transworld Skateboarding would become the other main skating magazine. It was started by Larry Balma, who also owned Tracker trucks. *Transworld* was preparing its first issue that summer, and a rivalry began to grow between the two magazines and truck companies. Adding fuel to the fire, Tracker was out of San Diego, in Southern California, while Indy was located in San Francisco. So there was a bit of Nor Cal versus So Cal attitude floating around.

I was paid a staggering fifty bucks a month by Indy, but to me it was pure gravy. I deposited my Powell checks and spent my Indy checks. After saving up for a few months, I carefully studied the models at Radio Shack and finally bought a medium-sized ghetto blaster.

360S AND RADIO STATIONS

I went home after winning a contest in Pomona, California, but a week after my sixteenth birthday I flew back to California to skate in the last pro freestyle contest of the year. It was held toward the end of the summer at the Del Mar skatepark, Tony Hawk's home park since Oasis had been shut down. Tony was the youngest kid on the Bones Brigade, two years younger than me, and his parents offered to let me stay at their house during the Del Mar contest. I flew into LA and hooked up with Stacy, who put me on a train heading south, where the Hawks picked me up. In the two years since the Oasis contest where Steve and I had watched him learning ollie to grab airs, Tony had turned pro, along the way developing the longest list of tricks in vert skateboarding. I watched him goof around at the park, and immediately I was blown away by the progress he had made in such a short time. He was peerless now.

I recognized that he was the future. You could spot his genius in seconds; he looked so fluid and relaxed, while other skaters seemed forced and unnatural on their boards. I couldn't believe that anyone could achieve such mastery as a skater, never mind in such a short period of time. He was an extremely smart guy, and you could see that skating was an extension of his intelligence just by watching the way he learned a trick.

Apart from winning contests, Tony and I had a lot in common. We were both called robots, and we both felt like outsiders in skateboarding. Being outcasts, we related to each other immediately, and I quickly discovered how smart he was. His whole family was sharp: his mom was on her way to earning her doctorate and his dad was a jack-of-all-trades. Tony also had a self-deprecating sense of humor that always made me laugh—especially from a guy who seemed so gifted.

Academics and intelligence were such focal points in my house that I automatically zeroed in on those aspects in other people. Here was a kid who recited the lyrics of songs he'd heard on the radio after hearing them only once, and who did math problems for fun. Even before I knew he had a 144 IQ (I read this in his book, he never told me) I could tell he was different from the average talented skater.

I noticed how most pro skaters didn't always embrace Tony as one of the guys. Here was this kid—*literally* a kid—who was destroying older skaters with his peerless vert skating. And that had to hurt the seasoned pros. Nobody could keep up with the tricks he created, and he cranked out one after another. He'd think of tricks while he was going to sleep and make a list of ones that he had to figure out how to land.

I also met one of Tony's friends, Greg Smith, who was an amateur freestyler. In my mind, Greg personified the California kid—he had dyed blue hair and wore quicksilver Jam shorts that went past the knee, which were quite avant-garde in comparison to the

Daisy Dukes most skaters wore at the time. His mom was an awesome half-Cherokee woman, one of the most giving and supportive persons I've ever met.

Greg eventually turned pro and became a successful chemical engineer later on, but what really blew me away back then was his porn collection. *Penthouses* stacked next to *Thrashers*; XXX videos stacked neatly beside his TV—right out in the open. Greg reasoned that everybody liked it, so why should he have to hide it away? Steve, Tony, and Greg all had a sort of freedom that I had never dreamed of. Granted, the porn collection seemed to be taking it a bit far—I cringed when his mom would walk right by it—but the way they lived seemed unbelievable to me. Whenever I noticed that free spiritedness of theirs, I felt like a fish inside a tank, looking out with curiosity at them.

Tony's home life was the opposite of mine. The condo his parents owned seemed like Disneyland to me, with people always laughing, cracking jokes, and poking fun at each other. (They all possessed an acute sense of black humor.) But more than anything else, the house was permeated with support. If Tony had been obsessed with lawn bowling instead of skating, his parents would have been behind him 100 percent. His mom even seemed happy that *I* was skating well.

To me it was the perfect family. The Hawk condo didn't have the Wild West feel that Steve's house did, but it was a free, open, wholesome place. I loved how the Hawk family members talked to one another. They seemed like friends talking, all of them on the same level, giving one another equal consideration.

His parents loved the fact that I was obsessed with skating, but they noticed what was going on underneath my surface. Mrs. Hawk once said, "Rodney was the most stressed-looking boy I ever saw." She did everything she could to make my time at her house relaxing. She also went to every skateboard contest she could and watched her son win that Del Mar vert contest and me win the freestyle contest.

Transworld Skateboarding covered the contest in their first issue. "Then came The Mutt to give another clinic," they wrote.

"One judge gave him a perfect 100. The rest gave him 98s and 99s. A voice in the crowd asked what he did wrong. As a trend-setter making all the new moves—which he created—he should have been given the 'Comaneci' score."

FLIPPING AT THE 1984 SWEDISH SUMMER CAMP.

Don't ask me what "Comaneci" means. I had to look it up in the dictionary but still couldn't find it. Steve placed second and Kevin Harris third.

Going home after the contest sucked, but I was getting used to regularly visiting California, which was like a massive decompression chamber for me. So long as I had the California carrot dangling in front of my nose every few months, the stress at home was easier to deal with.

Before I left for Florida, I recorded a few audiotapes at Tony's house of the local radio stations, commercials and all, so I could play them at home as I went to sleep or when I skated.

My father wasn't wild about my summer of victories. It reminded him that I was aiming my talents in the wrong direction.

"You're a big fish in a really small pond, Rodney," he said. "I know it means a lot to you, but before it gets too late, I think you should set your sights on something else."

That summer was the first time the life of a priest became attractive to me. I knew I could handle the discipline required of the priesthood, and I figured it would be possible to transfer my passion for skateboarding over to the church. I had already read the Bible three times, and the idea of studying all the time, obeying a strict code, and having all the extraneous stuff taken care of while I dedicated myself to God fit me well. What attracted me most though was the idea of not having to deal with anybody, being able to totally focus on my faith. I imagined I could just study, constantly intensifying my biblical interest, analyzing each page down to a microscopic level. That's what I've always loved—studying. Whether it's skateboarding, the Bible, or math problems, I love focusing in until the rest of my world fades away. I figured I'd take my Casio watch with me, the only remainder from my past life.

CHAPTER 13
SKIN AND BONES

ONE OF MY SISTERS WAS SOMEWHAT ANOREXIC FOR A SHORT TIME.

There wasn't a lot my folks could do about it, and it wrecked them. My father was visibly unnerved. I overheard him talking to my sister once, and it was the only time I ever heard a note of pleading in his voice.

An eating disorder like anorexia seemed tailor-made for my personality. I'm still not sure if what I went through can be called anorexia, but from what I know, I had the symptoms. Like skateboarding, steadily reducing my dietary intake provided a sense of control over my body. In the same way I had my skating and weekly running, I had to better my personal best with losing weight. If I ate two bananas one day, then I'd eat one less banana the next day—a simple incremental reduction that gave each day a sense of mission. Weighing myself a few times a day, I would graph my weight loss, charting it in the same way I had made a diary of my skating progression. Subtracting calories and denying my body nourishment gave me a sense of accomplishment, because it was so hard to have the discipline to squash my body's protests, especially while maintaining my skating goals. No one could reach in and change that.

A year earlier, when I was still fifteen, I had carried a bit of baby fat around my cheeks. Now, a year later, I could look in the mirror and see my cheekbones jutting out. I'd run my fingers over the smooth outline, impressed with myself.

I'd skip meals and often go an entire day without eating, but my skating schedule never deviated. Even if it seemed as if I was skating in wet cement because my ass was dragging so much, I'd hit that Casio start button and skate. This was another challenge for me. Sometimes I'd have to stop and catch my breath during a session, squeezing my eyes shut to focus on not passing out.

After a few months of losing weight, I developed a way to measure my progress aside from trusting what I read on the scale every day. My new weekly ritual was the "knuckle test." I'd encircle my hands around the thickest part of my thigh and connect my fingers on the bottom and connect my thumbs on the top. In the beginning, my thumbs connected at the tips. But later my fingernails would overlap, then still farther down the knuckle.

I began jumping rope for twenty minutes a night in my room, trying to be as quiet as possible. Each night I'd try to get a higher number, and very quickly I maxed out. My life was chores, skating, exercise, and as little eating as possible. Even sleep became a contest—how much did I *really* need? I began sliding down to three hours of sleep a night, taking twelve-minute catnaps throughout the day.

I had lost over twenty pounds in a few months when my father stopped me in the hallway.

"Rod, what's happening to you?" he asked. I shrugged and stared at the floor, but something in his voice made me raise my head and meet his eye. He was staring at me with concern, and the look on his face startled me. It was unusual for my father to reach out to me this openly, because we had always had a formal, father-son relationship. It was as if he was talking to me without that armor of demanded respect—really looking at me and wanting to help.

"What are you doing to yourself?" he said. I wanted to respond, but after I heard that note of concern in his voice, I could feel myself getting emotional. I had always wanted this concern, this love, from my father, but now every feeling inside me was churning faster and faster. It was the same genuine concern I had heard in his voice when he was talking to my anorexic sister.

He just stared at me. "Your knees are bigger than your thighs." I couldn't handle it, though, and started nodding at the floor.

He shook his head and continued walking down the hall.

I knew my father was upset and not angry because he never made an offhanded crack about weight loss. Growing up, he had often scolded me for not reacting fast enough. "You don't walk when I tell you to do something, you run!" he'd say, raising his voice. But I think he was afraid now that his temper might inflame my problem. Here was an aspect of me that he couldn't control, and he was confused about how to fix it.

After I had restricted my eating for four months, Mr. Henry, one of my eleventh-grade teachers, called me to his desk after class.

"Hey, Rodney, why don't you have one of these?" he said, as he handed me a banana from his lunch.

"I'm okay, thanks," I replied. I'd already eaten my daily five hundred calories. I'd usually eat a bowl of cereal with water in the morning, and only a banana and a plain potato for the rest of the day. At dinner I'd nibble a bit and move food around my plate so that my parents wouldn't notice.

Mr. Henry glanced at me. "Look, is there something I can do?" he asked. I could see in his eyes how much he cared about me. Me! Just another of his students. I shook my head and quickly walked into the hallway.

My math teacher, Mr. McCall, also asked if he could help me. I pretended that I didn't know what he was talking about, and he was sensitive enough to see that blunt questions wouldn't work with me. He was one of my favorite teachers, and I devoured everything in his class; I even did work that was grades ahead because I loved numbers so much. He appreciated my enthusiasm and decided to give up his lunch hours for the entire year in order to tutor me in advanced mathematics.

SKATE DEATH SENTENCE #2

My father's patience had its limits. After watching me steadily lose weight and shut down over a period of months, he decided he'd had enough and called a meeting in March of 1983.

"Get in here!" he yelled in a barely controlled outburst. "Sit down."

I automatically stood at attention. "Yes, sir."

"Get in here!" He pointed to the space in front of his chair.

"Look at you! Look at you! You are a freak! You don't communicate! You don't live a normal life! Look at you! You're getting worse and worse . . . everything bad is getting worse. You are *my* son. Why are you doing this? I can't communicate with you—nobody can!"

He was really worked up now. I knew something was going to happen—some sort of eruption was going to end this conversation.

"I've had it! It's over!" he said. "End of next summer, skateboarding's over. Get this shit out of your system because you are going to have to enter the real world and you won't know what hit you."

He rose out of his chair so fast that I backed up. He shook his hands in frustration, and I had no doubt that I disgusted him so much that he didn't want to have any contact with my skeleton-like body.

I didn't move for minutes after he'd vacated the room, which was still stuffy, full of anger, while I was empty and completely hollow. I staggered out the back door and walked down the long dirt road that ran in front of our house, so exhausted and depressed that I couldn't focus my brain, except to think *it's really over now.*

This was like nothing I'd experienced before. When this had happened in my younger years, I had been ignorant of what was at stake. Now that I had been to California half a dozen times, I had tasted the freedom that was there, right out in the open, available to anybody who wanted it. And it seemed to me that the skateboarders I knew had friends to talk problems over with and drew support from each other, and that being a successful skater provided control over one's life. I was acutely aware of *exactly* what I was losing.

I was going to graduate from high school a few months before my eighteenth birthday, but the fact that I could just move out on my own, as Sara had, never crossed my mind. I knew my father wouldn't want that, and I obeyed him, no questions asked. That was the way I was raised. If I did disobey him, I'd be exiled, as my grandmother had been.

I didn't have any concept of time or even what I was doing until I walked into my driveway. The sun had gone down hours ago and it was dark out now. I opened the door as quietly as possible and snuck upstairs and crawled under the covers of my bed with my clothes on.

I called Stacy up and told him that I only had half a year left before I retired. I couldn't help it, but I started crying. Stacy was completely supportive, caring more for me and my well-being than for losing one of his top pros. He had already learned that I was weird and had laughed at most of my little tweaks, but he was concerned about me now and asked if there was anything he could do. I told him there wasn't.

CHAPTER 14
FIRST-TIME LOSER

I STILL HAD TWO MORE CONTESTS LEFT. THE FIRST ONE WAS THE

spring contest of April 1983 at Del Mar. I had made up a new trick for it—the "magic flip," better known as the ollie kickflip.

Of all the moves I've made up, this is my favorite, because it was the starting point for taking all kinds of flip tricks off the ground. I popped my board into the air, kicked it into a flip, and landed on my board while it was still rolling. It was the most awkward setup possible. The idea for the ollie kickflip originated from watching how my board flipped and spun when I bailed out of an ollie at its peak. I'd often inadvertently drag my front foot off the edge of my board when I messed up on an ollie, and it would flip the board. It took me a couple of days to time the flip after the snap of an ollie, but I finally landed one.

It gave me a totally different feeling than any trick I had done before, because suddenly I could control my board after it was airborne midollie, similar to what Tony Hawk had done by ollieing into his airs on ramps. With my other tricks, all I could do was land on my board once it was airborne. Now it was as if I'd learned to skate on another plane, one that hovered above the ground. Immediately, possibilities for other tricks that could be done midair formed in my mind. I was more stoked about the possibilities that the trick introduced than the trick itself.

Excitedly, I called Stacy. I still ordered boards from him, and the highlight of my month was talking to him and explaining the new tricks I'd learned. He'd make me break down each step, repeating it until he had a clear picture of the mechanics. He'd do the same with Tony and other members of the Brigade.

STATIONARY HANDSTAND FINGERFLIP. THIS IS HOW IT WAS DONE TWENTY YEARS AGO.

People at Del Mar seemed more stoked on this trick than any other I had invented. They couldn't figure out how my board flipped—hence the name "magic flip." A lot of the "new" tricks I would do were just extensions of standard tricks. This was a totally fresh way to control the board.

I showed Tony the ollie kickflip at Del Mar and he was stoked on it. Then he showed me a trick he had invented.

"Watch this," he said, before dropping in and pulling a perfect fingerflip backside air. He had taken a freestyle trick and adapted it to vert. I knew then that he was heading in a direction nobody else was. As he popped out of the bowl he said, "I call it the 'Mutt Air.' "

I had just seen Tony doing a crazy trick that inspired me, and I had a new trick of my own. I was pumped for this contest.

I started my contest run well, but midway through I stepped off. I went to do a simple flip transfer—a set-up trick—and my board landed on the wrong side, wheels up. It fell on its back like a stranded turtle.

The whole crowd went "*Ohhhh,*" as if I were a dog that had gotten squished by a car.

Technically, Per Welinder was my closest competition, and he made a great run—as he usually did. When the judges announced their decision, only one thought blinked in my mind. *Are my parents going to think I'm a failure now?* It was followed by similar thoughts, until a whole traffic jam of them crowded in my head. *Will Stacy think I'm a failure? Will George Powell think I'm a failure now? Will Steve or Tony or Greg like me anymore?* I had come in second place. I had fallen; Per hadn't.

Kevin came up to me and told me how my run had blown him away. "Even if you fell five times, you should still have won," he said. I'd have loved to have been beaten by Kevin, because his skating impressed me with its naturalness—the very opposite of mine. I always appreciated the skaters who looked more comfortable skating than walking, and Kevin personified this quality. After watching him at contest after contest he became my favorite freestyler.

Kevin took his skating in the opposite direction from mine, with a style that came naturally out of his mellow and smooth personality. His contest runs were all one long flowing connected line with no broken sections.

Plus, I loved his whole vibe. I always felt a bond with Kevin, because he was so humble and mellow. He didn't care; he was just there to do his thing. There was some special quality about his skating—it was as if he wasn't trying. I appreciated his compliments, but I never thought of myself as being in a competition against him or really anyone else, stupid as that sounds. The sense of loss I felt was because I had failed to do what I set out to do. There was only one person to blame.

A few seconds after the results were announced, the thought of ending my career with failure sank in. As I accepted my second-place trophy, I was already thinking about how to redouble my efforts.

I had accepted an invitation to the Swedish Skateboard Camp that summer, and I made plans to isolate myself there. Free of distraction, I could skate all day long. I wanted to extend my time in Sweden and skate the hardest I could possibly skate. I'd return to America in August in time for the Del Mar contest, the last I'd ever enter. I didn't even allow myself to consider not giving everything to this contest. I knew the result would echo on long afterward, spilling into other facets of my life.

I thought a lot about Tony Hawk. Tony had entered the pro freestyle contest and placed seventh. Here was the vert ruler, and to see him goofing around at a contest made me reflect on how uptight I was regarding competitions. I knew how focused and determined Tony was, and I struggled to understand how he could do everything needed to win one contest and then turn around and goof off—but still try to do his best—at another. Contests weren't a joke! They weren't supposed to be something . . . fun? Or were they? I only thought about this because Tony was so talented and so dominant. He was able to unnaturally focus when he skated in a contest, pushing himself to another level, but he also had lighthearted ways to offset that strong will. He had found a way to strike a balance, and I realized that I hadn't.

EATING AGAIN

Second place at Del Mar combined with the impending loss of my skateboard privileges made me reevaluate my way of life. Being so desperate, I was uncharacteristically open. I met a girl at a demo who helped change my life.

She watched as I did my demonstration, and after everybody else had left she came up and talked to me. Somehow, she just knew what I was doing to myself. She told me a story of how she and a friend had both been highly competitive ice skaters. As they matured and their bodies developed, they tried everything they could to counter it and became hardcore anorexics. Being so close, they followed similar regimens. One of their exercises was to run up and down the flight of stairs in their apartment together. She returned one day to find her friend dead, sprawled out at the bottom of the stairs. That shock helped her recover.

I had never respected anyone else's concern for me, because I had always felt that others couldn't relate to what I was going through. But here was somebody who had pushed herself even harder than me and had managed to recover. I credit her for pulling me out of the hole I was in.

SWEDISH MONASTERY

The organizers of the camp built ramps, and they had some of the top skaters stay for two weeks or a month. The younger skaters were paying for the chance to hang out with skate stars, while the pros received a skater's dream vacation (at least in the 1980s)— expenses paid, cool ramps to ride on, a topless beach nearby, and a few hundred dollars. True, it was as low budget as you could get, but everybody loved it. We slept in dorm rooms, ate horrible food, and—most important—had a lot of fun. (In fact, the food was so bad that one trick Tony Hawk invented at the camp, "the stale fish," was named in its honor.)

If this was going to be my last skating summer, I wanted to maximize every minute. I made no bones about treating my time in Sweden like a stay in a monastery.

I'd only brought a week's worth of clothes and my toiletries, but I was deathly afraid of being stuck in the middle of the Swedish boonies with no books. *Electricity and How the Mind Works* and *Different Mnemonic Devices* were two of the twenty books I stacked into my bag.

Neil Blender, one of the funniest and most creative skaters ever to step on a board, walked over to me and watched me skate for fifteen minutes.

"You're going to tear Per a new asshole," he said and grinned before letting out a whoop that resembled a mad cow's mating call. I laughed and thanked Neil, but I was wary of falling into a competitive trap. Most people couldn't understand that I had fallen in a contest and that somebody else had won, but it was that simple, nothing personal, even though skaters and journalists wanted to make it so. I was so isolated as a skater and felt like such an outcast that the last thing I wanted to do was get into some sort of rivalry.

After that Magic Mountain contest in 1981, I had developed a fear of losing—I was terrified at what my friends and peers would think of me. My new runs had enough new stuff to slide me past the other guys, but nothing more. I played it safe and felt like a fraud. Everybody who patted me on the back and congratulated me for winning amplified what a fake I had become in my mind. My victories rang hollow. I wanted to go back to the Oasis days, when I had given it everything I had, and when my attitude toward contests had been pure. Losing made me reevaluate my contest thinking, and I felt like I had a new fire inside.

Neil Blender also wrote an article for *Transworld* about the summer camp. "Rodney was definitely on a training program of his own. Skating six, sometimes seven hours a day," he wrote.

MUTT

⚡SWAN SONG⚡

News had spread around the skate world that Del Mar would be my last contest. I had one thought in my mind—to land everything. I was seriously worried about what would happen if I fell again. Could I even survive the fallout of a psychological bomb so big as failing in my last contest?

I was feeling the most intense I've felt before a contest, equal only to the first time I competed, at the Oasis contest, where it all started. I stood in the middle of the freestyle area, whispered a quick prayer to God, and breathed slowly as I waited for my music.

The song kicked in, and I pushed as fast as I could and began doing my tricks as rapidly as possible. For the next minute I nailed trick after trick, not happy, not sad, just *there*. I was so calm once I started that I felt like I couldn't fall. It was like being on autopilot, and suddenly I just sort of woke up in the last ten seconds of my run.

The finality of it all hit me hard as I wound up for the 360s that ended my run. *This is it,* I realized, *when I stop it's all over.* I

IF I'D REALLY BEEN FORCED TO QUIT FOR GOOD, I'D HAVE MISSED OUT ON APPEARING IN VIDEOS LIKE THE ONE STACY PERALTA'S WORKING ON HERE.

tucked tighter to increase my spin. It was terrifying to see the end of something I loved so much speeding toward me. My mind was spinning out of control, my skateboard life flashing before my eyes—all that time in my garage, at the skatepark, on the road with Barry eating peanut butter and crackers with his dog, messing around with Steve, talking to Mrs. Hawk, Stacy's laughter, my first board, trying to stand on Jack's old Bonzai. When my wheels touched the ground all the memories slammed to a jarring stop, and the outside world rushed at me like a flood.

My last run was rated 99-99-99-99-98 by the five judges.

People crowded around me, congratulating me, asking me if it was true, was I really finished? I just nodded as I tried to hide the tears in my eyes. I walked over to the pro vert contest and watched Tony win. He included a "Mutt Air" in his run.

On the plane the next morning I was incapacitated, unable to deal with my emotions. I thought that this would be the last time

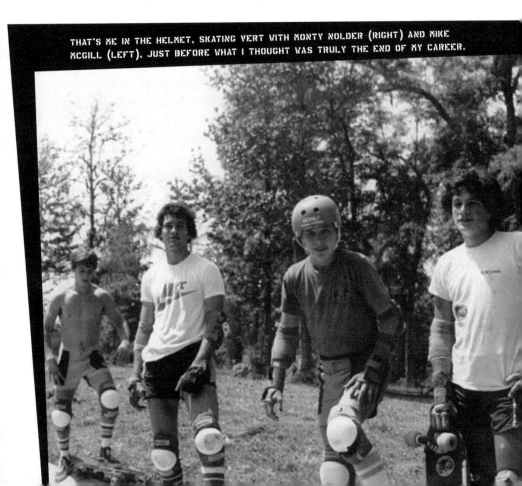

THAT'S ME IN THE HELMET, SKATING VERT WITH MONTY NOLDER (RIGHT) AND MIKE MCGILL (LEFT), JUST BEFORE WHAT I THOUGHT WAS TRULY THE END OF MY CAREER.

I'd ever come to California. I couldn't answer the flight attendant when she offered me a drink. I just shook my head.

"Don't cry about it, deal with it," my father said when I arrived home. I wasn't crying, but apparently he thought I was moping around, sulking.

I nodded and answered, "Yes, sir."

Fausto, the owner of Independent trucks, wrote my father a letter after that contest. I never saw it, because it was addressed to my father, but my mom saved it and told me about it years later. This intimidating man from San Francisco had gone out of his way to try to show my father how important skating was to me, and how important I was to skateboarding. It did nothing to change my father's mind, but I'll always be thankful to Fausto for caring enough to make the effort.

CHAPTER 15

WATCHING THE DECAY

I TRIED TO OBEY MY FATHER, BUT AFTER A MONTH OF SITTING BACK I

had to skate. I was a junkie. I had a secret board that I hid at school, and every Wednesday I used it to skate on the tennis courts. I was petrified of my father finding me—nobody had ever disobeyed him in such a blatant way.

Skating sucked. The one thing that powered and fueled me with energy was now my enemy, a reminder of my rapid decay. Every trick demonstrated what I was missing in life. Every week I witnessed my skills rotting, slipping.

My physical state began to deteriorate, as well. Though I was making an effort to gain weight again, depression had set in and I was headed toward my previous size. I couldn't sleep for more than a few hours at night, and I dreaded bedtime.

By the third month of my exile from skating I stopped talking. I'd go days without opening my mouth for anything other than a direct answer, and I had long ago ceased making eye contact with anybody. Only when my father was present did I make a real effort to maintain a show of normality. Teachers at school noticed my spark dimming. Even though I didn't talk to anybody, I had begun to mumble to myself occasionally, never anything meaningful, just nonsense that needed to get out. My emotions were running so high that odd phrases would seep out autonomously at unpredictable times. I couldn't follow conversations, and if people tried to talk to me their voices would lower until they finally drifted off and disappeared.

The really screwed-up thing is that I was still in mortal fear of failing in the more tangible parts of my life. Because there was nothing else to exert myself toward, I focused on school. Basic homework assignments turned into dissertations. Mr. McCall, my math teacher, took me under his wing, and for the entire year we went over basic number theory and got into the details of proofs that the textbooks skimmed over. His support meant more than he'd ever know.

By the fourth month of this, my father must have understood that his method of correcting my lifestyle had backfired. He was concerned that I wouldn't be able to function in society because of skating, but I was socially retarded to begin with, skating or not. At least before, people used to get a sense of who I was through my skating, but with my main form of communication severed, I was a wondering idiot.

He stopped me one weekend and forced me to make eye contact with him. Here was this incredibly fit, successful man staring at his son who weighed barely over a hundred pounds, had blotchy skin, bags under his eyes, and couldn't make eye contact.

"Rodney, look at me."

I tried to raise my line of vision, but it was hard. I didn't want to make contact with anybody or anything.

"Rodney," I could hear his voice crack with emotion, something I had never heard before. I looked up into his eyes, but for me it was like looking out of a filthy window. I couldn't really see him; there was no connection.

"I can see that this is taking a toll on you."

I didn't say anything or move. I didn't care what he did; if he hugged me or hit me, it didn't make any difference to me at that moment.

"As long as you don't get obsessive and crazy about skating you can skate again. But you can't compete because that drives you too hard; it'll distract you from school." My father thought that competition was the major force behind my skating, the reason I redlined.

"I don't want you to be so . . . so *into* skating, okay? It's not your life, but I'll let you do it. Just don't be so focused on it."

I nodded. I was so screwed up that it took a few hours for the news that I could skate again to soak in. I walked into the garage and plugged my boom box in and began skating.

My appetite returned, and soon I could sleep through the night again. Something in my spirit snapped and was reborn; I felt fresh. Thoughts organized themselves in my head. My energy returned.

I aced school and began doing demos again. Stacy had never pulled my board from production and was overjoyed when I told him I could skate again. I was worried, because competing had been a huge part of my success, and I didn't know if Stacy would be upset now. Fortunately, he said it didn't matter. Because I never told anybody in the skate industry the details of why I was retiring, nobody declared me dead. They thought I had merely stopped competing, for what reason they couldn't say. Luckily, my depression had also happened in the winter, when skate contests go into hibernation.

I continued to learn tricks, and Stacy asked me if I wanted to skate at a freestyle contest. Not compete, of course, just show up and skate for fun to show people I was still alive and kicking. The one thing that really changed my perception of skateboarding was how quickly the magazines turned on me once I stopped competing. Back when I was entering contests, the writers had usually praised me, but as soon as I was out of sight, they began saying other skaters had finally caught up with me and that, if I did come back, I might not even be able to win a contest again. Mostly they spoke of me in the past tense.

The praise had never blown up my ego before, but these new backhanded comments about my "retirement" bummed me out, forcing me to reexamine what contests and even the media meant to me. To an extent, my father's opinion was right—where had all this competition gotten me? I was already a has-been, even though I still skated as hard in those days as I had before, and my learning curve had accelerated, too. In fact, I was able to figure out a bunch

CAREFUL STICKER PLACEMENT. AS YOU CAN SEE, I'VE ALWAYS BEEN A FAN OF LANCE MOUNTAIN AND TONY HAWK.

of new tricks. (Two of them—half-Cab kickflips, where you turn your body and board 180 degrees while kickflipping, and 360 flips, where you rotate just the board 360 degrees as well as flipping it over a rotation—became staples of modern street skating.)

I skated at a Del Mar contest, as Stacy had asked, but didn't compete. This small action had a positive effect: the magazines stopped talking about how I was distracted by college and letting my skating slip.

Competing aside, I was back in the pro skater rotation, and the timing couldn't have been better; skating had begun to grow in popularity again. For some unknown reason, skating has followed a boom and bust cycle every decade since the 1960s, the time of the first real skate explosion. Popularity slowly grew, peaked in the middle of the decade for a few years, then declined. The next decade, the cycle repeated itself with a new generation of skaters who ushered in a more progressive style of skating. I started at the tail end of the last boom, in the 1970s, but now skating's sales numbers were increasing again.

I graduated from high school in 1984 and was awarded some sort of honorary prize for academics. It was supposed to be handed to me out in front of the school a month or so before the final ceremony. When the time came for me to accept the award, I was nowhere to be found. I had freaked out at the thought of standing in front of my school and ran away like a frightened child. Skating in front of hundreds, sometimes thousands of people, wasn't a problem for me, since I could just narrow my focus on my skating. But walking across a stage and looking out at people and having to say something? No way.

I'm not sure what happened at the ceremony, but a teacher later cornered me in the hallway and backed me into a wall by pointing an accusatory finger at me. She blasted me with both barrels, saying how disrespectful I was, how the school had gone to all this trouble to honor me, how it was a slap in the face to so many of my teachers. I couldn't even stammer out a word. I just looked down and walked away when her finger stopped jabbing in my direction.

I was essentially disengaged from high school and just handed in my work when it was due. I didn't even know if there was going to be a prom. I was already thinking ahead to Sweden, which I was booked to fly to for another skateboarding summer camp. Lance Mountain, one of my favorite skaters, was there when I arrived and he commented that I "had already put three days of skating in during my first hour."

Lance was always a positive reminder of the pure fun of skating for me. He was a top vert pro on Powell and was always goofing around—even in the middle of contests! You couldn't find two skaters who were bigger polar opposites in attitude than Lance and I, and I often envied his mixture of ambition to win and pure careless-ness. He never seemed to prioritize winning over the joy of skating.

Looking back, I think that skating used to have a fountain of youth aspect to it, at least in the mentality of the skaters. The enthusiasm skaters possess is often beat out of the average guy once he turns eighteen and has to enter the "real world" and start acting like an adult. But being a successful pro skater is like going on a summer vacation that stretches on for years. Grown men often act like mischievous kids, and Lance was the archetypal skater in this respect. He treated skating like a toy that provided him endless hours of fun.

After all the demos and traveling, my father felt comfortable that I had achieved some sort of balance in my life, and he finally allowed me to compete again. At the end of 1984, I won the N.S.A. World Open at Huntington Beach, and for the first time I felt like I had bridged the tension between my father's expecta-tions and my overwhelming passion for skating. *Transworld* wrote: "Rodney has got to be the most frustrating to skate against if you are a professional freestyler. It's good to have him there though. Welcome back Rodney!" It felt good to be back.

CHAPTER 16

"REAL LIFE" AND THE UNIVERSITY OF FLORIDA

NOW THAT I HAD GRADUATED FROM HIGH SCHOOL, IT WAS TIME FOR

my first step into the real world my father had warned me about. Ever since I was a kid, I had been frightened by his frequent warnings about life outside of P. K. Yonge, which to his mind was a coddling experimental school. In fact, I don't think he ever really trusted the grades I brought home. The University of Florida, on the other hand, would be a true measuring stick of my intelligence and work ethic. I signed up for basic engineering courses. They were designed to weed out the weaker students.

I was so afraid of how gnarly university was going to be that I devoured my text books. I'd complete my homework and keep going, doing whatever I could to squeeze more out of the lessons.

No one was more surprised than me when I got straight As and won the two freestyle contests I entered in 1985. After a year of school, I realized that I could handle competitive skating, no matter the burdens it added to my studies. College had always loomed over me—the black cloud on the horizon as I was growing up. I figured I would have to stop skating once I enrolled in college, that I'd have to devote all my energy just to passing classes. But in a way, college made it easier for me to focus and to succeed, because it forced me to divide my day into inflexible blocks of time. I had to be at classes at a certain time, I had to study, and I had to practice. On the weekends I did demos around the world.

PERFECTION? RIGHT.

The International Exposition was held in Vancouver in 1986, and a skateboard contest was set up in the middle of it. By then, skating was the most popular it had been since I first started in the 1970s. But unlike today, it was popular in an underground rather than mainstream way. Most ordinary people were still clueless about skating and couldn't name a single professional skater.

It was fun to be part of the Expo, because it was such a celebrated event and had a different flavor than the average skateboard contest. Countries sent teams to compete, and the team members walked in the opening parade, waving their country's flags.

Going to Vancouver for the Expo was more of a vacation than a regular contest for me, partly because we were there for over a week. The contest itself would include old-school events like high jump, slalom, and a 360 spin-off, as well as vert and freestyle.

Being there for a week allowed me to spend more time with fellow skaters than I usually could at contests. For me, it was the golden age of skating, when trick evolution and individualism blended seamlessly. I could look at the vert ramp and see Craig Johnson with his dreads poking out of a hole cut in the top of his helmet, or watch Tony Hawk skate next to the flamboyant Christian Hosoi, and all these different characters appreciated one another's uniqueness. There wasn't a cookie-cutter sense of style back then, no way a trick was "supposed" to look, and skaters often didn't even compare the way they did tricks. They just commented on how a certain skater's McTwists (a 540-degree midair rotation) had its own style. Skaters skated like themselves; there was no overwhelming pressure to conform to one particular standard.

Even though skating was hugely popular in the 1980s, the skate world was a closed community, a true subculture, so much so that mainstream coverage was still a novelty. If you saw a skateboard in a commercial, or even one leaned against a kid's bedroom wall in a movie, you were stoked. If you saw a skater on the street, you'd probably start talking to him and skate together. Instead of the many cliques that thrive in skating today, in the 1980s there was one massive clique that excluded nonskaters. We'd all go eat together, skaters from different teams with different interests outside of skating, and even though I was usually a loner, I never felt I was being judged by my peers.

That's another reason I loved skating—the almost universal acceptance one found in our insular community of outsiders. By being a hardcore skater in the 1980s, you were already a social reject, since the skate culture didn't permeate into the mainstream. Skaters had their own look, their own slang, their own way of looking at the world. We were like the population of the Island of Misfit Toys in the Rudolph the Reindeer claymation Christmas TV special. We were considered the bottom feeders by society: constantly chased by cops and security guards, harassed by pedestrians, and mocked by nonskaters everywhere. That persecution from the outside helped us bond.

Unfortunately, the Expo '86 contest was a nightmare. The vert ramp was shoddily built, and Jeff Phillips, a top vert skater, was its first victim—he had to have a two-inch long splinter removed from his foot. The freestyle contest was screwy, too. For some reason, they decided to cut the skaters to the top fifteen and to have a single run afterward. Usually, you did two runs in a final, and your lowest score was thrown out or the two were averaged together. Here we would have only one run. This got every freestyler sweating; one mistake and you could fall from first to fifteenth.

The organizers obviously hadn't thought ahead, because, with only one run to judge, there were six ties, and the skaters were forced to do runoffs. The crowd had no idea what was going on. Some skaters went once, others twice.

I was talking to myself, I was so nervous. To calm myself down, I found a notepad and began diagramming the synthesis of aspirin with stick diagrams. It was a good distraction, but I felt jumpy when my name was announced and I walked out and started my run. I could see Barry Zaritsky waving a towel on the side of the ramp. He

STEVE ROCCO FREESTYLING AT OCEANSIDE, 1986.

had been hired as the medical trainer for the contest and was always taping, icing, or stretching someone in his triage unit under the vert ramp. *Just like the old Sensation Basin days,* I thought.

I began my run with a few high-speed spins into one-wheeled spins and filled my run with handstand flips, the most difficult shove-it combinations I could do, and impossibles, a trick I had invented in 1982, but had only just recently felt comfortable enough to put in a contest run.

The name originated from one freestyler's opinion that it was "impossible" to land a trick where your board rotated end over end, in contrast to the usual quick sideways roll of the kickflip. I realized I had to use my rear foot as an axle so that my skateboard continued on a clean rotation as it wrapped around my foot. I liked the trick but realized its limitations. While the kickflip allowed me to expand, the impossible was a more awkward trick. But at the time, I was the only person who landed it, so it was a fairly big deal. I didn't think it was a perfect run, but I was happy to score a first ever perfect 100. For winning arguably the most prestigious world championship contest in the history of skating, I won a grand Canadian, which came out to about seven hundred bucks in U.S. currency. Nobody ever said I'd get rich from skating.

Near the end of that year, Powell and Peralta released their third and most popular skateboard video, *The Search for Animal Chin.* Stacy was a genius with his vision for skateboard videos, and he directed them on a scale that had never been done before. When he released *The Bones Brigade Video Show* in 1984, it was a massive success. He followed it with *Future Primitive,* an even larger success.

The main Bones Brigade (vert and street skaters) starred in *Chin,* traveling around the world and killing different hot spots. Kevin Harris, Per Welinder, and myself, arguably the three best freestylers in the sport, shared a few minutes of screen time in the film. We skated during a party scene in a converted garage.

I was never angry or bummed about the screen time. Freestylers have always been aware of their position in skating. We were nerds. We skated on the flat ground—how dangerous was that? The reckless vert and street riders got the chicks and glory, partying away those weekend nights while freestylers skated alone. Stacy always made Kevin, Per, and me feel that we were just as talented and well appreciated as the others, but it was obvious that from a business standpoint we moved a fraction of product compared to the street and vert boys.

Still, Stacy once told me that freestylers were extremely valuable, because we did demos all over the place. No ramp or huge space was needed for us. We could skate in everything from a gas station parking lot to the Macy's Thanksgiving parade, and in that way we helped promote Powell and Peralta to the mainstream.

ASPIRING PLAGIARIST

Dealing with people at the university was sometimes pretty daunting. My first semester, there was no room in English One, so they stuck me in an advanced English course, which I expected to be near impossible without the benefit of the first class. After our teacher had graded the first assignment, I watched him handing our papers back—everyone's except mine. "I need to talk to you after class, Rodney," he said. I wanted to curl up into a ball under my desk. *I knew it, I'm a retard,* I thought. *My father was right and I'm not ready for the real world. The guy's going to kick me out. Those stupid idiots over at admissions never should have skipped me up a class.*

After everybody was excused and the room empty, he held my paper in front of me, staring hard at me.

"This is very serious," he said.

I had no idea what he was talking about.

"Plagiarism is a very serious offense."

I nodded, still clueless. "Yes, sir, it is"—willing to say anything to ease the tension.

"Did you copy this?"

"No, sir." Nobody had ever accused me of cheating before. "No, with all my heart, I did it myself."

He handed me the paper. "I've never given an A plus before, and if you really did this on your own, it's excellent."

At the end of the term, as he was saying good-bye to everybody, he called me aside and told me that he was keeping my paper and would be investigating it over the summer.

"If I find out it is copied," he said, "I'm going to flag your record and your school career will be over."

BROKE

My father had always been talented at making money, and he wanted to help me capitalize on my savings. As far as I knew, my money was just sitting in the bank, earning crap interest. "I have a golf buddy who does life insurance," he said. "You can put in twenty thousand dollars, get a plan for a quarter million dollars. Once AIDS kicks in, life insurance could get a lot more expensive, and you may be glad you did it early." He might as well have been speaking Swahili, but I trusted him. I knew that my father loved the idea of his kids not being able to blow their money on stupid things like Members Only jackets.

His idea sounded good, and I trusted his business sense—it had made him a millionaire, after all. I agreed to do it. I figured I should have had at least thirty thousand dollars in the joint account shared with my mom. I barely made any money from my pro board, my biggest check being a little over three grand, but I had just signed with Converse and made five hundred bucks a demo for them. And I did a couple of them a month.

My mom had overheard our conversation and talked to me about it later. She looked terrified and began apologizing. "I'm sorry. I'm so sorry," she said.

"But what happened?" I asked. I didn't want to hurt her, but I needed to know.

She walked me into her room and showed me what she'd bought with the last of my money, a mink coat.

"See, Rodney? Isn't it beautiful? I just had to have it. I have a hard time looking at myself in the mirror, but I had to . . . you understand, don't you?"

I nodded. "It's okay, I understand. Don't worry about it."

There was nothing I could do about it. I understood right then that just as I had skating, she had her own way of dealing with things, and it was shopping. I knew how I felt under my father's pressure, how I did crazy things like starve myself to achieve some tweaked sense of control. In my mind, this wasn't something my mom did intentionally; I imagined that she had to do it or else she might have gone to some other extremes. My mom was my closest confidant in the world. I could never have felt bitter and betrayed by her. She had always done whatever she could for me unconditionally, and out of total love.

She knew there was no way I could back out of my father's investment without him finding out about her shopping.

"I can get you the money," she said, "I can swap some accounts around." I had no idea how she and my father handled their money, but I believed her when she said she could swing it. The less I knew, the better. She got me the money, and I invested the twenty thousand dollars into life insurance. Problem solved.

SWATCH

Swatch sponsored me and began sending me around the world for demos. This was the 1980s, and everybody had one of those neon-colored Pop Swatches. They paid me four hundred bucks a demo.

They flew me into New York for a big show at the Beacon Theater with professional models and dancers. At the time, my routine was as strict as ever. I studied the Bible twice a day, ran the stairs for twenty minutes every morning, barely ate any sugar, and skated two hours on every weekday and five on weekends.

After two days in New York, my head was spinning. All the performers had to take a bus out to a required dinner, and I'd hear nonstop chatter about their gnarly nocturnal activities from the night before. I was surrounded by models who snorted coke off fashion magazines and talked like bisexual sailors about their sleazy escapades and who on the bus was a better screw.

I had seen people snorting coke once before, but this was harsher. One of the times I went to the beach with Sara and her friends, there had been a party. I was ten, and I was superexcited that day because I had bought my first Pro-Tec helmet, just like all the pros in California wore. I was so proud of it and my awesome sticker placement that I put it on in the shop and wore it all day. I was wandering around some stoner-surfer's overgrown hut when I came upon a room where a group of strangers, a circle of older surfers I had never seen before, were snorting coke through a rolled-up fifty-dollar bill.

"Want some, dude?" a guy asked as he looked up with tiny pupils and a flaring red nose, like some distorted coke clown.

I could feel my helmet rock back and forth as I shook my head and wandered off to save some bugs in the backyard.

But here in New York, it seemed like the whole back of the bus inhaled coke before we even got moving. Every snort made me tenser. It was a roiling cesspool.

There was another freestyler at the show named Bob Schmeltzer, a top skater who often placed in the top five. The goofy French choreographer wanted to see what tricks we could do, because he wanted us to synchronize our skating on either side of the stage. Bob wasn't being lame, but he wasn't taking the skating seriously, and I equated that with "selling out." In my pretension, I was insulted that a skater could treat a public performance so casually. Skating meant so much to me that it freaked me out to see a skater disrespecting his gift.

"Okay, let me see what tricks you can do," the producer said, standing next to the choreographer. "You two have to do the same trick in sync."

Nosebone. San Francisco, 1987. I'd use a roll of hockey tape a week on my fingers so the griptape wouldn't rub them raw. J. GRANT BRITTAIN

One of the only decent shots I have of my mom, just after she watched me compete at Sensation Basin around 1978. PHIL CHICID

A slightly disturbing up-skirt shot of me skating the driveway ramp my father and I built. PHIL CHICIO

Steve Rocco—they look like hands, but they're really horns.
J. GRANT BRITTAIN

Kevin Harris, my favorite freestyler. J. GRANT BRITTAIN

Wedding day, April 2000. Traci and I wondering what our Australian friend, Gary, was doing with gold spray paint. BRUCE TALBOT

SOCRATES LEAL

Truck stand against a panoramic view of Wyoming. JODY MORRIS

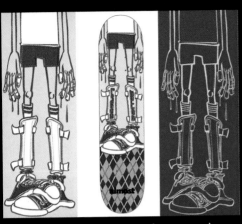

My first Almost deck, from graphic genius Marc McKee. MARC McKEE

Being featured in Tony Hawk Pro Skater saved me from a beating when gang members recognized me and requested tricks from the game. NEVERSOFT ACTIVISION

...rry about ...o show' mullen ...ot being at the ...wards ceremony.

his leather jacket wasn't back from the cleaners and he lost his shades, bro.

this is such a photoshopped enjoi shirt

RODNEY MULLEN IS MY DADDY

RODNEY

ROD IS GOD

enjoi

life is not a beach

my essence. ENJOI

What, me worry? *SEU TRINH*

I began firing off my tricks—all tricks I knew Bob couldn't do. Each trick deflated him a little bit more.

The producer told me to stop and took me aside.

"I know what you're doing," he said softly, "but you're killing his confidence and he's not going to be able to perform. You may be a great skater, and I can see that, but here, it doesn't matter. It has to stop. It is fundamentally wrong to be doing this."

I nodded. I knew I was being an asshole, and to this day I feel like an idiot for doing that to Bob, who was a talented skater and a nice guy. It had nothing to do with his skills. Skating was all about freedom to me, and here I was punishing another skater because he wasn't living up to my code. Maybe I was more like my father than I realized.

REAL STREET SKATING

Obviously rehearsal didn't count as *real* skating, so I had to skate my two hours at night. I cruised around and found a spot, hit my Casio, and started practicing. I drew a crowd, and suddenly a few black break-dancers started performing beside me.

"Hey, give it up for the man!" one of them said and passed around a hat that was quickly filled with change. Then he walked away.

The biggest break-dancer of the group walked over and nudged me. "Don't worry about that guy, I have a bucket of change and I'll give you some. Hey, watch my money for a sec, I'm going to buy the new L.L. Cool J tape," he said.

I couldn't believe this guy trusted me, some kid he had known for less than a minute. He returned a few minutes later and invited me to skate with his group the next night. I had to do the show and told him so. He left it as an open invitation, passed on his number, and gave me pointers on what I needed to do to improve my showmanship and make enough money to survive.

"You need an outfit and a name in order to perform with my crew," he paused and looked me over. "What about 'The Mighty Whitey,' " he laughed and patted me on the back.

We talked for half an hour, and then he shook my hand, looked me in the eye, and told me to take care. I couldn't believe that this tough street guy from Harlem had walked up to me on my own, tried to help me, trusted me with his money, and honestly wished me the best. It flipped my New York experience upside down. I wanted to be with this guy, on the street performing, not hanging out with coke-snorting dragons at some stupid production.

Meeting the break-dancer affected me so much that every night I went out searching for people to meet. If I saw somebody on the street who looked interesting, I'd walk up to them and start a conversation. It took all the courage I could muster, but it was worth it. There were gold mines of knowledge walking everywhere you looked. I met a schoolteacher who called himself Robert New York, who was walking around scribbling in a notebook. We strolled and talked for hours. I talked to hookers, one of whom offered me a rain check on a "free visit" next time I was in town.

The guy in charge of the show told me that I was considered "antisocial" by the other performers and strongly suggested that I attend another cast party. I sat in the bus as the models did more coke and taunted the black driver, who asked them not to do drugs on his bus. He was the coolest guy there, an old man who smiled at me with a face full of kindness. I was in a bad mood after I left his presence and had to wade through the room of excess.

At the cast party, I was hit on by this creepy older lady who worked in the "industry." She wouldn't leave me alone. My brain was boiling in my head. I walked out to the bus and hid in there until everybody else came out drunk and coked up.

We had to go through Harlem on the ride back, and I saw the area where the break-dancer lived. Here was an area that had sections resembling a war zone, but it had produced the coolest guy I'd met on my trip. We were driving by on our rock star bus, superficiality oozing out of every pore. I took off my Swatch watch and began smashing it on the metal part of my seat. I crushed the crystal, pulled the arms off, and was working on the straps. I didn't care what the people around me thought, didn't care that they were staring silently at me. That watch was symbolic to me of what I hated in life and what was sitting next to me—the waste and the arrogance.

When the bus stopped, I went back out to search for more people on the street.

CHAPTER 17

THE GREAT ESCAPE

AFTER MY NEW YORK MELTDOWN, I FOUND SOME SANCTUARY

when I returned home, in front of a country Baptist church. It wasn't spiritual sanctuary, since I never stepped foot in the church. Just as with my skating, my religious beliefs have always been very private. I was out one night driving, and I saw a church's parking lot illuminated by multiple lights. I pulled in and checked out the area. The pavement was smooth, the light perfect, and the feeling just right. It was quiet and isolated.

As I was casing out the joint I saw the pastor on the grounds as he was locking up. I walked up to him and introduced myself and immediately pleaded my case.

"You don't know how great your parking lot is!"

An odd expression pulled his eyes back and he stared at me. I knew that look. He was asking himself, *Is something weird about to go down here?*

I can only imagine what I must have sounded like, some intense-looking dude holding a skateboard and babbling about the redeeming features of a parking lot. *Is this fruit loop going to snap, whip out a shiv, and fillet me? Or, worse, am I going to have to listen to his internalized monologue for the next hour?*

But I pressed on. "Look, your parking lot is perfectly lighted up, and the pavement is smooth; you don't know how hard it is to find an open smooth place like this that's lit with the real white lights, not those new brownish dim bulbs. I need to skate at night, and this is the only place around. I promise I won't make a mess, I'll even clean up. I promise."

I pulled out my driver's license. "Here's my name and address and I'll give you my phone number and I'll never do you wrong, but if there ever is a problem, please, please contact me."

"Sure," he said, finally confident that I wasn't insane. "I can't see a problem with that."

Easy as that. Always being polite, just like Mom taught me. That parking lot became the most relaxing place in my life during that time. I skated there until one in the morning most nights.

ANARCHY IN THE MULLEN HOUSE

Steve Rocco was team manager for the popular skateboard company Vision, but he finally got fired in 1987 after torturing his boss one too many times. Confused, and I guess having nobody else to talk to, he drove over thirty straight hours from California to my house. I had told him about the church where I skated. It was almost midnight when Steve pulled into the parking lot. I glanced over to see who was invading my space, noticed Steve, and paused my stopwatch.

He popped out of the car, all hopped-up from the drive, which he had no doubt spent talking to himself.

"Rodney!"

"Hey, Steve, good to see you," I said.

"Rod, I just got fired from—"

"Hey, Steve, can you come back in another hour and . . ."—I looked down at my watch—"eighteen minutes?"

"What? I just drove over—"

I was getting antsy. I jerked my thumb toward the parking lot. "Steve . . . I have to get back."

"Okay, okay. Relax. You're like a skate Nazi or something. I'll grab my board and skate with you and we can talk."

I shook my head and tapped my watch, anxious that I was losing time, getting out of my rhythm. "Can you just come back in an hour and eighteen minutes?"

"Back?"

"Yeah, you have to go away."

He lowered his head, dejected, and walked away, no doubt muttering all the colorful names he had for people he disliked. All I could think was, *You drove over thirty hours and you had to show up during these two hours?*

We talked afterward. Steve was broke and almost homeless. He had saved no money; the only thing he had to his name of any significant value was his ex-boss's calling card number. I was tempted to tell him that if he had saved his boxes of wheels instead of throwing them at people, he could probably have sold them and covered his rent since he was no longer living with his parents.

I didn't tell my father that Steve had arrived. After a disastrous first visit a year earlier, I thought it better to hide him for the week he planned on staying. He had stayed at my house for a few days once, and he holds the distinction of being my sole friend to stay overnight at our house in the country. He wasn't exactly invited; I never really invited anybody over.

The information leading up to Steve's first visit had been fuzzy, but it seemed that he was on a tour with four other skaters, and by the time they'd reached Florida they'd made a unanimous decision to abandon Steve at my house, whether I liked it or not. Everything went smoothly for the first day or two until we all ate dinner together. My father started a conversation by asking us how much a complete skateboard cost. Steve and I started bouncing it back and forth and giggling at how clueless we had become—it was years since we had paid for anything. We had lost sight of the real intent of my father's question. He took this as disrespectful, so he got up and slammed his fist down on the table, ready to put us both in our places. We didn't argue, just excused ourselves and ran away.

For Steve's second visit to the house, my mom and I kept him hidden the entire time. When my father left for work, Steve would come out to play. We could always tell when my father was coming home, because he had a huge diesel truck and our dog would hear the engine revving and run outside, darting back into his doghouse where he belonged. He wasn't actually allowed to freely roam the house, but my mom let him anyway. He was petrified of

STEVE ROCCO (RIGHT), DOING WHAT HE DOES BEST: GOOFING AROUND. TOGETHER WITH NATAS KAUPAS (LEFT) AND MARK GONZALES (MIDDLE), WE HAVE HERE THREE OF THE MOST INFLUENTIAL GUYS IN SKATEBOARDING.

my father, because one time when he wouldn't stop barking, my dad fired a shotgun over his head. That had shut him up.

Steve and I often laugh about the visit and how my mom taught him to play piano. To show his appreciation, he taught her to "graze" at the supermarket. This was Steve's favorite way of dining out, you might say. He'd dip into the bulk food containers, grab a snack, and stroll the aisles, munching away. In twenty minutes he could devour a three-course meal.

After nearly a week, Steve decided that it was time for him to go back home, except, naturally, he hadn't given a lot of thought to his return trip. He pulled his empty pockets inside out to show me his savings.

"Hey, Rodney, can I borrow a hundred bucks to get back?" he said.

Whenever Steve had money, he spent money. Whenever I had money, I put it in the bank. I saved at least 90 percent of my money at that time.

With a straight face I said, "Steve, I don't have a hundred dollars."

"Yeah, you do," he said, and pointed to a hundred dollar bill in one of my drawers. I'd been paid in cash for a demo and had put the money in my sock drawer.

"Come on, Rodney, I know you're not that lame, you're just cheap. I'll pay you back," he pleaded.

I knew I'd never see that hundred dollars again, even if Steve became a multimillionaire in the future. I did want to help him out, but I also wanted that hundred, so I took out a piece of paper and began writing up a contract. Steve began mocking me relentlessly until I gave in and made him agree to a binding oral contract.

As I walked him to his car, I reminded him that an oral contract was just as binding as a written one.

Needless to say, that bastard still owes me that hundred dollars—with interest.

DUKES UP

I had aced my first couple of years of college, and during the 1987 summer break, I had no excuse to bury myself in books. But it was an easy escape while at home; I could say I was occupied and hide in my room.

On my second day of the break I was reading in my room when the back door slammed shut loudly. I heard my father stomping around. Instantly, my antennae registered what this meant. He had been outside working on the lawn mower. If he was inside banging around, he was probably in a foul mood. He opened my door.

From his stance I could tell that he was already angry, and that I was going to end up in trouble somehow.

"What are you studying for? School's over for now."

"I just thought I'd get ahead on—"

He cut me off. "Give me a hand with the mower; it's got a flat and I need help."

"Okay. Yes, sir."

I knew a confrontation was coming. We walked out to the mower, and the hair on the back of my neck prickled. It looked to me that he could fix the problem on his own if he'd wanted to. The lawn mower was on a slope and I was hesitant to start fumbling around and getting in the way before I knew exactly what he wanted me to do. I stood at attention beside it, waiting for orders.

"Don't just stand there; help me put that goddamn rock under the axle!" he yelled.

I nodded and said "Yes, sir," but it was too late. I was already sketchy from being so close to him while he was that pissed. I could see the lines squinting tight around his eyes. I backed away hurriedly, getting some distance between us. I could tell by his body movements how angry he was. I knew I was going to get it.

How to diffuse the situation? I thought. *Quick. Quick. Quick. What can I do?* I didn't want to do the wrong thing. In my head I was begging him to assign me a task, give me something to go find—a wrench or jack or something.

"Goddamn it!" he screamed. "Would you help me?"

Before I could reply, he threw his gloves down into the dirt and whirled around. His hands were already balled into fists. "Come on!" he shouted and bobbed his fist as if he was cocking it.

Adrenaline shot through me. All the bedtime stories he told me about his championship boxing in the navy came back to me vividly, crystal clear.

He was a few feet below me on rocky, uneven ground, and instinctively I pushed him back. He lost his footing on the down slope and stumbled back a step as I leaped away from him.

More surprised than anything, he stared up at me as I bounced on the balls of my feet, fists clenched and fuming with adrenaline. For the first time in my life, rage completely replaced fear and left me with an eerie clarity as I stared down into his dumbfounded eyes. It was as though every smothered ember of rage reignited and exploded out of me in a guttural voice that wasn't my own.

I screamed as I bounced and shook, tears streaming down my face. "Why are you doing this? Why? Why do you make yourself so hard to love? I know I'm not what you want, but I'm trying—that's what matters. I know I'm not there, but one day I will make you proud."

He just sat there with glazed eyes. His long arms dropped down his sides, and his body arched forward as if it were weighed down.

He slowly gathered himself up and walked over to me slowly. My feet shifted in the dirt, fortifying my stance with some unconscious strength that I didn't recognize as my own. My mind reeled at what might happen next. His hand slowly rose but his eyes stayed low. He seemed to be reaching to shake my hand. I faltered for a second, and tentatively met his. We shook hands as men, for the first time.

There was no question for me anymore. I had often told myself that I should leave, that something worse than this was bound to happen, but it took this incident to make it real enough to act on it. Next time I might not be this fortunate.

"Let's go for a walk," he said in a calm voice. It was over, and I sensed his remorse at letting his temper get the best of him. We walked to the barn that we had built a few years earlier. It was basically a concrete slab under a tin roof lined with fluorescent bulbs, but perfect for skating. It was where I did all my skating at home.

"We could build an enclosure so that when it rains the concrete wouldn't get wet," he said. I shook my head slowly. I already knew I wouldn't be skating there anymore.

"No, it's okay. It's fine as it is, thanks. It's perfect."

ESCAPE

That night, I told my mom I was going to leave. The next day, I had to do a Swatch demo in Corpus Christi, Texas. When the people organizing the demo picked me up, they asked if I was sick. I had barely slept the night before, and the color was drained from my face. At that demo a kid asked me to wear a bracelet he'd made out of wire with beads. I was in the middle of my demo in a fancy department store's jewelry department. Everything was glistening white, and expensive clothes racks had been moved out of the way to give me space. In the middle of an ollie nosebone, when I grabbed my board, the wire bracelet cut my wrist and blood began dripping all over the white floor. It was a long, deep cut, but I barely noticed it, and I tried to carry on the best I could as it continued to coat my hand in blood. I was so programmed to end my demos with 360s that I automatically whipped into a spin. I could make out the whirling blurred faces of people stepping back, waving their hands in front of their faces as the droplets rained out like a sprinkler, leaving a circle of red spray on the glistening white floor. That was the end of that demo.

I taped a couple of napkins to my wrist with hockey tape and flew home, thinking the whole time about how my life was about to change. I was so upset that the guy sitting beside me asked me if I was going to pass out—I looked so pale.

I sat in my car in Gainesville's small airport parking lot, listening to Mozart's *Requiem*. On the way home I thought about what my friend Hudson had advised me to do. He was the sole friend I had made at school after almost fifteen years. He was ten years older than me, and getting his PhD in chemistry. Instead of being a straight-up nerd, Hudson was into punk rock and photography. He saw me skating one day and asked to take some shots, and after that we began to hang out. Gradually I confided in him, and he brought an outside perspective to my life for the first time and encouraged me to move out. He provided the push that helped me overcome my inertia and make that decision.

I drove to my grandma's, who lived twenty minutes away from us. It was the first time I had really spoken to her since I was a little kid.

"Things are bad between my father and me," I said. "Do you think it would be possible for me to stay here, just until I get situated?"

"Of course," she said. "I'm sorry this happened to you. I usually rent out the basement, but you can stay there. I'll give you some advice, though, Rodney, don't cry about it. This is life and it's full of lessons; consider this part of your education."

I told her I was going to be leaving in the next few days and slowly dropping my gear off night by night, so that my father wouldn't notice and confront me.

I cried on the way home but managed to dry up before I parked the car. My father happened to be out front and asked me how my trip was.

"Fine. It was okay."

"You look sick."

"I'm fine. I've just been thinking a lot."

"Yeah? Well, don't think so much."

He walked off and I stopped sweating.

I waited until my father was asleep that night and told my mom, who always stayed up later, that I'd seen Grandma and was going to be staying at her house. I started crying because I was worried about her, but she shook her head. "This is good. It'll all be fine. I'm happy that you're doing this. Be strong and do not worry about me."

I strategically packed a load of stuff into my car late at night and drove to my grandmother's house. I only had to clear out my room, so it only took me two nights of trips. I left everything superficially the same, so that if my father happened to peek in everything would look normal. I even left all my skateboard memorabilia. On the third night, I packed up my car for the final time, unloaded it at my grandma's house, and went back to see my mom. I stayed up into the early hours, talking to her and writing my father a letter.

I wrote a one-page letter to my father, apologizing and thanking him for all that he'd given me and saying that one day I would make him proud.

My father woke up around seven, and I pretended to be asleep. When he left for work, I put the letter in his bathroom and said goodbye to my mom. She'd put on a Mozart concerto we both loved.

"That's it, Mom, everything is gone." She was strong and tried to remain chipper, talking about how exciting it would be for me to be on my own. She promised to bring me home-cooked meals from time to time.

We hugged and I left.

THE LONGEST DAY

I couldn't sleep once I got to my grandma's. I counted down the hours until my father returned home and found the letter. I only expected one thing—rage. It didn't take long for him to get the information out of my mom. She told me later that he yelled, "I know you know where he is."

She called my grandma and told us that he knew where I was.

I was exhausted, hadn't eaten, hadn't slept, and my mind began spinning nightmare visions of him breaking down the door and beating me unconscious. I tied a string to the knob that would release cooking pans to wake me up, and I slept with a piece of pipe under the covers. My fears had gotten the best of me, and they proved groundless.

DROWNING

My grandma's basement was so moldy that fungus was starting to grow in small cracks. I was grateful for her help, but the first night I noticed I was having trouble breathing. I'd never had any problems like this before, so I thought I had a cold or chest infection, but gradually my breath became more and more labored. I woke up to a squeaking sound deep in my chest. It took me a few minutes to realize that it was my lungs. At the very worst, I thought I was getting a bad cold, but it was the beginning stages of asthma.

My mom knew where I was, so we saw each other every week. I was doing more and more demos and still getting straight As in school, but it was taking me twice the effort because I couldn't focus. I had saved up almost eight thousand dollars since the insurance incident, and I'd eat crackers and peanut butter, macaroni and cheese, noodles, anything cheap that kept me full. I was less stressed than I had been at my father's house, but my breathing was so bad that I'd have coughing fits that left me wide-eyed and gasping most of the night.

On one visit when my mom came down to the basement, I could tell she was nervous about something.

"Rodney?" she called out.

"Mom! How's it going?" I was excited to see her.

"Oh, okay," she said. She looked horrible, distressed. "Remember that money I got you for the life insurance policy? I need it back. Not all of it, but half."

My mouth hung open. This time it would really hurt. I was on my own, scraping my pennies together, and it would all be gone in a moment. But I knew my mother had no one else to turn to because my grandma's family fortune had been spent years ago. She had her house and that was basically it.

"This is all the money I have in the world, and I still have to pay taxes." I'd been gutted.

"Sorry, Rodney," she said, "there's no way around it that I can see."

I wrote her a check that cleaned out my account.

My breathing got worse, and I'd wake up from sleep because of a scary combination of nighmares of drowning and my father coming after me. I made the same familiar wheezing sounds whenever I lay down now. I visited a doctor, and after listening to my chest, he told me I had asthma and gave me an inhaler and antibiotics. His bigger concern was my blood pressure, but I just cared about breathing. I had never had any breathing problems before. In less than two weeks, the basement mold, the dust mites, the stress, and whatever else was down there had trashed me. I felt lost and alone, and the worst part was that I'd experienced just enough freedom for it to sting.

My mom's brother came to visit, and he eventually moved into my grandma's house. Because of that, I became closer to him than ever before. At one time he had been a talented and successful dentist, and he liked to tell me the details behind some unique dental tools he had invented. He seemed to be as gifted as my mom; yet he was far different, and for all his brilliance, he seemed to be crippled by the pain of his emotional breakdown. I wondered about his stability as he compulsively wrote letters to the governor, advising him on how to correct Florida's health-care issues.

He had served some time for contempt of court and shortly afterward been declared mentally incompetent by the State of Florida. He laughed as he described scaring the poor young woman who had been dispatched to assess whether he was mentally incapable enough to draw a state disability check. He was proud of tricking her into believing he was crazy.

One night, we had a long discussion about mental illness, and he explained how it felt to have a breakdown. "It was an incredible feeling of disorientation. You can't see things for what they are anymore, to the point where you're physically dizzy." He told me detailed stories about what it was like in the mental ward, and the people he had met inside who were so incredibly insightful, educated, and capable—except for the occasional breakdowns that put them there in the first place.

I loved my uncle, and it scared me to see someone with that many gifts end up so broken. He had been a charismatic professional with a loving family. In a quick chain of events, he had descended into a depressive quagmire out of which he never escaped. What shook me most was that there were details he described that I thought were brewing in myself, and it made me want to run as fast as I could in search of balance.

CHAPTER 18
A NEW COMPANY

SOON AFTER, I MOVED OUT OF MY GRANDMA'S BASEMENT, AND THE

only place I could afford to live was a government-subsidized house at the edge of town. For two hundred and forty bucks a month, I lived on the other side of a wall from a wife-beating maniac. A couple of apartments down housed a bunch of bikers, and a suspiciously overt drug dealer. All I cared about was my music, so I taped the windows shut with black poster paper. I didn't want anybody peeking in and getting ideas about stealing my stereo.

The most positive aspect of my new residence was the grave-yard next to it. I'd wander around at night, relaxing in the wide open acres of grass and tombstones. In my room, I was always scared that my wife-beating neighbor would hear my music and come over and smack me around.

I would visit my grandma sometimes. Shortly after I moved out, my uncle parked his stuff in my old room at her house. Talking to him was always a wild and unpredictable ride, but seeing how he decorated that basement took the experience to a completely dif-ferent level. He would often read aloud passages from Aleister Crowley, who openly identified himself as the Beast. His room was full of stacks of books covering the Golden Dawn, systematic studies in magic, ritual witchcraft, and the occult in general. It was like Crowley fan club headquarters. Pictures of various symbols hung on the wall and vintage tarot cards were stacked everywhere, each deck dog-eared from constant use.

I related to his passion for the sciences. He had a deep background in physical chemistry, and higher graduate textbooks were intermingled with the occult ones. Our conversations would abruptly jump from spooky topics to technical discussion of fermion decay.

He freaked me out, because he really believed what he was talking about, and I could see that it was evil. His bitterness was growing by the day, and he told me that he considered me a worthy recruit because I was smart and driven. He began explaining the basics of the occult to me anytime I visited, as if I was attending some sort of inverted Sunday school.

I was never rude to him, and I was interested in what he was saying, but I realized it was that intrigue, that wonder at all the possibilities he was explaining, that pulled me into his world. I could see what it was doing for him, and it wasn't making him a better person in my eyes. I visited less frequently.

SKATEBOARD GREMLIN

Steve was living in his car and occasionally on his friend Natas Kaupas's kitchen floor. I had always been paranoid about being broke, about having to work a miserable job, and because of this I'd been saving every cent possible. Thanks to all the mixed-up events at home, I was now in the exact same position as Steve. Actually, I was worse off—I still owed taxes. I had to get a loan from the bank to pay fifteen grand off, demo by demo.

Steve had been talking to Natas and Skip Engblom. Skip owned Santa Monica Airlines, the company Natas rode for. Apparently, Skip had allowed Steve to use his company's name, in an effort to help Steve out of his jam. He told Steve to buy five hundred boards and said he'd show him how to sell them. Steve called it Santa Monica Airlines, *Rocco Division*. He got a cash advance on his credit card and spent six grand on his boards and began his life as a company owner and skateboard industry gremlin.

After he sold the boards, Steve and John Lucero started a company called Prime Time distributors, and each put in six grand. Lucero pulled out after Steve spent a chunk of money on racks, though. Steve was screwed. (Not that I blame Lucero; Steve would instantly develop a feverish look in his eyes the minute he had a wad of cash in his hands.)

For half a year, I hadn't spent money on dishes, used yogurt containers as bowls, and raided the condiment sections of fast-food restaurants. I paid back the bank and saved up ten grand. Then Steve phoned me and laid out his story. He had gone to a friend of a friend whom I'll call "Suzuki," who functioned as a loan shark. Steve, with no business background, no accounting background, no manufacturing background, borrowed twenty thousand dollars from him.

I was living in Dostoyevsky land in my government housing apartments. The group of bikers made odd noises all night long, probably operating one of the first meth labs in Florida. I had done such a thorough job with my window that no light came in.

Here was Steve's answer to my problems: "Drop out of college, come out here, and work with me."

I had to go to Tahiti with Tony Hawk for a Powell demo, and we had a layover in LA for a few days, so I said I'd think about it and at least talk to him. He spent a day trying to brainwash me into thinking his little company would work. How qualified, I asked myself, was Steve to run a company, seeing as he was fired as team manager and lost his pro model at the same time? To his credit, he knew a lot about dry cleaning, his father's business, and had sold used cars with moderate success for a short time. But most impressive was the fact that after years as a successful professional skater and entrepreneur, he'd saved up exactly nothing. True, he was smart, but solving *Omni* puzzles is a lot different from running a business.

At the time, skating was run by "The Big Five": Independent Trucks, Powell, Vision, Santa Cruz, and Tracker. They collected around one hundred million a year. Steve, penniless, already in hock with his credit card company and the local loan shark, wanted me to join his ship—a ship that already had holes letting water in due to a pending lawsuit over the name he was using. I knew enough about business to know that we'd have no chance of making it.

I spent all night thinking about it and it came down to Steve as a person. Yeah, he was an irresponsible bugger who still owed me a hundred dollars, but he had always looked out for me. And he was determined to make this work. For instance, when I asked him how he paid for the sales calls all over the world, he told me that he still had the numbers for Vision's company calling card.

I debated both sides all the way through the airport on my way to Tahiti, through the metal detectors, through security, and up to the departing gate.

"Why?" Steve asked. "Why not? Just do it. Look, I can make it on my own, I can do it with Suzuki, I can have people help me make it, but why? Why not do it with me?"

I wrote a check for six grand with trembling hands and gave it to him at the last possible moment before running onto the plane.

WHEN IN ROME

When possible, I'd extend any LA layover I had and stay with Steve for a few days or a week. I had met a girl at a demo about a year earlier, and we had slowly developed a long-distance relationship. She wanted to move to California, and I connected her with Steve. Since they both needed to pinch pennies, she rented a room from Steve, who lived with his girlfriend, a Mormon bishop's daughter from Utah who wanted to rebel and found an enthusiastic helper in her new boyfriend. I had the perfect setup now, with my best friend and first serious girlfriend all in one house. But I was used to spending most of my days in self-imposed isolation, which was not exactly good training for a relationship.

One night before I flew to Hawaii for a demo, my girlfriend, Renee, and I got into an argument about all the time I spent away from her. Of course, it was a perfect relationship for *me*—I was in control. I could fly in when I wanted to, see her, stay as long as I wanted to, and go back and nerd out with my schooling and skate with no distractions. She had every right to be frustrated with me, but at the time I didn't have any perspective other than my self-centered one. I couldn't deal with the pressure and resolved the argument the way I had resolved every problem since I was ten—I went skating. She yelled that she was going to take a bath. Before I left, I wanted to apologize, but once I heard the water running I just bailed.

I returned three hours later. Renee was still in the bathroom.

"Hey, Renee, you okay?" I knocked on the door. "You still in the bath?"

I jiggled the doorknob. It was open; I walked in. Blood was smudged all over the counter, Renee was lying in a tub of bloody water, staring at me groggily and trying to tape her wrists up. She looked up at me, unable to figure out who I was.

"Renee . . . you okay? Let me see your wrists." She stared ahead like a zombie.

I looked at her left wrist and saw the crisscross of cuts she'd made with a shaving razor. I helped her out of the bath, leaned her against the counter, and looked at her eyes, trying to get them to focus. I saw the razor on the floor and held it up in front of her face.

"Renee, this is wrong, so wrong. I love you. I don't want you to die. I love you." There was no reaction; she just stared ahead.

I needed to get a response out of her, so I lifted my hand and pressed the blade against my wrist, not cutting myself, just pushing it against my skin.

Her eyes snapped to consciousness, and suddenly a blood-curdling wail filled the bathroom. It was the most basic, primal scream I have ever heard in my life. Her eyes were wide open, like the eyes of an animal panicking.

It was as if that scream had pulled a plug in her, because she stopped and slumped down. But I could tell she was out of her daze. I walked her around gently. She was coherent and mumbled.

Renee's suicide attempt jolted me. I realized that she was the first person outside of my family that I had ever loved, the first who I let get close enough to hurt me. I was dealing with a whole new set of emotions.

The next morning, she was fine. I made sure she was okay, and she told me not to worry. She told me that she regretted what she'd done. I had to do a demo in Hawaii, so she drove me to the airport. I called her compulsively over the three days.

Renee was the first person who I trusted to provide the security that I felt on my skateboard. As much as I cared about her, though, I knew that skating was still my first and most intense passion. But opening up for that first time was a big step for me. I began to think about our relationship. It was moving much too fast, and I wanted an escape route, only I was petrified to disagree with her, scared that she'd kill herself if I broke up with her. She took care of that when she told me that she'd had a dream in which God told her to break up with me.

Even though I wanted to be alone again, I felt abandoned after our breakup. I had tried to open myself up, and that had left me confused and sorry. My boyfriend/girlfriend experiment felt like one more dead end.

SKATER IN THE CORN

I hung in with school and finished my fourth year. My grades slipped for the first time, but I didn't care; I knew I was finished with school. I had burned out. I spent a few weeks on the Powell summer tour working, trying to avoid a full-fledged anxiety attack. By the second week of the tour, I couldn't hang on. My nerves acted up, and I became moody, antsy.

Finally, I lost it and after my freak-out, I frantically called Steve. It was late at night.

"Corn!" I yelled into the phone. "Corn!"

Steve's confused voice crackled in the receiver, asking me to slow down and make some sense. "I'm losing my mind," I said. "I didn't know where I was; I just sort of looked up and saw all this corn whizzing past me."

That string of babble didn't exactly clear things up for Steve.

"I'm a prostitute," I continued. "I'm selling my gifts. All these people, all this hoopla. I can't relate."

One of the guys on tour who I was sharing a room with wouldn't let me use the bathroom, because he didn't want the steam to escape. His pants were in the bathroom, and he'd left the shower on full blast hot so he could steam his pants and press them before he went out in public.

"Rodney, calm down. Tell me what happened."

I pieced together my last few hours for Steve. I had been in the Powell tour van with a few other skaters. It was hot and sticky as we drove into some East Coast town. I had slowly been getting more and more anxious at the demos, and I knew it was only a matter of time before a meltdown. I couldn't deal with the mob scenes, people shouting questions at me, chanting my name, suffocating me as they squeezed in closer and closer trying to get an autograph. I dreaded getting out of the van at demos.

I finally flipped in Philly, pushing autograph seekers away and throwing my pen in the air, yelling like Charlie Brown in a fit of despair. It was a full-blown panic attack, with the air-raid sirens going off in my head. I turned on everybody and yelled, "I'm the same as you! I'm no different! Why do you want my ink on your skateboard?"

A huge body builder scooped me up and carried me over his shoulders, above everybody else, and walked me across the street to an empty lot.

"Sorry," I apologized.

He nodded his head at me. "Naw," he said, waving his massive hand. "I understand."

But there wasn't always a person to carry me away, and the thought of another demo and the constant whining in the van grinded like sandpaper on my mind. I started hyperventilating, staring out the window at the miles of harvesting corn, trying to concentrate on being anywhere besides this van stuffed full of people.

Didn't work.

"Hey," I said as calmly as possible, "could you please stop the car for a second?"

The driver pulled the van over to the side of the road. The skaters must have thought I was going to be sick. I stepped around people and walked casually around the side of the van. *Nice and easy,* I said to myself, *must not do anything to arouse suspicion.* I could see everybody in the van watching me.

It was as if a starter gun was fired—I sprinted as fast as I could into a row of corn, away from the freeway, the passing cars, the nonstop prattling, the music, the stuffiness of the van. I ran down a row, cut across to another one, cut back and ran in the opposite direction. Zigzags, squares, triangles—I ran all the patterns I could think of. My energy was blowing up inside me, I had to find a way to get it out or it would consume me, destroy me. I ran and ran until I collapsed, heaving, and lay down in the dirt, out of sight from anybody except the crows flying around wondering what in the hell was happening in their corn patch. I stared at the sky, still heaving, until I began to breathe normally.

After an hour I walked back to the road, totally relieved. I saw a 7-Eleven with a van parked in its lot. I walked up and nodded meekly to everybody. Nobody said a word.

"I'm okay now, guys. Sorry about that."

OUT OF STATE

I skated at a contest in San Francisco and won, and when I returned I packed up everything I owned—it all fit in my car—and

shipped it to California. I left Florida for good and flew into LAX.

I moved in with Steve and two skaters also working for the company. I had my own room and even my own mattress. One of the skaters knocked on my door as I was falling asleep one night.

"Rod," I heard him whisper. "Rod, I've got a hot one here."

I opened the door. The skater continued, "She's downstairs; let me use your bed and I promise I'll change the sheets."

I slept on the floor downstairs. A few times a week I donated my bed.

I drove in with Steve every morning, the two us like a married couple. I'd work, skate, and do demos on the weekends. I was in charge of doing the books, and, frankly, it's amazing that we stayed in business. The four of us, along with Jesse Martinez, did whatever was necessary to stay afloat. We'd all pack boxes, write invoices, clean up—whatever needed to be done. A favorite pastime for me and Steve was calculating how many boards we needed to sell to stay in business for one more day. At first it was sixty-six boards, and then, once expenses added up, it grew to eighty.

Everything was sucked into that money pit of a company. I made money from Swatch demos, but Steve wasn't doing demos, and he gave himself a salary that barely covered his rent. Every day he'd frantically open the mail, sorting out the dollars sent in for stickers, and he'd use that money to eat. If no dollars came, he'd go grazing.

Our sole treat was classical music. We'd hit the library and research various composers. We allowed ourselves one CD a week, and we went to Tower records, because it had the largest selection we knew of. We'd spend hours picking that CD, arguing about what to get.

"One day, Rodney, we'll be able to come through here with shovels and just scoop up whatever we want," Steve said.

Everything dangled by a hair; everything was timed down to the last minute. Steve would come into work every day and pack boxes, take orders, and try to sell a few more boards. Then at six he'd scrounge together whatever money we had and pick up blank skateboards. He'd buy as many as he could and take them down to Huntington Beach, to a friend who screened at night. He'd hang out for five hours, leave at midnight, and drive back with a van full of boards, praying he wouldn't have to slam on the brakes or get in accident, because then the boards would get tossed around and smear the paint, which was still wet. The fumes from the paint were so gnarly that he had to open every window and stick his head out. Even with that, he still got headaches.

BOULDER HOLDER. TAKEN IN THE EARLY 1990S—SHORTLY AFTER LEAVING POWELL AND PERALTA I STARTED RIDING FOR SMA/WORLD INDUSTRIES, A COMPANY I HELPED START.

I worked the most ill-suited job in existence for me—sales. I'd cold-call shops, introduce myself, and pitch our teeny company and pray for the owner to buy at least a board and a T-shirt. The worst part was how long it took to dial each store. We were still using Vision's old calling card, so I couldn't dial direct; I had to dial a 1–800 number and then punch in the code and then dial the shop's number.

We were pretty pathetic with only three pros, Jeff Hartsell, Jesse Martinez, and Steve. I still skated for Powell. While at the Long Beach trade show—an expo for the skate industry—O., the infamous skate photographer, told Steve to come outside and check out a kid skating in the lot. Immediately, he picked out Jason Lee for his talent. (If the name sounds familiar to non-skaters, it's because Jason is now a famous movie actor, starring in flicks like *Almost Famous, Chasing Amy,* and *Vanilla Sky.*)

Amazingly, my sales calls continued for a while. An absolute idiot, I never thought that skating for Powell and calling shops up to sell another company's boards was a bad thing.

This is a testament to how cool Stacy Peralta is—it was partly his company, yet he called to warn me that George Powell was going to be calling me.

And George did call.

"Rodney, irreparable damage has been done."

CHAPTER 19

LOAN SHARKS AND SKATEBOARD WAR

WHILE MY PROBLEMS WITH POWELL WERE STARTING, BUSINESS WAS

so rocky that we couldn't always pay Suzuki on time. The non-negotiable Louisville Slugger contract demanded that we pay back three grand a month for a year, but our company wasn't growing fast enough to cover us. So here's how two math nerds solved their numbers problem: we borrowed another twenty grand from Suzuki to pay back the first loan.

Steve was nervous about the idea of going to Suzuki for a second loan. Here was his rationale, as expressed to me: "I figure we'll spend ten thousand dollars buying boards, get a thousand boards with that, and then have four months worth of 'loan' payments, and by then we'll catch up." But things kept happening that disrupted our plan.

If we had a bad month and couldn't make the payment to Suzuki on the first, Steve always made sure we handled it like a "team." Here's how our teamwork worked out: an hour or so before the agreed-upon time for the money exchange, Steve would suddenly disappear. Now, I had no idea what to say to Suzuki. He was an intimidating dude—*really* intimidating. He'd ask how things were going and cruise in and look around to see our operation. He saw that we had money invested in product, and that must have reassured him that we weren't trying to screw him over. The fact that I was about three seconds from grabbing his legs and begging for mercy was also obvious to him, and he appreciated that.

Suzuki intimidated you in a way that wasn't straightforward. He'd tell stories about guys who hadn't paid him, and how he'd sent "Brick" to their house. A few had been put in intensive care. I prayed that I never met Brick, because if I did it would be too late. The loan interest was about to get painful.

SHOULD I STAY OR SHOULD I GO?

Steve was friends with Stacy and he respected George, but both of us hadn't really thought how our business affected anybody else.

I was still a full pro for Powell, doing demos all over Europe and North America for them, in addition to my Swatch and Converse demos. When George called with the opening greeting of "Rodney, irreparable damage has been done," it was two days before a demo I had scheduled in Germany. I tried to use that as an excuse to stall the meeting he wanted immediately.

"Come tomorrow. Wake up early, fly up here to Santa Barbara, and you can be back in time for your flight," he said.

I couldn't sleep that night, and for a few reasons. I liked George. I was one of the few on the Powell team who had a genuinely friendly relationship with him. The rest of the pros didn't dislike him; they just never dealt with him, because Stacy handled the team. But George and I clicked—he was an engineer and a math guy like me. The last thing I wanted to do was disappoint him.

I flew up to Santa Barbara and George picked me up.

We drove around and talked. "Look," George said, "Rocco isn't going to be around long anyway. His company is under litigation, and there is no way in the world he's going to be able to survive."

A month earlier, Santa Cruz had threatened us. They were a hugely successful company at the time, and I think they owned Santa Monica Airlines or had some deal with Skip. From what I was told, Skip really didn't have the right to let us use the SMA name. If they wanted to get serious, they could easily squash us. Naturally, my doomsday attitude kicked in, and I figured we were already dead. Steve didn't seem to be letting it bother him too much, though.

"Look, Rodney, you are bright," George continued, "you're Stanford material. Just work up here with me for a while and get some experience. Who knows? Maybe there's something I could do down the line that helps you get in. You belong there."

I was blown away by George's generosity and his faith in me. I knew he didn't want to lose me as a pro for Powell. I was aware that I was a famous skater and that I helped his company, but he also cared for me as a person.

"Thank you so much," I said. We drove around in his Mercedes and talked some more, and he showed me his Mac 2, which was a big deal at the time because it was a computer with a color monitor. Then he laid the bomb on me. He asked me if I thought I'd ever get the money back that I had invested. I told him I didn't know.

"I'll pay you that money back, and then Steve can make payments to me until it's all squared away. Do you think Steve will even give you anything on paper acknowledging that you even gave him the first cent? That's how much I wonder about Steve Rocco, Rodney."

I flew back to LA and met with Steve and told him about George's offer and that I was thinking about taking it. I expected Steve to be bummed at me, angry that I didn't support him, but he got all excited.

"That's great! Take it!" he said, hyper now. "We'll tell him that you invested twice as much as you did, and you'll make the money, and you can invest it in the company and he won't know!" By that time, I had invested what was to me a mind-staggering eighteen thousand dollars.

I realized that with heart like that, it was as true as it got. If I bailed and Steve had to pay George back, I knew he might eventually meet Brick. I also knew that skating was dwindling in popularity, with freestylers taking the hardest hit. I could see that my days, *any* freestyler's days, were numbered. I was an endangered species, but I figured I would at least have a job with Steve after my skating career died. Steve was the only real friend I had ever had, and if our ship was going to sink I wanted to be on it with him.

Steve also had an intuitive perspective on the skating industry that the old guards didn't. His ear was to the ground, and he knew that skating was dying. The industry was in a slump, board sales were dropping at an alarming rate, fewer people were becoming interested in skating, and the ones who were interested wanted rawer companies with more street credentials. Top vert pros on

Powell went from making ten to twenty grand a month to making a few thousand. I probably had the top-selling freestyle board in the world, and I cashed monthly royalty checks for a few hundred. Every day fewer and fewer people skated.

"You know, Rodney," Steve said, "it's not always safest to be on the *Titanic*; sometimes a little lifeboat is the only thing left in the water after the big ships go down."

I told George I would talk to him when I got back from Germany.

When I came back, things got a lot more complicated. Steve and I had moved into the house of RI, a pro BMXer, and Steve's friends would stay with us sometimes. One of them was Mike Vallely, an eighteen-year-old kid from Jersey who became an overnight sensation. Powell was largely betting its future on him, since he was the leader of the raw, new street breed. Freestyle was fading and vert was becoming less popular due to the lack of skateparks and ramps. If skating were going to survive, street skating was the only "style," because you couldn't take the streets away. It was raw and accessible, because the urban landscape suddenly had unlimited potential.

I never went near street skating. I was a freestyler, and if freestyle died, so did my skating career. A year earlier Stacy had tried to get me interested, pointing out that the top street skaters were taking my tricks and applying them on the street. Ollies, kickflips, 360 kickflips, half-Cab kickflips, and ollie airwalks were some of the the foundations of technical street skating. "Street skating needs you," Stacy said. "The vert guys are doing it right now, but it needs more technical expertise. You could do it in a second." I refused, considering myself a purist.

In just a year, street skating had shot light-years ahead of other styles. Vallely often skated with Mark Gonzales and Natas Kaupas, the two skaters generally credited with creating modern street skating. They were the first to do handrails, and they took the ollie to insane lengths. Steve had slept on Natas's floor and hung out with Mark, and he became friends with Vallely.

Powell was a clean-cut corporation, and you often felt you were supposed to be honored to be on the team. Back in the day, the company was so popular that it had that hold over people, but lately Powell seemed more and more out of touch, a relic of the old days of skating. One of the things that pushed Mike over the edge—at least from what he told us—was a manual that Powell gave to its riders, telling them how to operate, what to wear at photo shoots, and so forth. This rubbed Mike the wrong way. He felt it was a form of manipulation.

I didn't know Mike that well, but he knew I was going to be the first major pro ever to quit Powell. One night, Steve figured out where my conversation with Mike was going and left. "I can't be here," he said, "I'm out of here."

Steve was nervous about what would happen. Bringing Mike in could take our teeny company, teetering as it was on the cliff of bankruptcy, and make it one of the most popular over night. Vallely was huge, the biggest new star in skateboarding, and any team would have killed to have him ride for them. This was going to shift the skateboard industry seismic plates.

Mike and I talked for half an hour. "If you do it, then I'll do it," I said, and we shook hands. Steve was pacing around in the hallway like a caged rat. He froze when the door opened and we came out to see him.

"Okay, we quit," I said. "We're on."

I waited for the smile. I waited some more. A look of terror draped over his face, his eyes widened, and he said nothing.

"What's wrong?" Mike asked.

"You're my two friends, and now I feel responsible for you guys."

There was more to it. Steve realized at that moment that he was in way over his head. He knew how popular Vallely was, arguably the most popular skater at the time, and he simply didn't have the money to make the thousand boards immediately.

"His board sales for the first month alone were going to be more than all our board sales combined since we started," Steve

told me later. He finally had to ask Mike for a loan of fifteen thousand dollars, just so that he could make enough of Mike's pro model. I had another fifteen thousand saved, and Steve managed to twist that out of me. With that investment, I owned 10 percent of World Industries, and Mike owned another chunk.

I called Stacy and told him that I was leaving. I thanked him for everything he'd done for me.

"Rodney," he said, "you don't quit over the phone, you do it in person."

He was right. I was taking the easy, nonconfrontational way out, and in the process disrespecting our relationship. One thing Stacy instilled in everybody on the team was respect. (Once he left the industry, there was a gaping hole in terms of respect that hasn't been filled.) I drove up to his house, and after a brief conversation parted from one of the biggest influences in my skating life.

LEGIT

Mike Vallely's leaving Powell shook the whole industry. Not only was our rinky-dink company stealing arguably the most popular skater in the world huge news on the business side, but it created an underground buzz among hardcore street skaters. Vision, Powell, and Santa Cruz were humongous slick companies, but the kids liked our rawness—or rather, they mistook our ineptitude for rawness. We could barely figure out how to make ads for the skate magazines, and since we had no money, we had to make them in black and white. Sometimes Steve and I shot Polaroids of product for the ads.

Steve and I were still stressing over the litigation with Santa Cruz. They could sink us easily just by swamping us with legal bills. We knew we'd have to change the name, so we slowly began phasing SMA out and adding World Industries at the bottom of our logo. That wasn't going to appease anybody at Santa Cruz, though. Steve thought about it long and hard and came up with an ad that he felt would help the situation. I was sure this was going to be the end of us as he hacked away at the keyboard on the ancient Macintosh computer, laughing at his inside joke. After looking at it I could only protest. As always, he got his way. I trusted him, since it was his ass on the line, too.

The picture was of a kid in a coma lying on a bed hooked up to a machine. This was the text below the picture:

This is Joey. Joey doesn't have polio, leukemia or even AIDS. Joey has something much worse: he is one of thousands of children across America who suffer from a tragic disease known as Confusion in the Market Place. This horrible affliction strikes impressionable young skateboarders who for one reason or another just don't pay attention. Then one day they get hit by the cold, hard Truth. The results, as you can see, are not a pretty sight. In Joey's particular case, he was skating down the street with a friend. They ran into a group of hardcore skaters. They told Joey (riding a Rocco) and his friend (riding a Natas) that their boards were made by different companies. They said that while the Natas was actually made by Santa Cruz, the Rocco was made by those goofballs at World Industries. They went on to elaborate that while Natas, Theibaud, and Reyes rode for one company, Rocco, Martinez, Hartsel, J. Lee, Vallely, and what's his name (Mullen) rode for the other. Furthermore, not only did these companies have nothing to do with each other, they were at WAR. After pondering this, Joey's friend, enlightened to the situation, merrily skated away. Joey, on the other hand, was not so lucky: he lapsed into a coma from which he has not recovered. So, while there may not be much hope for Joey, there is a way to prevent this travesty of commerce from happening to others: we ask that, effective immediately, all World Industries purchases be halted. This way we'll go out of business, and kids like Joey can once again lead happy, productive lives.

I'm sure most kids didn't understand the ad, but everybody in the industry did. Everybody understood that it set the tone of an us-versus-them mentality, which seemed crazy to the big companies but attracted rowdy street skaters. Amazingly, we managed to settle with Santa Cruz, and in a way that wasn't nearly as traumatic as I had imagined while lying wide awake so many nights. Basically, it all came down to us not using the Santa Monica Airlines name. Steve delayed this for as long as possible, since it was our brand recognition, after all. But eventually we agreed not to use the full name. We had the artist O. draw a logo with the initials SMA, put a map of the world over them, which partially obscured the initials, and write "World Industries" underneath. Eventually the SMA disappeared and World Industries became our name.

Steve wasn't finished screwing with the big companies, though. He still had all his old contacts at Vision, and he wanted the mold for a double kick board they were coming out with as a model for our Vallely board. Steve met the guy who designed the mold, and it just so happened that this guy so disliked the owner of Vision that he was willing to share the mold with Steve. I worked with Mike and designed a huge freestyle board for him. No pro board had ever looked like it.

Then Marc McKee, our young (read: cheap) artist, who also happened to be a virtuoso—the most talented artist I had ever seen—drew Mike's graphics. Mike was a hardcore vegan at the time, so McKee drew a cartoon farm with various animals asking not to be eaten. This was a vast improvement from Steve's first graphics, which were photocopies of that Winnie the Pooh picture where Winnie has his hand in a pot of honey. Steve had changed the pot to read "Money."

My first graphic was a drawing of a dead horse with a halo and dog food cans floating around it. The labels depicted the ingredients—horse meat. It was a little tribute to my sister Vicki, the horse lover.

CHAPTER 20

JUMPING OFF FJORDS

IN 1989, JUST WHEN STEVE AND I WERE GETTING SUCCESSFUL, I LEFT

California to do a demo in Norway, and I ended up falling in love with the country. Now that I had some distance and objectivity, I was trying to make sense of my life, especially my family situation. I wanted to be alone, and in a big way. Just as I used to go up to my room when things got hairy at home, I went to Norway to think. It was a perfect plan, because I didn't speak the language and didn't really know anybody in the country.

The skateboard distributor who paid for me to come over was a cool guy, and we got on well. He was excited, because the Norwegian government had just made skateboarding legal, and now he wanted to get the word out and pump the country full of skating. He offered me a summer apartment and $800 a week to psyche kids up with my skating.

I called Steve about it and he said, "If that's what you need to do, Rodney, do it." I knew that he was bummed and that I was letting him down, but I was burning out from working and skating so much. I didn't think I'd be getting opportunities like this ever again. Freestyle was almost completely dead; maybe thirty of my pro boards sold a month. How much longer would people want to see me skate? Once again, I thought my career was winding down, finished.

I did demos at mall fashion shows for kids and skated at gas station openings and sporting goods stores. When I wasn't skating, I was completely absorbed in books or in seeking out odd people, thinking their unique perspective might offer me some answers. I hung out with a guy who had been an assassin for the Israeli army and claimed to have killed two people, which landed him in an Iranian prison. He told me he was put in solitary confinement, where he taught himself to play chess. At the time I met him, he was hustling chess games at an Oslo bar where all the Middle Eastern guys would hang out. But he saw something in me and took me aside.

I was still trying to figure out everything in my life, and I couldn't get my stupid face out of philosophy books. I had stopped reading the Bible and was running around in an intellectual maze, exhausting myself. My asthma was still acting up, which made me even more anxious. Norway was one of the most beautiful environments I'd ever been to, but for some reason that made me start thinking about killing myself again. My assassin friend must have noticed my depression, because he took me aside one day and told me about his three mock executions, when his Iranian jailers had taken him outside and fired into the air. He looked me in the eyes and said slowly, "It completely destroys you as a human being."

I appreciated what he said, but I still obsessed over the best way to kill myself. I bought some postcards of the famous Norwegian fjords and taped them to the walls of my apartment, staring at them as if they held secret answers that I failed to totally comprehend. Step by step I walked through the process. I'd hike up a fjord, examine the edge and the drop below, kneel for a quick prayer, back up, and then calmly run and leap off the edge. Everything I had done in my life amounted to nothing. I just wanted to disappear. I had a loving mom, fame, material wealth, but I had no feeling of belonging. No matter what angle I looked at myself,

I amounted to nothing. My skating didn't matter, my money was all gone or wrapped up in a company that would probably fail, and I was socially bankrupt, unable to function in the real world. I couldn't meet anybody normal, either, which was a reflection of my own mentality. Everyone I talked to was a freak. One guy I met wore earplugs because he said he was so sensitive that if he heard a wrong tone it sent an electric jolt to his brain. We started hanging out and he told me how his parents were both killed when he was a kid. I was inexorably drawn to damaged people like this—my true homies.

I skated for four hours a day, but in an empty way, as if I was automated. I was like some robot that can't stop and continues functioning until its machinery grinds itself down. All I could do was wonder if my skating was even worth it. The spark and creativity that had pushed me through my years of struggle were growing cold. Worse, I felt that all the energy I put toward fighting for my skateboarding had been an incalculable waste of time and effort. I was a failure in my father's eyes and had made nothing of the talents I was given. I had been the "best in the world" and felt like a fraud after most of the contests that I won. My faith in myself, in my passion, and even my faith in God was dissipating. But I knew nothing else; skating was the only constant in my life.

Years ago I had met a Swedish girl, and we'd been pen pals since then. Now that I was in Norway, we began going out. I had fun with her, but emotionally I was flatlining. Then she called me one night, drunk, telling me how she was going to kill herself. I called her parents, who casually told me that she always behaved this way. I took it as a sign, a warning that if I sat around in this dystopia with only Kafka and my memories as stimuli, I'd be dead.

The realization felt like a self-preservation alarm going off. I was more scared than I'd ever been in my entire life; a coldness seemed to be in my marrow, and I felt it for the first time.

This shock allowed me to step away from myself and instead of feeling that I was trapped in an unlit hole, I saw with objectivity what I was close to doing. For the first time, killing myself became real and it sent a shock through my body and brain. I had to get back home as quickly as possible, and I bought a ticket the next day.

On the plane ride back I read a book by the poet Rainer Maria Rilke, *The Diary of Malte Laurids Brigge*. The main character comes to the conclusion that his life is the sum of his memorable moments, and that he has had practically none. It pulled me away from my pity and allowed me to focus on how rich my life had been, for good and bad. I made a pledge to forget about the past and to stop trying to intellectualize everything. I would make something for the future, too. My thoughts turned to Steve, who had encouraged me to go to Norway even though our company was a crazy mess. *I'm going to be there for my friend,* I thought, *who's always supported me.* I also began reading the Bible again, for the first time in over a year.

Back in California I made an effort not to "hide out" anymore. I wasn't going to bury myself in books, I was going to try to meet people. I started by seeking out homeless people a few nights a week, and I recorded my conversations with them on a tape recorder.

INTERIOR DECORATING

World Industries was somewhat of a success by now, except that Steve and I could barely run a business. We couldn't keep up with demand and back-ordered shops for months at a time. Instead of hurting us, this made the need for our product shoot through the roof, oddly. Steve was still doing his ads, becoming wilder and more irreverent each month. There were older ads "selling" J. Lee for $9.99, and they looked like they were done by a sixth grader on the first day of computer science class. Sometimes, Steve just made fun of our customers, calling them "credulous saps we're constantly on the prowl for at World Industries." But it didn't stop there. "Yes, it's the mindless dolts which make it possible for new swindling corporations like us to stay in business. So, from the bottom of our Swiss bank accounts, thank you," he once wrote.

Skaters loved it. They were all smart-asses to begin with, and at the time you'd be hard-pressed to find a culture more self-deprecating. But the other huge companies could never connect in the dirtball, ghetto way we did. Years later, Steve explained the reasoning behind his ads in an interview with Miki Vuckovich in *SkateBiz* magazine. He said: "I just didn't think like Brad Dorfman [owner of Vision] and George Powell [co-owner of Powell and Peralta], so even if I tried I couldn't do an ad like them. My ads—being that I wasn't a businessman and had no background in anything—were so completely different, they just came straight from my brain, right to the paper, and right into the magazine. Most people do ads when they want to try and sell product. We did ads to make statements."

Steve bought some real desks when we moved into our new warehouse, and he thought it would be a fun idea to get skaters to help decorate, so we held a painting party. It took about forty seconds for people to start spray painting each other, the desks, the computers, and the toilets.

THREATS

No longer were we the pesky brats at the skateboard kiddie table; now we were taking food from the big guys' plates. At the time, the skating industry worked together—there were separate companies, but they often met behind the curtains and worked toward a greater goal (i.e., their image of what skating should be like and how to maintain control). This all made perfect sense and worked well—if you were one of the ones in control. Now, suddenly the big companies were taking shots at us in ads. (In all fairness, we had started the fight. But our ads were just funnier.) This strategy backfired for them, making us look more interesting to the growing number of new street skaters, who saw the polished professionalism of the big companies as phony and distant.

We hit a main nerve with our Gizmo wheel ads. Back then, most wheel compound came out of the same barrels, and from the same company. Steve wrote an ad saying that all these wheels were the same, and that bullshit marketing was the only thing that separated them. So why not buy our wheels, called Gizmos?

The companies freaked out. Obviously, we weren't working with them as one big family; we were mocking them. I got a little worried when one of skateboarding's heaviest guys threatened me, because I knew this guy could back his talk up with actions.

"Look, Rodney, I know you're a reasonable person," he said. "That's why I'm calling to give you a chance. No one can talk any sense into Steve, so I'm saying this to you. I'm calling with a warning—unless you guys change your ways, something is going to have to be done."

I was polite on the phone, and I said I'd talk to Steve, but I knew we were in the right. The heads of the other companies realized their decade-long stranglehold on the skateboard world was slipping.

These companies had massive overhead and monthly costs that they couldn't cut down. They were dinosaurs, slow moving and gargantuan—it hit a soft spot when they sat on thousands of unsold boards, whereas we still couldn't meet our demand.

Apparently, we became so much of a nuisance that the big board companies were having powwows to decide how to kill us. They devised a sleazy tactic, too. Steve had packed a huge order with an international distributor that moved as much of our product as we could ship. We waited for a week, but no money came in and no calls concerning our order. After another week Steve called the distributor and asked what was wrong.

The owner faxed over a letter from Powell or Vision. The two companies were pressuring the distributor not to sell our product.

Steve pinned the letter to the wall and stared at it for a long time.

"These guys are trying to *really* put us out of business," Steve said. I could hear the emotional tremor in his voice. He looked at me and shook his head in disbelief.

"I'm pissed off. Fuck you guys. We're going to give it to them every which way. They're going to get it so hard they won't know what happened."

He pointed to the letter and said to me, "You know what we're going to do? We're going to steal every skateboarder that means anything to them."

BLIND

Though Powell had marketed Mike Vallely into the hottest new star, the undisputed street skating king was Mark Gonzales. Rumor had it that he sold so many boards, one time he cashed a thirty thousand dollar royalty check for one *month*. That's the largest I've ever heard of for straight board royalties—and he was only making around a dollar a board, at most. Over thirty thousand boards sold in thirty days. I don't know if anybody has ever matched that.

While I had been in Norway trying not to kill myself, Steve had been at a contest in Arizona, talking to Mark about how easy it was to get things done with a small company. We had another ball in our corner, because the skate industry was choking all these extremely creative skaters. Most professional skaters had the same board artwork for years at a time, while Steve and I changed graphics in a matter of days and created a T-shirt for one of our riders in a single day. For a skater like Mark, who had unhinged creativity, we seemed like a good fit.

Riders had no minimum pay and were all at the mercy of variables they couldn't control. Board royalties were on a confusing percentage system that changed depending on how or where the boards were sold. Some skaters made less than a dollar per board. We doubled that and gave our pros a flat two bucks a board. This freaked out a lot of the industry heads. Pros could now ask their multimillionaire bosses why some podunk company could afford to pay that much per board while they got less than half.

Mark didn't care too much about the money talk, but he got excited about having creative control.

"Yeah, yeah, yeah! I want to start a company and call it Blind," he told Steve.

"Why do you want to call it Blind?" Steve asked.

"It's the opposite of Vision," Mark said and laughed. Vision was Mark's current sponsor, a massive corporation.

"Okay, let's do it," Steve said.

"I want one thing, though," Mark said. "I want Jason Lee."

This was pretty heavy. J. Lee was awesome, one of the most stylish young street skaters around, and even more than Mark he blended technical freestyle tricks with street skating. For the past few months Mark and Jason had been skating together and had become good friends.

Even though Jason was obviously on his way to being a popular pro, Steve agreed to Mark's terms and Blind was born. It was strictly Steve and Mark's deal, but by running it out of World's warehouse and having us distribute Blind, we moved up to the big leagues overnight.

CHAPTER 21
HICKEYS AND HOMECOMINGS

SWATCH SET UP A DEMO AT AN AIDS BENEFIT IN NEW YORK AND

invited me to go. I went and once again was surrounded by "hip industry heads," models, and drag queens. The skater Gator, who later became infamous for killing a girl, was at the show. Acting strange even then, he was all over one of the models, a California girl named Carrie who stood over six feet tall. He was trying to hook up with her, but she seemed more irritated than interested. Her bluntness forced me to stare down at the floor while Gator got shut down. With that same delicate tact, she later told me that I came off as an "antisocial, gross little pig." Who knows what she thought of *him*.

This was a serious show. The famous artist Keith Haring had drawn huge pieces of art for it, and a long runway had been set up, jutting out into the sea of photographers from all the major fashion magazines. Techno or house music, whatever it's called, thumped so loud that it gave me a headache. And to make matters worse, I had run out of chocolate. The California model noticed me freaking out, pacing around anxiously.

"You okay?" she asked. She was used to this circus, but I couldn't talk; I was totally overloaded. I excused myself and went to the bathroom to hide out, in silence, I hoped, but I heard grunting in the stall beside mine, and when I quietly bent down to peek under the stall I saw that there were two men in the one next to me. I fled the bathroom and found a safer, quieter place deep backstage.

Being so spun out, a wave of nerves hit me as I looked down the spotlit runway, lined with photographers' popping flashes. A few seconds before my cue, somebody grabbed my hand, and I squealed in fear as I looked at the imposing drag queen beside me, who shot me a look and then gave me a wink. But it was Carrie's hand in mine and she whispered, "You'll be fine." I snapped out of it, did a few tricks for the crowd, and got offstage as soon as I could. My lost puppy aura must have attracted her, because we talked for a bit later that evening and exchanged numbers. She was married and living in LA, she said, but she thought maybe we could all go out to eat when we got back.

FBI, DRUGS, AND INHALERS

A few months later I received a letter with dinosaurs screened on the paper. It was from Carrie, and she wanted to hook up when she was back in town. A week later the phone rang.

"Hey, it's Carrie. How's it going, Rodney?"

"Oh? Okay. You doing okay?" I asked.

"Yeah. You want to go do something tonight?"

"What about your husband? Won't he get bummed?"

"No. He just got busted by the FBI for drug trafficking. He's waiting to see what happens; besides, we're getting divorced." She had a gift for brevity.

"Oh . . ." Sirens went off in my head. What am I getting myself into, I thought? She had a way of saying things in the most shocking way possible, as if it was like a game to her. Her unbridled tongue was the opposite of mine, and I was attracted to her sense of freedom.

After we hung out for a week, she made it apparent that she wanted to stay over.

"I don't think that's a good idea!" I said.

"No, it'll be all right," she said. "Look, I'll call Ray up and it'll be cool," as she reached for the phone and started dialing.

"What!" The last thing I wanted to do was have an accused drug dealer pissed at me. "Where is he?"

"At my parents' home, sort of under house arrest until he goes in."

The next thing I knew she was arguing and yelling into the phone, "Why do you want to talk to him? Huh! What are you going to say?"

She handed the phone to me. I waved frantically, trying to shoo the receiver away.

"Here, Ray wants to talk to you," she said.

"You Rodney?" a calm voice asked.

"Yes."

"You'd better take good fuckin' care of her—that's all I gotta say."

"Maybe she should go home."

"No," Carrie spat out in disgust. I got dizzy.

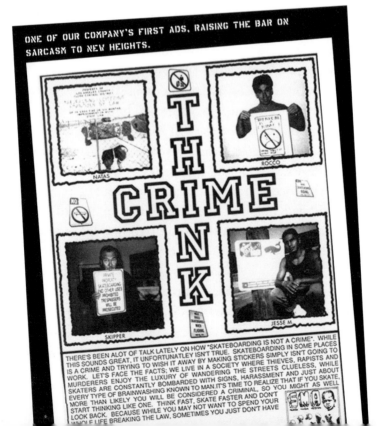

ONE OF OUR COMPANY'S FIRST ADS, RAISING THE BAR ON SARCASM TO NEW HEIGHTS.

"Look," I said, dropping her the phone as if it were a snake. "You should go. Drugs. Husbands. Parents. House arrest."

She ended up going home, but not before mentioning that she and Ray belonged to a gun club and describing their closet full of guns to me. She told me what had happened with the Feds. She said the FBI had been following them for months while Carrie did fashion shows around Europe. They showed Ray all these surveillance photos as evidence to be used in the case against him. There were pictures of Ray and Carrie interacting with a whole range of people—from their parents to underworld goons.

"And who is this guy?" the agents asked, when they showed Ray the pictures of Carrie leaving my house. It was a nice shot of me waving like a nerd. Then they showed him another one, of me standing on a curb to kiss her.

I can only imagine how Ray replied. They were divorced just before he went into federal prison.

HICKEYS AND DEATH THREATS

I flew to Japan to do a demo and found Jay Adams sitting beside me. He was a legendary Z-Boy from skating's late-1970s heyday, and some considered him the most gifted ripper of that generation. We knew each other casually and got along. He was in Japan as an honorary judge for a contest, and we started talking about the legendary Dogtown days of skating. Then he paused, as if remembering something.

"You know, my friend Ray wants to kill you." I gasped, wondering where I put my inhaler. Hadn't he said on the phone, in a roundabout way, that everything was cool? I assumed that "You'd better take care of her" was a hall pass of sorts to date his future ex-wife.

"I know you're all right, Rodney, but you should watch yourself," he said, tapping my chest, in a caring rather than threatening way. He saw a hickey on my neck—actually, a patch of them—and nodded knowingly, putting his arm around me. "You know," he said, "we have the same taste in women."

At the end of 1989, just as America was invading Panama, I reasoned that my relationship with my father might be on repairable terms. So much time had elapsed since I moved out, the last time I had seen him, that hopefully the bad feelings had mellowed with age. I had done a demo in Malta, and at the airport, as I was waiting for my return flight, I suddenly had a tremendous urge to see my parents. It was Christmas time, it had been two years since I'd seen them, I had a new girlfriend, and I was feeling strong and secure enough to see my father.

I changed my flight, and that very night I flew to Florida. I knocked on my old front door. Nerves were charging through me in anticipation. How would they react? Would my father smile or be angry? Would my mom run up and hug me? Would . . . would somebody please answer the door? I stopped knocking after five minutes and sat against the door and read a book from my travel bag.

My parents had been out eating, and when they drove up, they were visibly shocked to see me sitting on the porch, waiting for them. It was as if nothing had ever happened between us. We had two of the best days of my life, really a perfect family experience, one that I cherish to this day.

It was such a magical time that I returned two months later with Carrie and spent four days with my parents. My father was excited to see us. He seemed to want to make amends for any problems we had had in the past, even suggested that we go partners in a land project he was working on, and that I eventually move back to Florida. "This could be your future, Rodney, you know," he said. I appreciated his offer, sensing that it was his way of showing his love for me, but also feeling an enormous amount of pressure.

Once I got back to my old house, I started sliding back to the scared child who yearned for his acceptance. I knew that if I went with him and looked at the property, I'd have to tell him that my decision was no. My own weakness and fear of a confrontation acted like gas on flames by never giving him a straight answer.

I should have simply said no, but I kept making excuses, saying I had to go skate, or spend time with Carrie. By the third day of this, I was aware that I was irritating him by not answering. I had an inkling that he'd appreciate my answering squarely, but I couldn't get past the indelible memories where he'd blown up if I gave him the "wrong" answer.

I could see a confrontation coming. I drove Carrie to the airport and put her on a plane home. I felt it was important to get her out before the anger I could see bottled up in my father exploded. I was still a product of my father's house, and when I was home I reverted back to the obedient child I had been. I had said I was going to stay for four days, and I did.

Before I drove Carrie to the airport, I hid two metal bars in the shrubs by the front door. I figured if I was chased out of the house, all I had to do was make it to either side of the shrub. Crazed by fear and memories of our lawn mower confrontation, my backup plans grew more desperate.

On my way back from the airport I stopped by my grandma's and said good-bye. She pulled some food out of the fridge that looked a little too old for human consumption, but I thanked her and ate it so I wouldn't be rude. By the time I was five minutes away from her house, my stomach was gurgling so loud I could hear it over the engine. It was hard to stand up straight as my stomach knotted.

My father wanted to talk when I got home, but I was ready for a bathroom session and begged off, explaining that I had food poisoning. When I heard my father go to sleep, I walked downstairs to talk to my mom.

"Mom, I'm really scared that something is going to happen."

"No, Rodney, it's just your imagination. Don't worry about it," she said.

Later she came in to say good night to me and set off my booby trap. The dental floss tied to the doorknob yanked my board off the table, and I leaped out of bed, eyes wide with fear, adrenaline shooting through me.

She looked at me and shook her head sadly, "Oh, Rodney . . ."

At breakfast I could tell once my father sat down that he wanted to fight. I tried to end the conversation.

"No! You listen to me! I can't believe what a mess you are, that you're my son. You're disrespectful, you're—"

"I'm sorry. I'm really, really sorry and I'll just leave. I have to go upstairs and pack and then I'll be gone."

I grabbed my bags, and when I came down he was standing in the driveway. My mom pulled the car around, but he positioned himself between me and the car.

He stood glaring at me, clenching his fists. "I just want you to know, I'm ashamed of you; you're nothing but a leech on society."

I thought that when this moment came I'd go nuts and be all nerves, pee my pants or something. But I was overcome by an eerie calmness in exactly the same manner as with the lawn mower confrontation.

"You disgust me!"

"I know, and I'm sorry."

"Sorry—my ass. I offer you a legitimate deal, and you don't show any interest in it. You don't even have the respect to give me a straight answer."

STEVE ROCCO, AS USUAL, UNABLE TO BE SUBTLE.

"That's okay, it's for you. Thank you for offering, but . . ."

"Shut the fuck up!"

"I'm not going to fight you, sir."

"What are you, gay? You a faggot?"

"No, sir."

I nodded slowly, staring him in the eyes. He was getting wilder with rage. As he pumped his fists in a rhythmic boxer stance, I could see in his eyes that he was getting flustered because he couldn't get a rise out of me. He almost seemed confused as he faltered for an instant.

"You know that girl is going to leave you. I can see it. She doesn't give a shit about you," he spat. Then he suddenly seemed disheveled, as though he had just forgotten where he put something.

The realization swept into me like a cool wind: the calmer I became, the more he lashed out. Our opposite reactions simultaneously weakened him as they strengthened me—we both saw it. *Was this really my father? My God . . . Was this really the man whose respect meant more to me than my life itself? How could I have missed this, all these years? My bloody remains would be at the bottom of some fjord right now as God Himself would shed a tear at the absolute waste of my life—everything He'd given me.* My blindness nearly cost me my life. I had never been able to truly separate him from what he became once he lost his temper. His every word had always sunk into me.

I fought back an untimely urge to smile as I marveled at the recognition of what had emerged: In a weird way, I felt peace.

I looked past him and saw my mom behind the wheel, her hands gripping it. She couldn't even look at what was happening. I worried for her.

"Yes, sir, I think you're right." Carrie was so wild that in my heart I also thought we'd break up eventually. It was fun while it lasted, I mused.

"Yeah? Well, you're not getting a damn thing out of us. You are thoroughly disowned."

"Yes, sir," I nodded.

After a few seconds of silence, he spat, "Aw, I can't believe you," waved his hand in disgust, and walked around the side of the house.

When I was sure he was far enough away, I threw my bags in the car and calmly and emphatically told my mom to drive. "Drive! Drive, just drive, Mom. Drive fast. He could change his mind and come after us."

"He didn't mean it; he's just been under a lot of strain," my mom said. She was so busy trying to reason with me that she was driving ten miles an hour. I kept nodding, looking over my shoulder, telling her calmly to drive faster. I imagined my father stewing over this confrontation and snapping, driving his truck after us and having a second go at it.

"Take the back road to the airport; don't take the main road in case he does come after us."

I got to the Gainesville airport two hours before my flight. I saw a cop making a patrol and felt relieved. *Good, I thought, I can just position myself around him.*

My mom dropped me off. She didn't get out of the car. I could see the dazed look in her eyes that rendered her emotionally blank. I was calm once again because I was concerned for her. I could tell she wasn't going to get out, so I snuck up and took a picture of her and tried to get her to smile, but there was so much going on inside her head that that was impossible.

I said good-bye and watched as she drove off. She was in another world, and her distractedness scared me—would she be okay enough to drive?

Until I got on the plane, I sat in a hidden part of the airport, my heart finally returning to a normal rhythm once we were airborne.

CHAPTER 22

THE MOST ILL-EQUIPPED BUSINESSMAN

AT THE START OF THE 1990S, STEVE RECRUITED A TEAM OF RIPPING

amateurs like Jeremy Klein and Ron Chapman for our company. Their smart-assed cynicism fit perfectly with our image. They were purely his discoveries.

Guy Mariano and Rudy Johnson were two amateurs from the LA area in the second generation of pure street skaters. They were still in their teenage years, and anybody could see their potential, especially Powell, who not only sponsored them, but promoted the hell out of them in ads and videos. But Powell had a huge problem: Stacy Peralta had just stepped back from his team manager role, and it now seemed to him that the number of riders he had was overwhelming.

Steve summed this up simply by saying, "Nobody's watching the henhouse at Powell." Guy and Rudy looked up to Mark Gonzales, and they were stoked when he asked them to skate for his new company.

Not only did we have the attraction of our famous pros, we also had Steve, who spoiled all of our amateurs—dangling incentives in front of their noses and coddling them like his own demon offspring. He'd take them on shopping sprees, drive them to contests, and offer them Nintendo video game systems if they won. They were treated better than any other amateurs in the history of skateboarding. Once, I freaked when I saw a bill for almost a thousand dollars from Toys "R" Us.

Losing their hottest skaters was a huge blow for Powell. First I left; then Mike Vallely, the most popular new generation pro, left; and after that their most popular ams moved to our companies. The shift in power was apparent to any skater, even if he was clueless about the industry. Powell was left with a team of talented but older pros, while we had a bunch of fresh faces. Though they still had their big gun, Tony Hawk, he was halfway out the door to start his own company.

Powell countered, incredibly, by running an ad attacking "small companies." First they had ignored us, then they had tried to backdoor us, and now they were going public. But it was a bad strategy, because it made them seem old and "big"—two traits that repel skaters. They were hammering the nails in their own coffin.

I've always appreciated what George Powell did for me and will never forget what an influence Stacy was on me. He had always been there for me, and I wished then that there was some way for both of our companies to have prospered with no ill feelings. But regardless, Stacy was out the door; he was concentrating on making movies in Hollywood. (He'd eventually make the award-winning *Dogtown and Z-Boys*.)

MUNSTER MASH

Finally, we had money rolling in. For our first big celebration, we took a trip to Germany for the Munster Mash contest. Steve called up Natas to see if he wanted to hook up in Europe, but Natas said he wasn't going over.

"What? Come on, we'll pay for you to fly over and hang out."

We rented two Mercedes for our group and went on a tour of the countryside, driving through France and Switzerland as well. We stayed in five-star hotels. Symbolically, those stars meant a lot, because skaters were usually made to stay in budget hotels.

On the way back from Europe, Natas asked if he could start a company with Steve, and Steve replied with a glowing yes. Now we had the three most popular street skaters in the world connected to us. How did we celebrate? Steve stole one of the last remaining ripping amateurs from Powell, Gabrielle Rodriguez, and he skated for 101, Natas's new company.

HIGH-FLYING EXECS

"Close to five million dollars."

Steve and I froze, staring at each other. We'd finally hired an accountant, since the books had been getting too confusing of late. He'd added everything up and told us what we'd just done in sales for 1991.

In our first complete year, we'd sold over a million dollars worth of product. That doesn't mean we'd made a million. We didn't make any money, because of the cost of running a company, buying product, paying rent, dealing with crap that doesn't sell, and so forth. But five million in sales meant we had finally made a profit. A lot of it.

"Rodney, you're getting a raise," Steve said. I hadn't been taking money out of the company, because I was able to survive on the forty thousand or so I made on demos each year.

"What do you want?" Steve asked. "A hundred thousand a year?"

I protested: "No, no! Don't do that! We can't waste that much money."

"Why not?" Steve asked seriously.

"You guys are high-flying execs now," the accountant said with a smile. I reconsidered Steve's offer.

It was around this time that the rumors of Powell declaring bankruptcy circulated. They'd be confirmed shortly, and Powell would not emerge until years later, as a far smaller company.

EVIL INK

"Come up with something radical," J. Lee said to Marc McKee, now our full-time artist. At another company this would not have been safe to say, but there were few fences at World, and if somebody really wanted to do something, we weren't going to stop him.

At the time, J. Lee thought organized religion was stupid, and he often had graphics mocking the negative aspects of American life. One graphic was called "Official dope" and consisted of drawings of a beer, a TV set, and cigarettes, all the narcotics Jason felt Americans were addicted to. But now he really wanted to make a statement; he wanted a graphic that was a sledgehammer of his views, something that would force people to take notice.

"Give it to me, McKee. I want the gnarliest thing ever. Give me devils, Satanic stuff." It was obvious that Jason wanted some seri-

CHICAGO, 1989. THE LOWEST COMPETITIVE FREESTYLE EVER SANK WAS WHEN IT WAS A "DEMO SPORT" AT A VERT CONTEST. THE ORGANIZERS SHOULD HAVE PLAYED CIRCUS MUSIC.

ous shock graphics. Marc silently nodded, ideas already churning inside his head.

Mark Gonzales, Jason, Steve, and I were there at the "unveiling." Marc had just finished inking the picture, and he was obviously proud of it. It was an intricate picture of a floating devil, levitating upside down, of course, with decapitated people hanging in the background, the pope burning, babies mutilated, skulls littering the floor—and the largest pentagram ever to grace a skateboard glaring out from the top with the name Lee emblazoned in it.

Jason stepped back.

"Ahhh, that is pretty gnarly, isn't it?"

"Yeah, but you wanted gnarly, right?" McKee said.

Gonz started freaking out. "Jason, you take that graphic and somebody is going to put a hex on you! Your skating life will be over! Don't do it!" It was hard to gauge, but Gonz seemed to like the fact of toying with Jason more than anything else. Steve, on the other hand, wasn't hard to gauge at all—unbridled entertainment like this was priceless.

Steve got excited. "Jason, how much is this going to take? I'll give you a thousand dollars to take it. Forget that, I'll give you ten thousand dollars to take that graphic!"

I could see Jason's head spinning, the graphics, the money, all of us barking back and forth. Steve ran to his office and sprinted back with a check, grabbed a felt pen off McKee's desk and scribbled "Ten Thousand Dollars" across it. "Here. It's yours."

Jason looked as if he was hyperventilating. "Okay, I'll take it. It's just a stupid picture."

Steve was overjoyed. He looked like he'd just given birth to a beautiful baby; he was glowing. He loved investigating the price of people's ethical values.

I was living with Steve, who had bought a house by then, and a little after midnight we heard a knock at the door. "I can't do it, guys," Jason said, his voice muffled behind the door. "I can't have a devil worship board with my name on it."

Before we could open the door, the ten G check slid under. Natas eventually heard the story and had no problem using the graphics for himself. This was even crazier, because Natas is a Lithuanian name, but if you read his name backward in English, it spells Satan. We got a lot of hate mail over that graphic, almost as much as for Gabrielle's graphic of Jesus Christ. Gabrielle had a strong Catholic background, and he wanted a picture on his board that would show his devotion. To Steve this was all a big joke. He kept score between "good" and "evil" to see who won in the complaint department, and more important, in the sales department.

Blind did a series of boards that took Powell graphics and tweaked them into caricatures. The skull-and-sword graphics were redrawn, so that a peeling banana replaced the sword. And Jason had Tony's hawk skull transformed into a dodo bird skull. This was all done in jest. Jason and Mark were good friends with Tony and often stayed at his house and skated together, even after the board was out. But I was still bummed and pleaded, "Don't mess with Tony, please! He's an icon." I even had a temper tantrum that resulted in nothing. The next time I met Tony, I felt self-conscious, but he never acted anything but cool.

There were some rough ones that we wouldn't do nowadays, such as the naked lady graphic that had to be shipped in black plastic bags. It seemed kind of funny thinking of how a giant black bag would look hanging on the board racks next to all the other graphics in shops. One I did love was the 1970s-looking drawing of a sexy girl with an Afro. We figured out how to apply velvet on a board and screened it in the background for that one.

Steve, who was behind most of the graphics, wanted to use skateboard graphics to address modern-day social issues. That's why he was excited about releasing a board with a crack pipe drawn on it, or about mocking the tobacco industry by including a free smoke with every board that depicted a cartoon cigarette character. It was Steve's way of mocking some of the tobacco companies for denying they were marketing to kids—his way was a

THE MOST ILL-EQUIPPED BUSINESSMAN **211**

little less subtle. Some people assumed that we were encouraging lighting up, when it was just the opposite. There was a lot of criticism of what we did, most of which was pretty lame, because the sarcasm seemed so obvious, like on the cigarette board. Some, like Gabrielle's icon deck, were done with good intentions but were misunderstood. Others were rooted in inside jokes and were in fact quite offensive. There are also a few I simply regret.

HOLD HOLD HOLD

We had an account at Wells Fargo Bank, a smaller branch, and I always got one of these two ancient ladies handling my deposits. You'd think that after a few months they'd get used to me, perhaps even be cordial to me, but they always hexed me with the worst stink eye, and on every single check—and I mean *every* one—they stamped HOLD. We never had problems bouncing checks, but I didn't look the part of a money man, wearing baggy scuffed pants and using a shoelace as a belt.

We shifted banks after our accountant recommended an Asian institution. When I walked in the first time, I saw that all the tellers were Japanese. I was so stoked—no more overly suspicious hags behind the counter. A month later, though, as I stood in line to deposit World Industries' checks, I noticed that there were five teller windows, and three of them were staffed by Japanese women. The two white-haired new hires were working the other two. I hung my head in defeat as I walked up to one of them who instantly recognized me as she took out her stamp. Hold. Hold. Hold. It was as if I was starring in an episode of the *Twilight Zone.*

TAXTARDS

For two guys who loved math, Steve and I were the most retarded guys with taxes. We never intentionally deceived anybody, but the business had gotten way too big for us to keep winging it. I did the books and payroll for the first years. In the beginning I was surprised to discover that there was a thing called payroll tax. It was all supposed to be paid weekly. I sometimes went weeks without paying it, though. Our accountant, an expert in traumatizing idiot skaters, often freaked out. "They'll put a chain on your door! You don't understand!"

The IRS audited us in our second year. Big surprise. But we had an intelligent accountant. This is how smart he was: he made Steve promise not to even be on the premises when the audit was going on.

It was good advice. Let Steve and his sarcastic ass in a room with a stuffed shirt who has the power to seriously screw with you, and I'd be forced to do demos in the street to pay those taxes back. After the first day, the auditor told our accountant that he was sure we were criminals. "I think there's drug money laundering going on here and I'm going to nail these punks."

Naturally, we freaked. We weren't criminals, just idiots. The auditor dug through everything trying to pinpoint a huge coverup, but he looked so hard for a big glaring clue that he missed almost all of our honest, stupid mistakes. He ran out of time—agents get

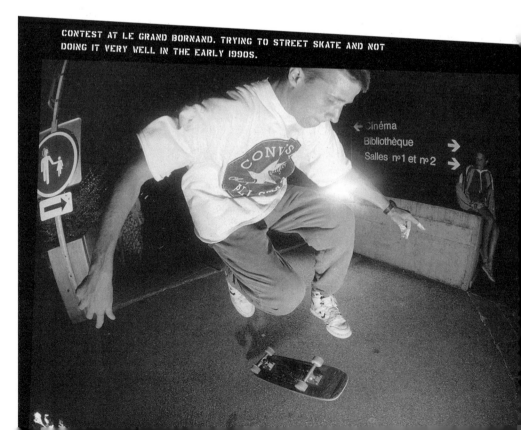

CONTEST AT LE GRAND BORNAND. TRYING TO STREET SKATE AND NOT DOING IT VERY WELL IN THE EARLY 1990S.

a set amount of time to audit—and finally, all he could do was slap us with a feeble thousand-dollar fine for filing forms late.

CEASE AND DESIST

With our guerrilla business tactics and learn-as-you-go attitude, we began taking a liberal approach to board graphics. From the start, with our Winnie the Pooh graphics, Steve had had no problem "borrowing" images. At first, his definition of clearing copyright was taking something to the photocopying machine. We went hog wild, tweaking well-known images for our own use. For some stupid reason, we thought that if you changed an image 10 percent it was okay. Having Winnie the Pooh roasting in hell with a snowboard seemed to be changing it 10 percent. That got a laugh out of the judge. Over the years, we collected stacks of cease-and-desist letters from lawyers representing everybody from The Hell's Angels to Disney to the Church of Scientology.

At first, Steve and I crapped ourselves, thinking we had jeopardized our company by goofing around with graphics. We talked to our lawyer, who did an excellent job of keeping me awake at night stressing about a life of poverty again. But after two or three or ten of these complaints, we grew used to them. Usually, companies or artists just wanted us to stop using their trademarked property. We got so casual about the complaints that we didn't even show them to our lawyer. We'd use the graphics on our boards only for a matter of weeks, then we changed them, so that by the time the letters hit our desk, we had already ceased and desisted on our own.

CHAPTER 23

TERMINAL DIAGNOSIS

SIX MONTHS AFTER THE CONFRONTATION WITH MY FATHER,

I was at work designing a board when my mom called me on World's 800 number, as she did every week. She told me that she'd been at the grocery store earlier and had suddenly felt woozy and passed out. While getting examined at the hospital, the doctors discovered something was not right.

"They ran some tests, and one of the doctors noticed I had white gums, a symptom of leukemia."

"What!" Everything blanked out. "What did you just say, Mom?"

"Leukemia. But I'll be okay, Rodney."

I had a hard enough time keeping my doomsday imagination under control with something as mellow as not being able to learn a stupid skateboard trick, but this was the worst news of my life. My mind reeled uncontrollably.

My mom continued to try to blow it off, but I could tell that she was concerned, and that she wasn't positive she was going to beat the disease. We made plans to meet at my grandma's the following week.

Chemotherapy is like napalming someone's insides, and my mom immediately felt its effects. She was more upbeat once the sessions were over, because being zapped slowed the progress of the disease. I stayed with her for almost a week. She'd spend the days with me, while my father was working, and return before he arrived home.

I visited her every month or two throughout the duration; she went through various rounds of chemo and was able to fight it off for a couple of years. Every new visit, her appearance changed because of the dual attack of chemo and the disease ravaging her body. Her energy was gradually draining out of her.

During my visits, my mom looked on the positive side of things, making her illness easier for me to deal with. I still don't know if she really felt that way, or if she just wanted to help me through it. I think she did it to help me cope with life now that she wouldn't be around to help. "I'm fine," she often said, beaming a smile at me. "This is actually neat because it's a little escape for me—it's like taking a vacation. All the doctors are so good to me, and people send me more roses than I know what to do with. I never knew I had so many people who loved me."

Her optimism reminded me of why my mother was the strongest, most beautiful person in my life.

She said my father was taking it hard, but he was making sure that she received the best care. To her, one positive aspect of her suffering was that it brought them closer. She boasted to me about how he kept the doctors on their toes.

And though my father never contacted me—and I didn't call him—I was glad to hear that he was showing my mom how much she meant to him. She was the central hub of life and love for our family. That was obvious regarding me and my sisters; though we weren't tight with each other, we all were connected through my mom. And as strong and hard as my dad seemed, he counted on her warmth, strength, and stability almost as much as we did. In a way, I was most concerned for him when she would inevitably pass away.

MY PERSONAL DECADE

At some point in time I arbitrarily decided that ten years of contest domination would give me some closure, allow me to relax and not push myself so hard to keep progressing. Like a timer going off, I thought I'd be happy and satisfied. The 1991 San Francisco contest marked the finish line, and I was excited to see how my life would change once I crossed it.

I had skated in thirty-four contests and lost only once. I had the best record of any professional skateboarder in history and had been lauded in every skate magazine and even been featured on the TV show *That's Incredible!* as some sort of wonder kid on a skateboard.

I nailed my run at the San Francisco contest and achieved my goal in front of a small crowd at the bottom of a dry fountain in front of the civic center. After the trophies were handed out, I walked around, holding my golden plastic skateboard man mounted on a faux wood podium, thinking about what a hollow goal I had set for myself. The ground was covered with blown trash. It was basically a garbage bucket, and as I walked around in it, I felt it was the perfect metaphor for what my contest wins amounted to.

I reviewed the past decade of my contests, and I was able to look more objectively than ever before at how my attitude toward them had affected me. It was as if I was finally able to strip away the deluding veneers I had glued on after every "victory." I liked winning, but I hadn't counted on developing such a terrible fear of losing. People would joke with me about how easy it must have been for me to win, or how it was a given that I'd win and that the real contest was to see who could come second. And on one rare occasion, my father even made a joke about skateboarding, the only one I can remember, when he chuckled and told me not to bother coming home if I ever lost.

TERMINAL DIAGNOSIS **217**

People laughed about how many contests I won or how dominant they thought I was, but I'd always cringe and either change the subject or get away. I couldn't think of a way to escape the corner I had painted myself into. I pressured myself to win, and I realized that other people put the same pressure on me to win. One judge had told me casually that I was making contests boring; everybody knew who was going to win and a lot of people hoped somebody would just beat me.

"I'm just waiting for that one slip," he said, "just that one that will give somebody else a chance." He wasn't saying this to be lame. He spoke in such a matter-of-fact way, it was as if we were discussing a menu at lunch.

My fear grew to the point that I'd go out and do the safest run possible, and still win. No more, no less, and it sucked all the fun and satisfaction out of skating contests. It was as if I had a big empty castle that I could never actually live in because I had to stand out front and guard it. Worse, I was a fraud. I knew I could skate in a more creative and therefore satisfying way, but I pussed out just to make sure I'd continue winning.

My first competitive goal had been to win a contest. I did that. Then I wanted to win two contests in a row, then three, then sprint ahead of the pack regarding technical tricks, then see my name on a sticker, shirt, and board—and I did all that, too. But was I the "best"? It struck me as so silly right then. Was I as smooth as Kevin Harris? Was he the best natural skater, kicking my ass in that respect? The attractive part of skating for me had always been the unlimited creativity, the artistic and inventive side of it, but I'd fallen into a trap where I regarded it as a result-driven sport where you either won or lost.

Losing perception of what skating meant to me, I had made it my goal to dominate freestyle for a complete decade. The very word *decade* sounded awesome. Ten years of domination! The Mullen decade! The Mullen Nothing was more like it. I hadn't told anybody about my goal, but I knew there was one person who'd understand my motivation behind it.

Barry Zaritsky was working at the San Francisco contest as a sports therapist to help injured skaters. I had seen Barry throughout the years at contests, but ever since Sensation Basin had closed and I'd moved to California, we hadn't been consistently in touch. In fact, I wasn't consistently in touch with *anybody* from that time except for my mom. Because of my lifestyle, people would often make a major impact on my life and then exit the picture quickly. It didn't mean that I didn't care about them or appreciate them, though. Barry was a good example of this trend. Whenever I saw him we comfortably clicked back into our relationship, as if it had only been days since we last saw each other, even though it might have been years.

Nobody would understand my drive as well as my disappointment better than Barry, who was there before it all started, and who was responsible in so many ways for helping me develop my contest skating. I hunted him down and took him to dinner.

We talked about that Oasis contest eleven years ago, and I realized that it had been the highlight of my competitive career. I had learned so much that weekend, when the tension with my father had been added to the anxiety of skating in my first real pro contest in California, the birthplace of skateboarding. But I had also felt like a purist then. It was the one contest I came into with no expectations to live up to, and no burden of victory on my shoulders. I'm not blaming other people, because nobody had raised the bar of expectation more than me, but I hadn't noticed that, like a leech, this sense of expectation had been slowly sucking all the pleasure out of skating. That scared me, because skating was the only consistent thing in my life for a long time, and if it soured I wasn't sure I would have been able to handle life.

Not bad. It had only taken me ten years to figure that out.

None of this stopped me from skating two hours every night, still timing myself, still stopping my watch for drink breaks, but it did give me the perspective to look back on how serious I'd taken contests, which weren't the true motivation for my skating.

I needed that realization, because skating was losing popularity again, following the same cycle it did in the 1980s. Every contest would be attended by fewer pro skaters and even fewer spectators. Companies were in financial dire straits, many going bankrupt and sitting on warehouses full of skateboards gathering dust. Because we were smaller and still didn't make enough boards to meet demand, World wasn't in that predicament, but Steve and I were concerned with the dwindling number of skaters. Sooner or later, if the downward trend continued, we'd start feeling the pain. In my mind, my future was uncertain, and skating was once again a loser activity.

There would be one more contest that year, in Savannah. World Industries was near the top of the skateboard sales heap, but it was a small heap, probably a quarter of the size it was five years earlier. And the Savannah contest was the lamest contest I had ever experienced. For some reason, the contest organizers moved the freestyle event to a different area than the street contest and never announced it. We had to skate on bumpy cracked asphalt in a crappy parking lot, and most of the spectators watching were carrying fishing poles because they'd stumbled upon us returning from a fishing hole.

Kevin Harris, who placed second after me, remembers it as his "first real bummer for a professional freestyle contest." It would also be the last one sanctioned by the National Skateboard Association.

Kevin later told me how he went out with some skaters to eat after the contest and happened to sit within earshot of the table where the organizers of the National Skateboard Association were dining. They were talking about next year's contests and one of them said, "We probably shouldn't do any more freestyle contests because Rodney wins them all, so what's the point? Why don't we just have the freestylers do demos at contests?"

And that's exactly what happened at the next vert contest in Chicago. Want to feel like a dork? Stop a raging vert practice session so you and some other pros can skate the flatbottom of the ramp. I felt like a bad circus act, like I should have started juggling. My life involving contests was over. To hammer the last nail in, some announcer introduced me as "The Eddie Van Halen of freestyle."

Freestyle was gone. Vanished from the earth, the first casualty in the recent drop in skateboarding's popularity. There were no freestyle boards being manufactured, and every freestyle pro had moved on in life, some, like me, to industry jobs. All that I had worked for, the thousands of hours of practice, the nightmares with my father, the contests I won—it all meant absolutely nothing. I figured I'd be an office boy at World, still skating on my own at night by myself.

Steve thought this was funny. He had seen the street craze coming in the mid-1980s when Natas, Gonz, and he skated together. He had happily made the transition, whereas I had never even touched a street board back then.

"I've seen what those guys are doing," I told Steve in the beginning. "Eventually it might turn into something, but right now it's not that appealing. I can't just abandon what I've spent all these years refining to try to join these guys doing footplants and an occasional shove-it or slappy." Primitive street skating hadn't created a basis of tricks of its own yet. But over the years it had evolved rapidly and was clearly the fastest-developing part of skateboarding.

After fifteen years on a freestyle board, I couldn't imagine starting from scratch all over again. I was twenty-four, the age at which a lot of skaters retire. Tony was the only pro my age who continued to dominate contests and push the boundaries of tricks. Besides him, almost every skater from my generation was going through the out door.

My mom getting sicker and sicker also gave me a healthy perspective on my dumb skateboard problems. Instead of feeling bitter about the death of freestyle, or dwelling on contests, I tended to reflect on my life and to think about her illness.

By 1992 our company was the biggest company in skateboarding, which wasn't saying much considering the state of skateboarding. It was a lot easier to do things and to summon up energy when we were striving and starving, but now that we were on top, it was hard to keep burning that much fuel.

Things had begun to crumble, and some of our top skaters left to skate for other companies.

Mike Ternasky didn't have a skateboard background—his was Foosball—but he was involved with H-Street, a strong rival skateboard company. He wanted to start a company called Type A, like the personality classification, which, interestingly, describes the exact opposite behavior of most skaters. He was busy cherry-picking an all-star roster of the hottest young pros in the industry, most from his old company, H-Street.

At the same time, Gonz, who never cared much for Ternasky—talk about a personality classification difference—was leaving Blind to skate for another company. Jason Lee left, too, and started another company, Blue, with a couple of our previous riders.

The "Type A" name was deemed busted, and Plan B became the new company that we distributed. I wasn't involved in the business end of this deal, but Ternasky had an odd request.

"What are you doing with Rodney?" Ternasky asked Steve.

"Nothing really," Steve said. "His boards don't sell, and he doesn't want to street skate."

"Let me take him."

"You're just going to be banging your head against a wall. No one is more stubborn than Rodney—not even me."

What happened next was comparable to the dollar bet in that movie *Trading Places,* where they take a panhandler (Eddie Murphy) and see if he can be transformed into a success.

"No," I told Ternasky. "I'm done. Do you realize what I do? I freestyle, and I'm going to keep freestyling at night, by myself. That's all I'm good at. But if I skate for Plan B, I'll be the biggest anchor, dragging your company down. I'll look like an idiot."

He was undeterred, so I tried again.

"You know what I am? I'm a geek loser in the eyes of skaters. Ternasky, I *freestyle.* Do you know what that means?"

"You'll start street skating."

"No, I won't."

"Yes, you will."

"No."

This went on for a long time with slightly different variations, much like the "Duck Season!" "Rabbit Season!" exchange between Daffy Duck and Elmer Fudd in the old Looney Tunes cartoon, until I finally caved in and agreed to at least try.

"Good. First thing we're going to do is design a street model for you."

Sheer futility. I hadn't set up anything other than a freestyle board for over a decade.

I was embarrassed to have a board and appear in the first Plan B ad next to a superstar team of Danny Way, Sean Sheffey, Colin McKay, Mike Carroll, and Rick Howard. I was a relic, half buried in the sand already. Freestylers were the Nerd Herd that street skaters hunted down until they were almost extinct. In World Industries' first video (directed by and mostly filmed by Academy Award nominee Spike Jonze), *Rubbish Heap,* Jeremy Klein broke my freestyle board into bits in front of my eyes. That pretty much sums it up.

Ternasky already had a strategy to convert me, one I couldn't wiggle out of. He said Plan B was going to make the ultimate skateboard video, and he wanted everybody to push the envelope; every single trick had to blow the viewer away. Up until that point, I'd shot my video parts in a few days. Now Ternasky told me I had over a year to prepare and assigned me a video shooter. Ternasky would tag along on the shoots, slowly beginning to dissect my freestyle board. I rode skidplates on the bottom of the tail of my board, and he made me take them off while he watched. Nobody rode skidplates anymore, but freestylers used their tail so often that they had to, or their boards would literally be bashed apart. Once Mike was gone, I'd put the skidplate back on. But gradually, over a few months, I got used to skating without one.

I still rode skinny freestyle boards, and Ternasky forced me to get used to wider boards, millimeter by millimeter. I'd shave a regular-sized board down and every week switch to a board wider by a millimeter, until I was comfortable with a normal-sized street board.

I filmed a few pathetic street tricks, and Mike contacted some of the gnarlier skaters on the team and must have paid them to call me and tell me that they were impressed with what I had filmed. If there was one gift Ternasky excelled at, it was making you feel ten feet tall.

Etnies shoes sponsored me and also tried to jump-start my image when they ran an ad of me doing a noseblunt slide on the lowest curb I could find. They shot it at night with low light, so everything blurred slightly and made it look as if I was skating faster than I was. "Just another gay freestyler" was the caption.

I was embarrassed to skate with anybody else. I couldn't skate fast. I couldn't skate on anything higher than a curb. In freestyle, there's nothing to run into; you skate on an open, flat surface: all you watch is your board. Street skating is all about using obstacles, but I couldn't gauge distance and had no clue how much space my board needed to land on an obstacle. For the first year of trying to street skate, I'd run into whatever I was skating. I looked like I had no depth perception. I was petrified of skating on something as high as a ledge. It wasn't long before I sprained my knee.

For seven weeks I couldn't skate. The rest of Plan B put together one of the gnarliest skateboard videos of all time. I saw unbelievable footage, years ahead of what most pros were doing.

I called Ternasky and told him I was quitting.

"Rodney, I extended your deadline for the video."

"I can't do it. Pull my footage. Take my board off the shelves."

"No. I'll give you an extra month, maybe two. You promised me you'd do this, Rodney."

I had made a commitment, and I had to honor what I promised. I filmed my part every night after work for the following six or seven weeks.

I was scared to death at the premiere for the video, *Questionable*. The theater was filled with hardcore pros from every com-

pany in the industry. I sat beside Ternasky. When *Questionable* started, the crowd cheered at each of the skater's names, until mine showed up. Nobody clapped. The room was silent. My stomach started churning, and I just wanted to sneak out the back door and throw up. *I warned Ternasky.*

During my part, which I'd worked the hardest I could for, maybe three people clapped. The part ended with a Casper slide, a pure freestyle trick where you flip your board upside down and slide on the tail and then flip it back onto its wheel, except that I did it up a curb and slid it across a sidewalk. No street skaters did that, but I made it streetish by sliding it over the sidewalk. It could have gone over either way—nerd trick, or inventive. The crowd waited until the trick was finished, then everybody screamed and clapped. Ternasky grabbed me around the neck. "See! I told you, you could do it! In the next video, we're gonna kill 'em!"

But I still had the worst-selling board on the team.

STEALING BIBLES

A year and half after her diagnosis, anybody close to my mom could see she was losing the leukemia battle. I had continued going back month after month, and after a while I was used to the routine of the visits. One day in June 1993, she called me at work and gently announced that this whole ordeal was going to be over soon. She seemed relaxed and at peace with dying, and because we had been slowly working toward this on every visit, I fed off her calmness. I have a tendency to stress over things, and it amazes me to this day how my mom helped me prevent the breakdown I surely would have gone through without her careful preparations.

I flew to Florida and had my best visit yet with her. We walked to the budget apartment I used to live in, with the graveyard beside it. Ironically, she would soon be buried there. We walked around the graveyard, and I made her laugh by telling her all my dumb stories about living down the hallway from yelling drug-dealing bikers and fighting couples. My method of dealing with crazy neighbors—

TERMINAL DIAGNOSIS **225**

taping my windows over with black paper and listening to classical music nonstop—made us both laugh. She was at ease with dying, and we were able to joke about my overactive anxiety.

We walked to P. K. Yonge and strolled through the courtyard, where I had gone since I was a little kid. We laughed about all the things I used to be afraid of, and I told her all the places around the world I wished I could have taken her. How awkward I felt when crowds would follow me for autographs—she seemed so proud, so content. We laughed about the fun things we'd do on Wednesdays, especially how she dove into the pool after me with all her clothes on.

"Rodney, it's as if you hopped on a giant rainbow and landed in the pot of gold on the other side in the one place you always dreamed," she said in her soft southern accent. She kept emphasizing that my life had only just begun.

I showed her the tree that I used to climb up and play my recorder. "Funny how small it all seems now, isn't it?"

She nodded, looking at the tree, perhaps imagining a young version of myself sitting in it, hiding from the world. "I was the same way at school," she said as she patted a branch.

"Mom," I said. "I'm not coming to your funeral."

"Of course not," she said, smiling, looking at me with calmness. "Why would you? Funerals are for the dead, Rodney."

She had brought some of her favorite mementos, which she stored in a fancy hatbox, and we sat down under the tree to look at them. She showed me folded, yellowed old piano recital programs that had her name, as the star performer, embossed at the end of them. She lightened up and started laughing as she showed me a stack of old childhood pictures. She paused on a picture of her award-winning roses and began telling me again how beautiful the rose was in her hospital room.

Two months later, on July 11, 1993, I was on tour in Indianapolis, trying to keep some World Industries amateurs from having fire extinguisher fights in the hotel hallway, when a family friend called and told me the news.

I had an expectation of how I would react to this news. Similar to something I had seen on TV, I'd maybe crumple into a curled-up weeping mess or silently wander around like an emotional zombie. But neither of these things happened. I was calm, though. Surprisingly calm.

I walked into the skaters' room and announced flatly, "My mom just died."

Silence. These were teenagers; they didn't know how to deal with this. Kareem Campbell, who was always wise beyond his years, said, "Whatever you need, Rodney, I'll be here."

I nodded and went back to my room.

I stole a gold Gideon's Bible from my hotel room and sat on the side of the bed and inscribed "July 11, 1993 The day my mom died" in the back of it. I continued to write my feelings and portions of a prayer my mom and I said together when I was a kid. I carried it with me almost as a talisman and walked around downtown Indianapolis all night long. I didn't know where I was going, was completely unaware of my surroundings, but as long as my feet kept moving and the memories kept flowing, I felt at peace just remembering my mom. I found myself walking into my hotel room as the sun was coming up and the streets were filling up with lights and noise. I had no control whatsoever of my emotions. It was as though I was along for the ride. Waves of them would rise and fall on their own accord.

When I walked into my room, I saw a care package on my bed with a card. All the skaters who had been throwing exploding firecrackers in the van and setting off fire alarms a day before had all written personal messages to me.

CHAPTER 24
STARTING OVER

I NEVER WENT TO MY MOM'S FUNERAL, AND I STILL WASN'T

communicating with my sisters or father. I think my grandmother had had a similar good-bye with mom; I don't think she went to the funeral either. We got together with my uncle and had a private ceremony of our own.

A few weeks later the three of us were standing in front of my mom's grave. I thought again about my life with her and how much those Wednesdays we spent together meant to me. I guess I was too quiet, or that my uncle expected some sort of speech, because once he realized I wasn't going to say something, he took it upon himself to help me out. He started by extolling my mother's virtues, then digressed into a long series of Crowley gibberish that would have terrified any self-respecting man of the cloth. My grandma and I quietly smiled to each other out of the corners of our eyes: Mom would have found it amusing, too.

Later on my mom's best friend told me a story that made me feel as if I was with my mom when she died. I had finished my part for the second Plan B video and ended it with a fade-out. Before the screen went blank, "I love you, Mom" appeared. Her dying had been in my mind during the entire filming of my part. It felt like a good way to wrap it up.

She was in the hospital and even though she was unable to speak, her best friend who was always at her bedside put on the video and they watched. My part ended and my message appeared on the screen. I hadn't said anything, and it came as a surprise to the both of them. My mom smiled and a few minutes later passed away.

Carrie and I broke up in 1993. Our relationship had been slowly unraveling for years, and I knew it wasn't going to work out in the long run. It had been my most significant relationship with a girl. But, like my last one, I was never able to give her the attention she deserved. Plus we traveled in different orbits. She was hanging out with rock stars; I was a nerd uncomfortable at parties. (The one Hollywood party we went to that I enjoyed was when I huddled up with Timothy Leary one evening and discussed everything from quantum physics to relationships.)

I didn't go through much of a moping stage, because I had so many other distractions. I was buried in work at World Industries, and I was skating with renewed intensity, focusing on the Plan B videos. I was getting better pretty quickly, but the guys still poked fun at me. One of them even "complimented" me by saying, "Rod, even though all those guys laugh behind your back, I think you're a pretty good skater."

These put-downs were bush league compared with what I had gone through with my father. While I wanted to be accepted, and suddenly felt like the nerd thrown into the school weight lifting club, it was a feeling I was used to. Though these insults were impotent, I still couldn't help but use it to kindle the fire that was growing in me again. It felt invigorating to go after something new.

I really hated the social climate of skating at that time. The 1980s had been relatively open and accepting. The early 1990s ushered in a new regime that felt a greater responsibility for policing the perimeters of what would be considered "cool." Like kids in high school, skaters created cliques that dictated what was "in" and what was out. Even shoelaces tied the "wrong" way were suspect. You might as well have been wearing dorky glasses taped in the middle. Even though I lived in the most populated area in the world for street skating, I skated alone. Part of this was habit, but another part of it was a conscious effort to avoid the strictures of the current scene. The freedom of skating I felt the first time I stepped on a board was in large part due to the lack of rules back then. Peer pressure had grown to be such a corrosive force on skaters. By now I was comfortable on the outside, even outside the only world I dared to call "my own."

In a way, it was ironic that freestylers—the much-disrespected nerds, remember—held some of the most powerful positions in skating. True, street skaters may have been the cool guys of skating, but they didn't control it. Nobody could argue that freestyle wasn't dead, but rather than disappear, a lot of us hung around the industry, exacting revenge. Kevin Harris had been operating Ultimate Skateboards, the most successful skateboard distributor-

A FREESTYLE TRICK ON A CLUNKY BOARD.
THIS WAS IMPOSSIBLE AT THE START OF THE 1990S.

ship in Canada. Pierre Andre and Don Brown were running Sole Technologies, the most successful skateboard shoe company. Steve and I were heading World Industries, and Per Welinder had started Birdhouse Projects with Tony Hawk, another successful company. Revenge of the nerds.

SEARCHING

One day I was walking down Hollywood Boulevard past the Church of Scientology when the propagator stopped me and asked if I wanted to take a personality test.

"Yes!" I replied heartily.

Five minutes after questioning me, the guy was backing away slowly, but maintaining eye contact. I started asking him questions, my voice getting louder as I became more frustrated by his double-talk. My questions spewed out, rapid-fire.

"Don't try to placate me with something you memorized from some comparative religion book. I need somebody to look me in the eye and *tell* me how it will all change. I need to know how my life can change. Can't you see I need help?"

The guy made a signal to somebody, and a security guard appeared out of nowhere and escorted me away.

"Look, I can see it in your eyes—you need help," he said, once I was on the sidewalk. "Why don't you go down the street to our auditing station?"

It was around nine at night when I knocked on the plain door and was let in to meet an auditor. The auditor was in his midforties and struck me as a gentle, sincere man, who seemed desperate himself.

I looked at him and asked if he could help me. I wanted to hear his story, to hear what had changed him. And by now, I had the confidence to really talk, and to really listen. My days of looking at my shoes and mumbling were over. I had done over a thousand demos and signed autographs for literally miles of people lined up to meet me. Each one of them wanted some connection, so I had learned to look right into their eyes and do just that. I had done interviews and TV and radio appearances. I made trips to children's hospitals to meet dying kids who were fans. In short, I learned to connect under all kinds of an intense circumstances. Now I was freaking out. I could feel that disorientation my uncle had felt before he was committed, and it turned on the adrenaline. I was amped and wanted the tester to realize the gravity of every word he spoke to me.

He was a mathematician and computer scientist, and he quickly recognized the same abilities in me. He told me he had given his life to Scientology after his wife had succumbed to schizophrenia.

He held up what seemed like a lie detector box that registered electrical impulses on your skin. "I would give up all my learning to operate this box," he said as he hooked me up to it.

He asked me how I liked my job and the needle barely bobbled as I answered. I could tell he was seeing how each question affected me.

"Father," he said, and then did a double take at the box. That one word made the needle look as if it was fighting to break out of the meter.

"Have some issues with your father?" he asked. I nodded, surprised that I hadn't blown the building's fuse box. We talked through the night, but I left feeling worse because I wished there was a way I could help *him*.

I began hitting all the religious centers I could find and talking with practitioners. I went knocking on the Mormon Temple doors. I got signed up for the United Atheist Society, which somehow made me smile the most. I chilled at a Buddhist temple and was fed by the Hari Krishnas. During one of my strangest mealtime conversations, a bald woman stared deep into my eyes and asked if I was on drugs. I attended a meeting of the Lost Twelve Tribes and begged to differ on their Bible interpretation. Not a good idea. A circle of very dedicated black men, dressed in brown military-looking uniforms glared at me, the speaker yelling, "What the fuck did you say, Gomer Pyle?"

I checked out a reclusive chapter of the Church of Satan, and oddly, they were nicer to me than the others, preaching a weirdly liberating religion that sounded attractive in the short term, but I wasn't taken by their rhetoric. I did become interested in all the stories they told, though. I hung out at occult stores and if I saw somebody who looked serious, I'd offer to take him out to eat and question him. The gnarliest black magic devotee took his jacket off at dinner and had tarot cards taped all over his arms and chest to protect him. He explained that his old occult group (the O.T.O.) was after him and that these cards helped deflect their spells.

I wondered what possesses a killer like Jeffrey Dahmer and reckoned that there must be some "power" that takes hold of people. I wondered if there was a force that somehow resonates with some more than others, which naturally led to a study of exorcisms. After a year or so, I had read piles of these dark books and talked to anybody I could find who'd had Ouija board or ghost experiences. I'm not sure why I went to such lengths to investigate evil, but it may have had something to do with developing a fuller understanding of the opposite of it. I had taken a long enough look to see the details of this dark force and it truly scared me.

After a lifetime of Bible reading I still wasn't settled. Yes, I believed, but why all the rules about blood sacrifice that even God has to obey? Those rules cost Him His son. In physics, quantum systems are irreducibly complex and we're still stuck with the imaginary part, too. That imaginary value in Schrödinger's equation is a gentle reminder that we can't see everything we want. Heisenberg concurs. The real world is happening in the depths of the complex frame, but we can't "touch" it or see it until it gets squashed, "flattened" into a real plane. We settle for shadows and silhouettes. I thought there had to be concrete answers and structures for everything—but there aren't, as far as we can see. So maybe I won't ever logically understand exactly what the cross is all about, but the hard look I took at darkness brought the gospel story to life for me; it made me value my free will. Without fully comprehending it, I felt fulfilled.

All that anger that I carried around from my relationship with my father dissipated for the first time. I had moved out of his house, but I still lived as if part of me was stuck there in my room, the obedient child who could never make his father happy. Rather than dwell on the negative aspects of our relationship, I knew I had to try to free myself from my cycle of depression, in which I was overwhelmed by the fear of failure despite the contests I won, the tricks I invented, or the successful companies I helped start. Whatever aspects of my character my father was responsible for molding were now my own responsibility.

I knew I couldn't do it on my own and so I asked Jesus for help. I started reading the Bible, not as before when it had sometimes felt like homework, but now in a way that felt refreshing. It seemed like a brand-new book because of my new perspective.

THE B BOMB

I've been a member of two elite teams, Powell and Plan B, and have learned that a delicate balance must be maintained if a team isn't going to implode. Stacy's talent was for spotting diamonds in the rough, and for helping skaters develop their talent over the years. Naturally, skaters appreciated what he was doing, and this also helped keep their egos in check.

Ternasky wasn't a talent scout in the way Stacy had been. Since he had picked skaters who were already popular, and incredibly talented, he had to deal with some determined personalities. His type A personality rubbed some skaters on the team the wrong way, and one time a difficult situation came up when Mike sponsored a skater that the team didn't like. This skater had filmed an incredible amount of amazing tricks, and to solve the problem Mike told the team that if they could duplicate the filmed tricks, the skater would be dropped from the team. Turning a skater into some sort of motivational tool was gnarly, but this was how Mike approached some problems. Perhaps he felt he had to do this to keep the rest of the team content, and maybe from that perspective he was right.

Skateboard teams are collections of people who don't belong in any sort of collection, so it's natural for them to spring apart, and it takes a lot to keep them together and happy. Powell killed it for almost a decade with a team that almost always placed in the top five, a mind-boggling record. Plan B, at its strongest, didn't last half that long.

In September of 1993, there was about $100-worth of confusion over a wheel invoice, and it became the straw that broke the camel's back. Some skaters had felt they were getting ripped off, and their anger was like a snowball rolling down the hill, gathering problems on the team until it was huge. Rick Howard, Mike Carroll, and top pros from Blind decided to quit to start Girl Skateboards.

It was a crippling blow for Plan B. We still had talented riders like Colin McKay, Danny Way, and Pat Duffy, but the team felt gutted.

World was also losing popularity, and we had made a few mistakes that were costing us now. Skating was in a lull, but as the top sellers in a small market, we had been forced to expand to keep up with demand. Now that sales were receding, we had overstock, and, to make matters worse, shops—which were also suffering—couldn't afford to pay us for the product they received. With the lack of payments, we were running out of money.

Ternasky was still the fire behind Plan B, but he suddenly found a new priority. In case anybody wasn't aware of his conversion, he showed up at a major contest in Vancouver wearing a baseball cap with a huge cross screened on it. He'd become a born-again Christian and wanted everybody to know it. On top of that, he and his wife were going to have their first child in a few months. There had been friction between Girl and Plan B, but at the contest Ternasky went up to everybody who had left Plan B and wished them the best. He wanted to make peace with everybody he had a problem with. To every skater who left he said, "I wish you the best of luck. Whatever happened before is water under the bridge. God bless you."

He flew home to go back to work on rebuilding Plan B. On the next day, March 16, 1994, he was almost at work and was making a left turn when an old lady ran a light and smashed into him going full speed. The impact was so severe that it burst his heart, killing him instantly.

My mom had walked me up to her death, and I had been prepared for it the best I could have been. I had said and shared all that I needed to with her. But Ternasky's unexpected death unleashed so much grief and confusion in me that I didn't know what to do. I was paralyzed. Not only had he been my friend, but I owed him so much for giving me a second life in professional skating. Did he know how grateful I was for that? Even more, had I made it clear how much he meant to me as a friend? I was stunned into a stupor that took me months to recover from, and when I did recover, I understood that Ternasky had done more than I ever realized. He had made me believe in myself.

CHAPTER 25

NERD LOVE AND DEVIL MAN

WHILE I WAS DEALING WITH TERNASKY'S DEATH, MY FUTURE WIFE

entered my life. This was in the following year, 1995.

World's sales slowly began to pick up in 1995, and the industry as a whole was on the upswing. More and more kids were starting to skateboard, and just as in the previous two decades, skating was becoming a cool thing to do again. I was hunching and punching on my computer at my office at World when I was interrupted. It was a new sales girl, and I had to stop to give yet another pep talk. World hired girls for sales, because it seemed that guys stuck in a skate shop all day already knew what products they wanted and would like talking to girls better than dudes.

Our new hire, Traci, was tall and dressed in her own style. She also had an aloof, funny air about her. I was immediately attracted to her, so my mind, always objective, calculated my chances of getting a date. *No way this girl would go out with you,* I thought.

For half an hour I walked her though the warehouse, showing her skateboards, explaining what concave means, different wheel sizes, wheel hardness, and why skaters ride different-sized trucks. I taught an abbreviated Skateboarding 101 in thirty minutes.

For the next few weeks, I'd see Traci cruising the hallways with another sales girl. I could tell these two had a bit of pirate in them and actually had lives outside of the office, unlike me. Stories about Traci's life began to circulate. She had lived in New Mexico, Seattle, Arizona, and on a Black Crowe Indian Reservation in Montana. She drove a big truck or a van or something tough that would go over dunes and up glaciers. (I drove a dented Toyota Previa van that the company didn't use anymore and could leave unlocked without fear of theft.)

TRACI AND OUR MUTT, DAISY, 2004.

Traci had also lived on the frontiers of Alaska, and I had images of her wrestling bears just because she was bored—that's how cool this girl was. If I saw her coming down the hallway, I'd dash into my office and pretend to be doing some humongous math equation.

Vince Krause, my work buddy, was chatting with Traci one day, and he asked her who her three dream dudes would be. She blabbered the typical, "Chris Cornell, Sean Connery—" but then refused to go on. Vince bugged her until she admitted her third was "Rodney."

"Who's Rodney?" Vince asked.

"You know, Rodney, Rodney who works here."

"Him?" Vince blurted. "That Rodney?" He thought about it for a while, his face scrunched up in thought, probably trying to imagine that he was a girl and wondering what could possibly be attractive enough about me to put me on the Sean Connery level.

After he had promised Traci not to tell me, he came and told me. "Rodney, trust me, I'm her boss and I know she likes you. She hangs out after work and she's not that dedicated to work; she wants to talk to you."

So I stalked her around the office to feel the situation out and make sure Vince wasn't setting me up like in some high school movie where the nerd thinks the hottest girl likes him.

After months of stalking, I was still too scared to actually ask Traci out on a date, so after seven months I employed the geeky we're-on-a-date-but-she-doesn't-know-it method. We went out to eat together, and after that night we started hanging out. She lived in Long Beach, and I'd skate there and hang out with her.

I'm sure she thought I was weird, because I made it clear that she couldn't watch me skate. I'm so used to skating alone that I get uncomfortable and self-conscious and usually can't skate with anyone when I'm trying to learn tricks. I can do demos fine, and skating in front of people is no problem, but skating *with* people is hard. The only person who regularly sees me skating is the filmer I use for shooting videos.

Traci never cracked on me for any of my eccentricities. I think she was actually amused by most of them. She never pressured me to include her in my skate world, and it often seemed like she was happy doing her own thing and letting me do mine and then meeting in the middle.

I'd come to her house, stinking of sweat and with a few new scabs on my legs, and we'd eat and talk. I was hooked on her after three weeks, and for once in my life I didn't dissect something, analyze it to death, and create a million variables. Traci had broken my internal computer. Six weeks after our first date I knew I wanted to ask her to marry me.

MY NEW FAMILY. TRACI'S PARENTS, CHUCK AND MINNIE HALLOWELL, WITH TRACI AND ME ON OUR WEDDING DAY.

Now I'll break it down and explain to you how a skate nerd proposes marriage.

STEP ONE: Dance around the marriage question like an idiot, asking hypothetical questions, such as, "Ever thought about getting married?" Make absolutely sure—99.9999 percent isn't good enough here—that there's no chance of rejection.

STEP TWO: Arm yourself with absolutely zero knowledge about wedding rings or what your prospective fiancée wants in one, and walk into a Robin Brothers' ring store at a minimall with a giant plastic ring bolted to the top of the building.

STEP THREE: Beg for help from the clerk and supply minuscule amounts of information. Talk like a nervous idiot: "Know nothing about rings. Know she doesn't wear gold. Please help."

STEP FOUR: Buy a ring with an "unusual setting," so unusual that it eventually breaks.

STEP FIVE: Go skating and take the ring out of its box and place it on a curb so that every five minutes you can stop skating and stare at it.

STEP SIX: Buy books on nerd subjects like gravitation, prophecy, particle physics, and the Bible. Live in a monastery-like puny beach house with only one chair, one small table, piles of books, a stereo, and one light. Invite prospective fiancée over and offer her the chair, like a gentleman, and then start the geek blitzkrieg. Talk fast because you're nervous.

"I want to show you something, the way my life works. There's a little bit of me in all these books. This here is a particle physics book, right? Some particles, antiparticles are represented as things that go backward in time." (Here show her Feynman diagrams.) "Look, there's so much to the world we don't see; what we see is the exception. If you get particles moving fast enough, they turn into energy and back into other particles under a whole shitload of conservation rules. The particles start springing or disappearing like a zebra changes into a frog. There're a gazillion different particles that happen, and there are recipes and rules that govern that. The Standard Model's messy as hell, so you don't want to go into the rules—trust me on this one. Incidentally, that's why some guys say it can't be the true. . . . Anyway, I'm just saying if you were to be on that scale and see things vanishing in and out"—deviate here into a non sequitur about the Bible—"Look at prophecy! If you go to Genesis and the way the Hebrew is, it's the only scripture book that says there is a beginning of both space and time—everybody else considers time to be infinite, as well as space. What does the universe expand into it? Space? No, it's outside of space. God the eternal one, seems to be outside of it all because anything with mass is affected by gravity and therefore trapped in time. But God is outside of time and he shows it to people. Look at this, for example. This is what made Cyrus the Persian say, 'I don't know anything about you Jews, but I see my name in the scripture in Isaiah 45 and you guys scare the shit out of me, so I'm not going to take you guys as slaves. Just go back and build your temples.' Same with Alexander the Great. It's scary! He's detailed in Daniel. Cyrus is mentioned by name coming in under the water and he actually dried up the water supply to Babylon and walked in under the city. It has to do with a perspective—there's something outside of space and time. The point I'm trying to tell you is that I have never felt that I belong with somebody, that there is a sense of purpose beyond myself. I feel that with you. I expect that our souls are immortal, and I want ours to be bound together for all eternity."

STEP SEVEN: Give girl the ring and then suddenly get nervous and say, "You can take it back if you want! I don't know shit about rings."

Traci walked to the one light in my place and looked at it. She was crying. I was crying. Everybody was happy.

Then it took us three years to get married.

DEVILMAN

By the mid-1990s, a new, younger batch of kids was getting amped on skating. Marc McKee, World's artist, was doodling, trying to invent a new logo and drew a cartoon devil stickman. You could tell right away it was perfect. The character looked so mischievous. He figured that this wave of kids had spent the past few years glued to TV sets watching cartoons, so that World would have a better chance of attracting them with a cartoon mascot than with some mature, edgy statement made through graphics.

Devilman became the new World Industries logo, and the theme that the company revolved around. The market was oversaturated with pros, and their selling power had become diluted, and Steve wanted to do more logo boards focusing on Devilman instead of relying on pro riders. Most companies had one or two logo boards, but McKee took it to another level, eventually drawing Flame Boy (Nether World minion) and Wet Willy (Holy Water) who battled each other on boards and T-shirts. Once these boards were released, World's sales increased, and later they blasted past any expectations as McKee drew a series of graphics that kids ate up. There were over ten million skaters in the United States and the numbers were increasing each year. In less than two years we had gone from almost filing Chapter 11 to sales in the multimillions.

CHAPTER 26

PHONE CALL TO MY FATHER

PLAN B STRUGGLED FOR A FEW YEARS LONGER, BUT IT WAS NEVER

able to run properly with the void left by Ternasky, and I finally left at the end of 1995. Other people, including some of the skaters on the team, had tried to run it, but it was a losing proposition. I was supposed to be in the fourth video, but I pulled my footage immediately after the premiere and quit.

This video part meant a lot to me, because it was the first time I felt as if I had moved on from my freestyle past. I felt that I was able to street skate at the same skill and comfort level that I used to freestyle at, because I was inventing my own tricks once more. I used the pulled footage from the Plan B video to make a video with one of my closest friends, Daewon Song. We jokingly called it *Rodney vs. Daewon*. Back in the dark ages when I was learning how to street skate at local schools, literally trying to land a basic tailslide, Daewon was ripping the place apart, killing me. I was almost twice his age. I felt as if I had escaped from the retirement house. But Daewon never passed judgment on me and was always

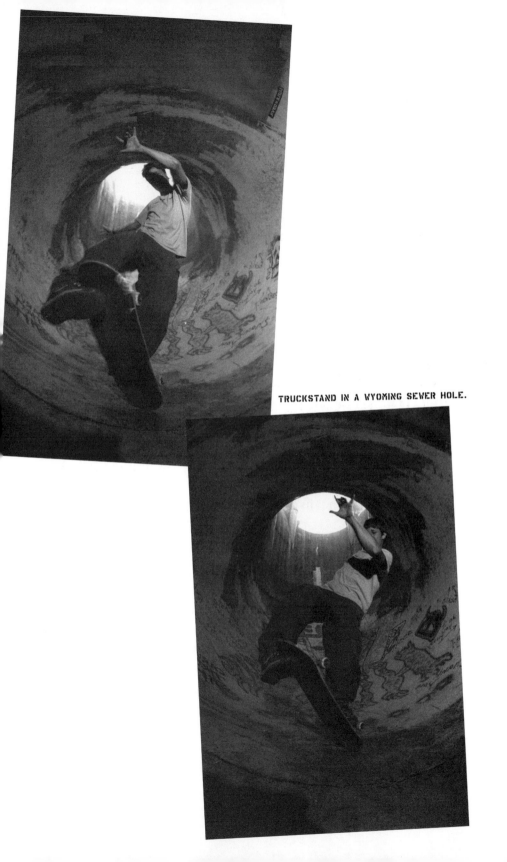

TRUCKSTAND IN A WYOMING SEWER HOLE.

psyched to be skating with me, even though he was an unsponsored kid who shredded ten times better than me.

I asked for his number and talked to him about riding for World. I wrote him a letter after we'd been skating for a few months telling him that I believed he had it in him to be a top pro. After hanging out for years, we were both finally at the same level, so everybody would understand the joke of the title.

A-TEAM

Given how big World Industries was, it was fairly easy to create a splinter board company. The head honchos at World decided that I was popular enough to draw the kids to a company of my own, and so I started A-Team at the start of 1997. The CEO of World and Steve Rocco appointed me figurehead and told me, "Go get some of your friends and start a team. We'll take care of the rest." I picked Gershon Moseley, Chet Thomas, Dave Mayhew, and one of my favorite skaters, Marc Johnson, for A-Team. I had been so stoked on Marc—not just because of his fluid street skating, but because you could just see the creativity flowing out of him in anything he did. He was always painting, writing short stories, and making hilarious droll comments on the state of skateboarding. He didn't skate or act like anybody I had ever seen.

MR. AND MRS. DAEWON SONG WITH TRACI AND ME ON VALENTINE'S DAY, 2001.

Putting me in charge of a company, even just figuratively, was a very bad idea. A-Team was a bummer. It was marketed as my company, but I had nothing really to do with it, outside of picking the team and helping write the first few ads. And nobody else at World stepped in to pick up the slack.

Marc summed it up perfectly when he once described it as "everybody's side project," because the artists, ad layout people, and T-shirt graphics designers all did A-Team work when they were done with their main projects.

Everybody on the team ripped, deserved much better, and was dissatisfied, including me. But it was as if we were all adrift, floating around without direction. We never had meetings, and the only time we saw each other as a team was when we went on tour for a week or two in the summer.

MILLIONAIRE DEMOLITION DERBY

While A-Team was dissolving and the millennium was coming to an end, Steve and the other business heads at World decided it was the right time to sell. They hired a management group that met with people gnarly enough to throw close to twenty million dollars around. I was out of the loop, but there were a few memorable meetings in LA skyscrapers. Over and over, I had to explain to the suits why skating wasn't going to die and why we "had our fingers on the pulse."

I sat in a mahogany-lined room for my first meeting with about twenty other suits and the World Industries' CEO and CFO. I had used a shoelace as a belt that morning and wore baggy skate jeans, because I had no idea what to wear to a real business meeting. I didn't own anything nicer, anyway. Luckily, the suits took it in stride. One of the guys patted me on the back and said, "Great tactical move, you look like the real thing."

The second memorable meeting was when the sale went through. Again, we had to do the transaction in a stuffy office. I had a decent share of the company and was in shock when I realized that I had become an instant millionaire, a couple times over. Steve and I looked at each other, he no doubt thinking about how far he'd come and everything that he'd gambled to make it this far, and I thinking that he'd finally be able to pay me back that hundred dollars I lent him years ago, with interest.

Steve wanted to get his share in a cashier's check, because he wanted to have some fun depositing it. He suggested we both hunt down those rotten tellers that used to hold our checks, or maybe just slide it through the automated teller. The suits refused and did a wire transfer.

I asked if I could use a phone in a private office. I took out a carefully folded piece of paper with my father's phone number written on it. I had been thinking about this call for some time but didn't have an excuse to dial him up until now. I took a deep breath and slowly dialed my father's phone number. As it rang, I rehearsed what I was going to say, how I'd control the flood of emotions that would surely overtake me, but once he answered I started talking naturally.

"Hey, Dad, something pretty major just happened and I'm not supposed to tell anybody yet, but I want to tell you."

"Oh, yeah?" he answered. We talked as if it had been a week since my last call.

"You're the first person I'm telling," I said. "We have something else in common."

"What?"

"We're both multimillionaires."

He started laughing. "I can't believe it . . . you kids," he said.

"Okay, I'll talk to you later. Take care of yourself."

"Okay, bye."

That was it. Maybe a minute-long phone conversation. But it was enough to pull the cork out, and I felt the years of disappointment and failure in my father's eyes rush out of me. It was a better feeling than being rich.

Steve was still bitching about not being able to get a check as we walked to his Land Rover. He had made sure to get his ticket validated and was understandably shocked when he handed it to the attendant, who asked for a dollar fifty.

"What! What are you talking about? My ticket is validated."

"Sorry, sir, but the validation only lasts four hours."

I checked my trusty Casio digital. The man was right; we were twenty minutes over four hours.

"No" was all Steve said.

"Pardon me, sir?"

"I'm not paying," Steve insisted.

I began digging around in my pocket for change. Steve turned on me. "Stop. We're not paying for this! It's a rip-off!"

"Who cares?" I asked. "Steve, we're millionaires now." He wasn't listening, as usual.

The attendant told Steve he'd have to call his boss to see if he could override the extra minutes.

"Don't do that," Steve warned. "If you walk away, I'm going to drive through your guard rail and smash it to splinters."

"I'll be right back, sir."

"Steve, don't—"

It was too late. Steve gunned it and the guard rail cracked into pieces and blew up all over the windshield. Instinctively, I ducked down to the floorboards.

"Steve, this is Orange County, there are cops everywhere around here! Get on the freeway!"

Steve, as calm as if he'd just left the meditation hall, looked at me, swerving into the carpool lane. "Rodney, you need to chill out. You're rich now."

"Yeah," I said to myself. "I can't believe it, I'm a millionaire."

"What? We're *multi*millionaires, you idiot."

We passed a Tower Records and I thought, *Now we can go back with shovels.*

BORDERS

Even though I now had more money than I ever thought I would, it scared the crap out of me. I just dumped it all in the bank and ignored it. My only perk was allowing myself a weekly shopping spree at the local Borders. Traci, who had agreed to marry me before I was rich, took it all in stride and didn't let it change her life, even though we were living together in my crappy minihouse. I lived on my salary and felt I already had everything I could ask for—except for maybe a bigger stereo.

Steve went hog wild, fully enjoying his newfound wealth. He bought tons of fun toys, a few houses, and fixated on tropical islands—he knew how to enjoy his money. I rented the same house for three more years, afraid that I'd buy when the market was high and then lose money.

Steve would come over and shake his head. Forever math geeks, we calculated how much interest we were earning. We both made spreadsheets running through various scenarios. I was satisfied looking at the number and relaxed by the sense of security it brought. Steve calculated how much he'd have to spend per day and per hour to go through it all. After that it became a running joke, and when it was time to leave he'd say, "Gotta go, I've got work to do."

CHAPTER 27

DOOMSDAY

WILL I NEED AN AXE? I THOUGHT. IF ALL THE POWER IS OUT AND IT

gets cold, I might have to start a fire. Yeah, but the looters and rioters will no doubt be burning half of the world up, so I can probably get a light and some kindling from them.

It was December of 1999, and I was locking up the storage shed I had rented. I was worried I might have forgotten something, so I went back in and double-checked. Sixty gallons of purified water, hundreds of tins of canned food, at least a hundred batteries, walkie-talkies, hand-powered radios, bolt cutters, and two bicycles. The bikes were important, because cars would undoubtedly be rendered useless after their computer chips went nuts, turning the roads into a scene from *Maximum Overdrive,* with cars madly accelerating, power steering malfunctioning and crashing vehicles all over the streets. Gas stations would be rendered useless, too, because most of them, like most everything in the United States, were run by computers.

At the end of 1999 my dreams were haunted by an apocalypse engineered by Bill Gates and his PCs, which everybody feared would fail to recognize the date 2000 and go bonkers. Experts were screaming their opinions left and right, some saying that nothing would happen and some predicting that planes would fall out of the sky. I went to the bank and emptied my accounts, bringing home bundles of cash and locking them in the industrial safe I had purchased and putting the rest in T-bills. I videotaped everything in my house, every book, and locked the tape in my safe. I wanted evidence in case my house was robbed. I couldn't sleep well, could barely talk without drifting off thinking about how my beach town was going to be turned into *Escape from LA*.

Steve, being the rich bastard that he was, had bought land on a private Hawaiian island and built a house there. I made him invite me and Traci to it for New Year's Eve. It was the only place I knew of that was run without computers. I had my long-distance windup shortwave radio with me, so that I could listen to broadcasts of the rest of the world exploding into chaos. I wouldn't talk to anybody that night as I listened to the newscasts. I was terrified.

Nothing happened.

Traci, always ready to humor me, was glad that I could finally stop stressing. Her ability to calmly deal with my "End of the World!" mentality was proof positive that I married the right person. Steve was used to my kooky behavior, so he wasn't even sur-

HANGING OUT IN HAWAII, 1999.

prised by my level of paranoia. But I just sat there, exhaling with enlightened relief and doing the calculations in my head of how long it would take me to eat the sixty cans of tinned spaghetti I had stacked next to the forty tins of canned peaches.

SKATING ON CLAY AT THE HOUSE STEVE ROCCO OWNS IN LANAI, HAWAII. I HID HERE WHEN I THOUGHT THE WORLD WAS GOING TO GO BERSERK ON NEW YEAR'S EVE, 2000.

Daewon and I began filming our second video, *Round Two*. It wasn't until a few months before the digital doomsday I envisioned, when I started skating tables and creating tricks on and off them with the comfort level I had had with inventing freestyle tricks, that I felt like a real street skater. I was still in my bubble, skating mostly alone, but I realized that I could skate tables better than a lot of these pros who mocked me. I felt free. I'd lost most of my stiffness, I didn't have to think so much while skating, and with my new confidence my creativity was finally back on track. I saw a change in how a lot of the "cool guys" treated me.

Round Two was also a turning point because I thought *I'm getting old and I don't have the energy in me to do another video.* (I can't break the paranoid feeling that skateboarding is going to be taken away from me.) In my eyes, it was the video where I emerged, where I showed that I finally had something to offer street skating.

Then I broke my ankle doing nothing. A kid at a demo asked me to do a 360 flip ramp to ramp. I did it lazily and landed with my back foot off and heard a deep "thunk." My body flushed and instantly I knew *I did something bad.* I went to the hospital and got X-rays and learned that my fibula was snapped.

I flew home, and Dr. Feder came to the rescue and put a plate and five screws in my ankle. (Dr. Feder quickly became a hero of mine, not just for his ninja surgical abilities, but also for his heart. He runs a program called Team to Win, which offers sports, medical, comprehensive, and specialized care for inner-city kids, regardless of their medical coverage insurance. Dr. Feder rules.)

I took it as a sign that maybe it was time for me to quit. (A lot of skaters seem to think the same way. Instead of reading tea leaves or tarot cards, we "read" injuries. Stacy Peralta retired from contests after he broke both of his arms, and in the late 1990s Tony Hawk considered retirement when he had two jacked ankles sprained so bad that he couldn't walk without pain for three

CASPER VARIATIONS
AT TERMINAL ISLAND.

months.) My ankle broke for no reason—no slam, no twisting. I just landed a trick normally and felt it go.

Jamie Thomas, one of the gnarliest skaters ever, paid a visit, and started yelling at me as I sat in my TV room with a cast on my foot talking about retirement. "What are you talking about? Are you crazy? You just came out with your best video part."

But I couldn't get it out of my head. I called Tony and we went out to lunch. I've always respected Tony and looked up to him, and I thought that he was the only skater who could understand the pressures I felt, because he had been at the top for so long. To this day, he is still doing tricks nobody else can do.

"Look, I think I'm going to quit," I told him. "You can understand where I'm coming from. Where are you in your life right now and how do you deal with it all? How can you skate knowing what you've done, knowing how good you have been, how can you skate just for the sake of rolling down the street again? I don't know if I can. I think I have to skate at that level or nothing."

"Just go have fun," he said. "Half the places I go to, kids ask me to do kickflip backside lipslides. I can't do those. That's okay, I'm just having fun skating. Don't worry about what others think, just do whatever you want."

I nodded. If that advice came from anybody else, it would have just breezed past me, but from Tony Hawk it was the Gospel truth.

"By the way," he said, "you want to be in my video game?"

This came out of left field. We'd never talked about it before, never talked about anything business-related before. I knew how popular Tony Hawk's Pro Skater was with skaters, but I didn't find out until later that it was one of the most popular video games series ever made.

"You want me?" I blurted. "You kidding?"

"No. I'd be stoked if you were in it."

"Yeah! I want to be in it."

Traci asked me how my lunch had gone with Tony. "You guys have a good retirement meeting?"

"Retire? I'm so stoked right now, I feel like I have a three or four solid years in me," I replied.

"That's what I thought," she said.

That was my pathetic attempt at retirement. I went into a restaurant thinking that my skating career was over, and I left pumped up and about to be involved in a project that would make me more popular than I ever imagined. In less than a year, I was being stopped on the street by nonskaters who told me what types of tricks they made me do in the game. Once, I was about to be beat up for skating in a schoolyard in a sketchy neighborhood, but the gang guys recognized my face as they circled me. The biggest guy stepped up to me and smiled.

"Hey, man, you're my favorite character in Pro Skater. Can you do some tricks for me?" he said.

NEAR BRAIN DAMAGE

My asthma had chilled out over the years, a lot of the credit going to Traci, who was the world's largest Valium pill for me. She went

MINI ME.

to New Mexico for a week and I was left alone, skating, reading my Bible code book, checking my e-mail. Steve had stepped back from his role at World, and I had become more involved as businessmen came in to help run the show, since they needed some-

body connected to skating to make sure everything was legit. I was sort of a utility man, doing a bit of whatever needed being done. I designed boards, helped pick skaters to sponsor, and generally gave my opinion on any big decision.

In my e-mail Inbox was a note from World's CEO. It was a harsh, straightforward letter about my obligations to the business. There had been circumstances in the past few years where my position as a pro skater and a shareholder had caused a conflict.

Chet Thomas, my A-Team teammate and a good friend, had introduced me to Matt Hill and Gary Valentine, two Australians who ran Globe shoes, and they wanted to sponsor me. No other footwear company was interested in me, and I always appreciated their supporting me before my popularity increased. My shoes became their best seller, and one of the best sellers in skating. Skate shoes had become the gold mine of the industry, and World wanted to start its own brand, using me and Chet as cornerstones. This would have gutted Globe of its two best-selling shoes.

Matt and Gary made me feel more at home at Globe than I felt in my own company. They had become two of my closest friends, and now I was being pressured not only to quit and take another rider with me, but to potentially ruin another company.

I was tearing myself apart, torn between what I knew was right and what I was told I should do for loyalty to the company. This e-mail hit when I had the flu, and my lungs were already heavy. It resurrected my unresolved angst. After an hour, I was having a hard time breathing. But I knew the trouble I was experiencing this time was different. Usually my chest got tight and I felt like I was drowning, even as I stood. I had had my most intense attack a year before, when I was away from home and wobbled into a drugstore, opened an inhaler, and curled up in the aisle sucking on it like a baby with a pacifier.

But this time was ten times worse. I started getting groggy and confused and went to sleep. I woke up a few hours later reaching for my puffer. I did at least ten or fifteen pumps—though the recommended dose was two puffs every four hours. I woke up a few hours later feeling worse, thickheaded. I could only take slow steps, because I couldn't breathe deeply. I called my doctor's answering service, then passed out again. When I awoke, I felt a little clearer, and I called again. Immediately the secretary said they were waiting for me.

I crawled to the car and drove myself to his office. I don't remember the drive at all, except that when I walked in the nurses rushed at me. It was just like on that *ER* show, people running around, calling for drugs, wheeling me into a room. They gave me one drug that didn't do much. They gave me another drug that worked, but that one was like speed, so now my teeth were chattering and I was all jacked up. Then they stuck a big-ass needle of adrenaline into me, and I felt I could have blasted through the roof. They tested my lung capacity and then released me.

I went back the next day for a follow-up, and my doctor asked me a few questions. He wrote the answers on a sheet on his clipboard.

"Two points," he said.

"Pardon me?" I asked.

SHAPING A BOARD WITH JEREMY WRAY.

He banged the clipboard down on the side of the bed. "Two points, Rodney. Two more points and you could have suffered permanent brain damage from lack of oxygen. You were at 11 percent lung capacity and once you reach 9 percent you risk brain damage. I don't know how the hell you managed to drive to the hospital. Pretty stupid."

It was good in a way though, because it made me step back from some of the hardcore business aspect of World. These days I do product research: I mostly design boards and concaves and trucks—all the fun nerd stuff. I also work with some of the riders and develop ads and marketing concepts.

CHAPTER 28

ENJOI!

BY 2000, A-TEAM WAS FINISHED. MARC JOHNSON WAS THE FIRST

to bail, and his exit started a chain reaction that disbanded the team. It wasn't a bummer, though; it was a relief for everybody involved. Being as creative as he was, Marc wanted to steer his own ship. He called me up one night, and we talked about our future. Marc had tons of creative ideas.

"Skating should be fun, full of characters, not faceless competitors," he said.

I agreed.

"You want to do something?" he asked.

"Yeah, I do," I said.

From the very first ad, I knew enjoi was going to be maxed out with Marc's sense of humor and fun.

Matt and Gary from Globe (along with Marc) encouraged me to merge my freestyle roots with the street skating. I had a part coming up for Globe's newest video, *Opinion*. I felt I owed it to Marc to tell him what I planned, in case he thought I might contaminate his company with my unconventional skating. I confessed my plan for the video to him while we were out skating.

"Marc, I hope you don't mind, I don't want to spoil enjoi, but I want to do goofball tricks," I said.

"Like what?"

"Like frontside crooked grind monkey flips."

"Do it!" he yelled. "Rodney, at this stage of the game, you don't have to prove anything. Just do what you feel like doing."

In *Opinion,* I have a part where I basically freestyle on my street board. I wasn't worried about what anyone thought anymore. I did exactly what I wanted for that video, and never enjoyed "working" so much. I was comfortable with the fact that I'd never fit in with what the majority of pros thought was cool. I'm probably the only pro skater who has studied the guidance systems of ballistic missiles and has a collection of Bible commentaries programmed into his Palm Pilot. I often listen to physics lectures while I drive and always have at least one book on quantum theory in my car in case I get stuck somewhere.

I can't hope to cover all that up.

ME, TRACI, AND MATT AND CHRISTINE HILL AFTER THE BEST VIDEO PREMIERE OF MY LIFE—*OPINION*—WHICH CAME OUT IN OCTOBER, 1999.

Once I allowed myself the freedom to finally skate the way I wanted to, I expected people to be less interested in me, since I'd be doing freestyle moves on street obstacles. But I was fine with that; in fact, I expected it. But I wasn't prepared to be on the *Transworld Skateboarding* readers' poll ballot for 2001. (The award would be given in the spring of 2002.)

Grant Brittain, the photo editor for *Transworld* at the time (he now works for the *The Skateboard Mag*), set up a photo shoot with another photographer, my friend Seu, to get some shots for the award issue. I was skating on a forklift blade, trying a crooked grind heelflip shove-it when I landed a little off. My body flushed again, and I could feel the muscles in the back of my knee tighten. It had been bugging me for months, but finally something tore.

I went to a masseuse that night because my leg still felt locked up. She could feel that my knee was jacked and recommended that I see a doctor.

I moped all the way to my car. I checked my messages while I was driving, and listened to six drunk skaters, who happened to be my friends, congratulating me on winning Skater of the Year. I felt uncomfortable going to award ceremonies, so I never went to them. Once Matt Hill heard I'd won, he called me and we talked on the way home. He was one of the few who knew about the struggles I'd gone through to just keep skating all these years.

Traci was at home, asleep, Court TV still flashing on the screen in the movie room. I woke her up and told her I had good news and bad news.

"I'll give you the bad news first, I think I have to have surgery, so can you call Dr. Feder tomorrow and set up an appointment. And for the next year I'd like for you to address me by my proper title, 'Skater of the Year,' instead of Rodney."

I was so thankful to all the little skate rats out there who had validated my choice in just having fun when I skated. To celebrate, I watched one of my favorite movies, *Ghostbusters*. Nerds battling ghosts—is it any wonder why I love that movie so much? (My wife, Traci, tells me that a more appropriate movie to watch as I reflected on my life would be *Revenge of the Nerds.*) I stayed awake until the sun came up, thinking of all the times when I had thought I'd have to give up skating. My knee surgery made me think about what would happen if skating were taken away from me. I looked over at Traci and saw my future, and even without skating I knew it was going to be all right.

#6 443 474 B

In the fall of 2002, my father organized a family reunion. He had moved to Arkansas and bought a huge piece of land that he developed shortly after my mom passed away. He had just finished a new house, and he was making an effort to bring the family together. I hadn't seen my family together for over fifteen years, and I had doubts about how good of an idea this was.

Traci encouraged the visit. She thought it was time that I dealt with my family issues and knew the only resolution was to visit my father. In Traci I finally had a solid foundation, which gave me the strength to agree to the visit. For the first time, I would have somebody by my side who understood my past and the convoluted emotions regarding my family. Traci wouldn't let me change my mind once I had agreed to go to the reunion. She knew I was finally ready for whatever happened.

I was quiet during the drive from the airport to my father's ranch, and I got a little nervous as we pulled into his driveway. My father was standing in front of his house with his new girlfriend who nodded and smiled at me.

And then . . . nothing. For the most part, the trip went well. Sara has kids who did funny Austin Powers imitations. Vicki was . . . well, she looked physically fit.

My dad seemed a bit nervous being the host, which was surprisingly endearing; it showed how much he wanted the reunion to go smoothly.

I waited until the last evening to show him the square of thick paper with a golden seal on it. I had rolled it up carefully in my backpack, and it was the sole achievement that I was positive he'd respect. The excitement I felt about earning my first patent was due to the expectation I had of showing it to my father sometime.

In 1999, I had designed Tensor Trucks and developed some stuff that was new to skateboarding. Tensor became the fastest-growing truck in skateboarding, according to Board Track, a company that monitors the skateboard industry sales numbers. But earning the patent mattered more to me than the sales. Once I had it, I began fantasizing about showing it to my father, though I didn't know when I'd have that opportunity until the family reunion came up.

I waited until I was alone with him in the kitchen and said, "Dad, look, I have something I want to show you." I unrolled the patent certificate where my name was written in calligraphy.

He looked at it closely. "Hey, this is a U.S. patent."

I nodded and pointed to my last name. "Look at that, that's our name."

He called his girlfriend in and showed her. They examined it and he asked me what the process was for applying for one, what my patent covered, and how I had thought up the innovations for the trucks.

For the first time I can remember, my father looked at one of my accomplishments and beamed. He was proud of me, and I could see it in his eyes.

"Ah, it was nothing," I said, downplaying it, reversing our traditional roles. "It's just a skateboard truck."

He read the entire document and then shook my hand.

I felt for the first time that he looked at me proudly as his son who had accomplished something legitimate. He offered to build Traci and me a house on his ranch where we could live. I thanked him and told him I was happy in California, but I still appreciated the offer and he respected my answer, even though it might not have been the one he'd hoped for.

I'm not going to pretend that the sun was shining and that we all sang "Kumbiya" around the campfire and had a group hug. There were arguments between family members, some crying and stomping off, but I'm glad I went to the reunion. My relationship with my father hasn't changed much—we only talk a couple times a year—and I'm still a bit frightened of him, but I feel at peace and I think he does, too. I am finally mature enough to appreciate the subtleties of his strict code of conduct and the degree of integrity that he holds everyone accountable for, including himself.

ENJOI!

CHAPTER 29
ALMOST

I LIKED SKATING FOR ENJOI MORE THAN ANY OTHER TEAM I HAD

skated for, and it was because of Marc. But he invested so much energy into the company that it drained him. Burned out, he left enjoi in 2002.

Marc and I were so close that it felt weird being on enjoi without him. But it was a blessing, in a way, since I could now join forces with Daewon and start a company with him, called Almost. Our relationship is like brotherhood, and he even honored me by making me the godfather of his son. I've always wanted to do something with him ever since I skated for Plan B. Ryan Sheckler, a thirteen-year-old who had already won some of the biggest pro contests, was the first rider we put on the team. I marvel at how much he shines, at how together he is for his age.

It's a dream team for me because I'm surrounded by friends who are just as driven as I am. For the first time I feel like a part of a complete team instead of just a stranded piece of a puzzle. And I feel like a father figure in a way, which makes me laugh. But I'm proud of Almost and protective of everybody on it.

GHOSTS

At the beginning of 2003, I flew into Tampa, Florida, for the Skatepark of Tampa Pro contest, to scout for Almost. There were a couple of skaters I wanted to get on the team, and I talked to them during the event. After the contest wrapped up and most of the skaters were off partying, I spent the night in a Denny's drinking coffee and watching people by myself.

What would my life be like if I hadn't started skateboarding twenty-seven years ago? Would I be slinging hash in the back of this Denny's after my mental breakdown? Would I be sleeping so I could wake up and develop nuclear warheads, as a few of my friends at the university were doing? Would I be like that lady I saw in Norway who made a duct tape uniform and wandered the streets, complaining about having her "sick" money taken away? Would I have killed myself?

Working on this book has stirred up a lot of memories for me, and sitting there in Florida added more to the mix. The following night, I drove my rental car to my old hometown. After a couple of hours driving, I stopped down the street at my grandma's old house. She had died a few years earlier in a nursing home and the house had been sold.

It was almost one in the morning, and I poked around the property, remembering where I used to run around, where my grandfather would meticulously edge the lawn. Everything was overgrown now, and the place looked like a confined jungle. Some areas were so overgrown that I couldn't recognize them from my memories. I walked around the property, careful not to make any loud noises and scare the current occupants. I wandered down the street to the park where I remembered running around in a forest, trees arching overhead, bugs and lizards and snakes crawling around. My make-believe forest had been an empty lot with a few bushes maybe five feet tall. Everything that used to seem so mysterious and humongous now looked like a badly constructed facade.

I checked into a Holiday Inn near my old school, P. K. Yonge. The receptionist recognized my name as she typed it into the computer.

"Are you Rodney Mullen, the skateboarder?" she asked.

I nodded.

"My dad got you on Converse; do you remember him? He went over and had dinner with your parents once."

It all flashed back. Her father owned a shoe store and had seen me skate in Converse shoes and lined up a sponsorship by talking to a sales rep.

"Hey!" she yelled to the other workers in the hotel, "we have a star in our presence!"

I signed a few autographs and dropped my bags off in my room. But I was too wired to sleep. All these memories and feelings were like ten cups of coffee. I walked a few miles over to P. K. Yonge. A full moon was out, and it was misty, as if a cloud had slowly lowered onto the street and just sat there. It was neither cold nor hot—the temperature was so moderate I couldn't feel it. The moonlight on the mist lit up everything in monochrome.

I walked around the school property for hours. Unlike in the Los Angeles area, where schoolyards are fenced in and locked tighter than jail cells, schools in this part of Florida are open. Some of the classroom doors were unlocked, surprisingly. It emphasized the innocence of my time there.

I looked in the windows of my old classrooms, and if the door was open, I'd walk in and sit at my old desk, or at least wherever my desk used to be. I walked to the gym and suddenly remembered skating there. My P.E. teacher had asked me to do a halftime show during a few basketball games. There was a trophy case in the entry of the gym, and I peered through a door window, but I couldn't see everything in the case. Sara had asked me to sign a board and send it to P. K. Yonge, because they wanted to display it. I peeked in the case to see if it was there, but it was unlit and so deep that I couldn't see anything but shadows inside.

I walked around the corner onto the tennis courts where I had skated in secret after my father made me quit, where I had

watched myself decay. I walked around and around in the same area where I used to skate. I sat down in the middle of the court and felt the ground, digging my fingernails in the ground. The court used to get soft under the Florida sun.

I remembered sitting in this exact location and watching bus-loads of students going to school football games, the cheerleaders laughing and goofing around with the guys. I was almost fifteen then and getting interested in girls, wishing there was some way I could fit in on that bus, some way to have both a skating and a social life. But I could not stop skating, and on that Friday night it hit me extra hard for some reason. I could not stop. *I'm just going to keep skating,* I thought then. *Life is passing me by.*

I had felt helpless and instantly worthless. *What am I doing with all these hours?* I remembered staring after the bus. *Look at them, they're going somewhere, they're the high school champs.*

I walked through the fields where my mom and I had our last talks, when I had told her I wasn't going to her funeral. It was the same area where the school would come out to watch the space shuttle launches at Cape Kennedy.

I came back into the school, walking the hallways and peeking in classrooms. All the posters had changed. Life today is so much gnarlier than life was back then; now they have posters on sexual harassment on the walls. The nurse's station was in the same spot. I had practically had a reserved seat from self-induced "stomachaches."

I sat down where I used to wait on Wednesdays for my mom. I could smell the leather of her car, hear her voice as she opened the door and said hi, see her smile beaming as I scooted over onto the white leather seat.

I walked back to the Holiday Inn and slept until noon. I skated to my old college, cruising around studying people to see if they were as insecure as I had been. I walked into the chemical research building to see a favorite old professor, Dr. Zoltewicz, who taught me organic chemistry. He was out, and I asked for some paper to write a letter. I just wanted to thank him for his inspiration, for loving what he did and passing on the importance of that to me.

I gave the letter to his secretary and she asked if "I was the famous skateboarder he often talked about." He'd boasted that he'd taught a champion skateboarder once, she said. That remark meant as much to me as winning the Skater of the Year award did.

I drove over to our first house, where I had got my first board. The whole area was developed, houses rising up as far as I could see. I stood at the top of the hill that I used to bomb down and set up plastic plant containers to slalom through. Our old house looked slightly worse for the wear, and like my grandma's home, it was totally overgrown with plants and trees.

I stood on the street, just staring and remembering, when I noticed a lockbox hanging on the door.

"Oh my God, it's empty," I said, so surprised that I blurted it out loud.

I walked up to the porch area where I skated those first few nights I had my skateboard. I kneeled down and felt the scuff marks where I'd imitated the pros in *SkateBoarder* grinding pool coping.

I walked around to the back and hopped the fence, not thinking about what I might encounter. I landed on the pool deck and was hit with memories.

I walked over and looked in the pool, full of dead bugs floating on top, while live annoying ones buzzed around. A memory slammed into me. The swarm of insects brought back a time I was on the porch when I was nine. Our family had gone out to eat, and I hadn't looked up at the waitress when I ordered. I was absorbed in coloring my kid's menu with some crayons. My father took this as disrespectful and called me a punk kid under his breath. When we got home that night I had to wash the pool deck as punishment. I finished the job, and reported it to my father, who inspected it and informed me that it wasn't clean enough. I was getting tired, and it took longer to clean the deck the second time. When I was finished, I reported back to my father who checked every corner, shook his head, and made me do it again.

"This time the right way," he said.

I had to do it all over again and had no idea what time it was when I finally finished.

It began raining, so I jimmied the door into the back room where the dog's space had been. I was amazed at how small the house seemed now. It was empty and hard to recognize. I started breathing hard, feeling I needed to get out.

I walked outside and by now the storm had moved in and it was pouring. I ran into the poolhouse where I used to change before I swam. The walls had a dark wood finish that sucked in any light, making it gloomy, and a musty stink filled the place from being unused for months. I turned on the light and the fan whirled on noisily. There was a closet where all the pool chemicals were kept, and I crawled into it like I used to sometimes when I was a kid. I just stared at the rain splashing in the pool and began crying. *I made it,* I thought. *I really did make it out of here.*

PHOTOGRAPHY CREDITS

COLOR INSERT

page

1 © J. Grant Brittain
2 © Phil Chiocchio
3 © Phil Chiocchio
4 © J. Grant Brittain
5 © Bruce Talbot (top); © Jody Morris (bottom)
6, 7 © Seu Trinh
8, 9 © Seu Trinh
10, 11 © Socrates Leal
12 © Jody Morris
13 © Seu Trinh
14 © Seu Trinh
15 © Neversoft Activision (top); © Enjoi (bottom)
16 © Seu Trinh

BLACK & WHITE

ii © Seu Trinh
vi © Seu Trinh
x © Socrates Leal
10 © Marc McKee
20 © Marc McKee
34 © Phil Chiocchio
39 © Phil Chiocchio
47 © J. Grant Brittain
48 © Phil Chiocchio
56 © Phil Chiocchio

59 © Phil Chiocchio
61 © Phil Chiocchio
67 © Phil Chiocchio
73 © Phil Chiocchio
77 © Phil Chiocchio
79 © Phil Chiocchio
86 © Phil Chiocchio
88 © J. Grant Brittain
94 © J. Grant Brittain
96 © Phil Chiocchio
99 courtesy of author's collection
102 © Phil Chiocchio
113 © J. Grant Brittain
120 © J. Grant Brittain
128 © J. Grant Brittain
133 © J. Grant Brittain
134 © Phil Chiocchio
139 © J. Grant Brittain
145 © J. Grant Brittain
157 © J. Grant Brittain
176 © J. Grant Brittain
181 © World Industries
182 © World Industries
198 © World Industries
202 © J. Grant Brittain
205 © J. Grant Brittain
209 © J. Grant Brittain
213 © J. Grant Brittain
230 © J. Grant Brittain
238 courtesy of author's collection
240 © Bruce Talbot
245 © Jody Morris
246 courtesy of author's collection
252 © Jody Morris

253 © Jody Morris
255 © Seu Trinh
257 © Seu Trinh
258 © Bruce Talbot
260 © Jody Morris
263 courtesy of author's collection